ANNALS OF COMMUNISM

Each volume in the series Annals of Communism will publish selected and previously inaccessible documents from former Soviet state and party archives in a narrative that develops a particular topic in the history of Soviet and international communism. Separate English and Russian editions will be prepared. Russian and American scholars work together to prepare the documents for each volume. Documents are chosen not for their support of any single interpretation but for their particular historical importance or their general value in deepening understanding and facilitating discussion. The volumes are designed to be useful to students, scholars, and interested general readers.

Dimitrov and Stalin
1934–1943
Letters from the Soviet Archives

Edited by

Alexander Dallin and F. I. Firsov

Russian documents translated by Vadim A. Staklo

Yale University Press

New Haven and London

This volume has been prepared with the cooperation of the Russian State Archive of Social and Political History (RGASPI) of the State Archival Service of Russia in the framework of an agreement concluded between RGASPI and Yale University Press.

Designed by James J. Johnson and set in Sabon and Melior types by The Composing Room of Michigan, Inc., Grand Rapids, Michigan. Printed in the United States of America by Vail-Ballou Press, Binghamton, New York.

Library of Congress Cataloging-in-Publication Data

Dimitrov and Stalin : 1934–1943 : letters from the Soviet archives /edited by
    Alexander Dallin and F.I. Firsov ; Russian documents
    translated by Vadim A. Staklo.
        p.   cm. — (Annals of communism)
    Includes bibliographical references and index.
    ISBN 0-300-08021-2 (alk. paper)

    1. Stalin, Joseph, 1879–1953 Correspondence.   2. Dimitrov, Georgi,
1882–1949 Correspondence.   3. Communism—History Sources.
4. Communist International—History Sources.   I. Dallin, Alexander.
II. Firsov, Fridrikh Igorevich.   III. Series.
DK268.S8A4 2000
947.084′2—dc21   99-39083

A catalogue record for this book is available from the British Library.

The paper in this book meets the guidelines for permanence and durability of the Committee on Production Guidelines for Book Longevity of the Council on Library Resources.

10 9 8 7 6 5 4 3 2 1

Yale University Press gratefully acknowledges the financial support given for this publication by the John M. Olin Foundation, Inc., the Lynde and Harry Bradley Foundation, Inc., the Historical Research Foundation, Roger Milliken, Lloyd H. Smith, the Soros Foundation, Keith Young, the William H. Donner Foundation, Inc., Joseph W. Donner, Jeremiah Milbank, Karen Pritzker, Robert Pritzker, the David Woods Kemper Memorial Foundation, the Daphne Seybolt Culpeper Foundation, Inc., the Milton V. Brown Foundation, the Patterson Foundation, the Forbes Foundation, and Jim Schwartz.

Contents

Documents

Documents Reproduced in Facsimile

ИНФОРМАЦИИ ЦК ВКП(б): ВОПРОСЫ ВНЕШНЕЙ ПОЛИТИКИ
(Bulletin of the information bureau of the CC VKP[b]: Issues of foreign policy), January 1945

Illustrations

Preface

This volume reproduces in English translation letters and memos sent to Joseph Stalin from Georgi Dimitrov, the secretary general of the Communist International, from 1934, when Dimitrov returned to Moscow from a German prison, until 1943, when the Comintern was disbanded, along with Stalin's responses. The documents are currently housed in the Russian Center for the Preservation and Study of Documents of Recent History (RTsKhIDNI), which was established in 1991 to hold the files of the Comintern and of the Communist Party of the Soviet Union (CPSU) that had formerly been held at the Institute of Marxism-Leninism in Moscow. Most of them come from a larger collection of 211 documents identified by a team of archivists working under the direction of Fridrikh I. Firsov, the Russian co-editor of this volume, in the archives of the Comintern and of the Central Committee of the Communist Party of the Soviet Union.

Most of the documents were originally written in Russian; the exceptions are primarily radio- or cablegrams sent to the Comintern (from China or Yugoslavia, say) and translated before being submitted to Dimitrov and others, and communications from agents and representatives abroad (for instance, Spain) written in German or French. Unless otherwise indicated, the documents reached us in typewritten form. A number of reports from abroad were transmitted to the Comintern in code and decoded in its Coding Section; at times the decoding presented difficulties to the staff and produced gaps and errors. In many instances what we have are carbons of letters from Dimitrov to Stalin, but they bear notations (signatures, dates, archival numbers) indicating that they were sent; some originals may have been kept in Stalin's files, which remain inaccessible.

For reasons of space we have had to omit a number of documents of interest; some of these are cited in the notes. Dimitrov and his staff forwarded a variety of reports to the Kremlin, but we include here only documents that were accompanied or preceded by a note or letter specifically from Dimitrov to Stalin. Some of the enclosures were filed elsewhere in the archive or were located as attachments to copies forwarded to other recipients; we include them only when their authenticity can be confirmed. In a few instances the enclosures mentioned in Dimitrov's letters could not be found in RTsKhIDNI; where relevant this has been noted.

This book is not an exhaustive account of the contacts between Dimitrov and Stalin, let alone between the leadership of the Comintern and the Soviet state (or the Communist Party of the Soviet Union). Leaving aside the likelihood that some of the documents exchanged between the two men never made it into their files or into the archives (we indicate below where we think this was the case), there were a number of other forms and channels of communication between the leaders and their staffs. Dimitrov's diary not only testifies to his superb memory and capacity to reproduce conversations and documents accurately; it and other sources make reference to or imply the existence of letters that have not been located in the archives. Where pertinent, we mention these in the notes.

In addition to sending letters and memoranda, Dimitrov and Stalin held conversations. Some of these are recorded elsewhere—for instance, in Dimitrov's diary—or are reported by third parties who were present (Viacheslav Molotov, Dmitry Manuilsky, and others). The two also held telephone conversations, for which we have no systematic record, but some of these find reflection in subsequent memoranda and decisions.

Another channel of communication between the Comintern and the Kremlin was Dimitrov's Soviet deputy Dmitry Manuilsky. Indeed, some of the enclosures sent with the letters to Stalin were located not in Dimitrov's files but as copies in Manuilsky's records. It is also clear that

Manuilsky had extensive personal contact with a number of Soviet officials (including the NKVD), a fact that may help explain some of the surprising gaps in Dimitrov's written contacts with Stalin and those around him.

The Comintern was fully dependent on, and controlled by, the Soviet leadership. It could hardly have been otherwise. The Comintern's role as a source and transmitter of information to Moscow and of instructions to Communists abroad is amply illustrated in the following collection. But it is well to remember that by and large, for the Soviet leadership the Comintern was only one of several channels of information. It remains to be studied in what ways information received in the Kremlin through the secret services and military intelligence—during the Spanish Civil War, say, or concerning the Yugoslav partisans in World War II—or via reports by Soviet diplomats stationed abroad, differed in quality, reliability, bias, or policy orientation from those transmitted through the Comintern. We know, for example, of instances in which Communist leaders abroad preferred not to communicate with Moscow through the Comintern residents assigned to their country. José Diaz, the head of the Spanish Communist party, chose to send a letter to Stalin through the Soviet ambassador to France, rather than through Palmiro Togliatti, Ernö Gerö, or Vittorio Codovilla, the Comintern representatives in Spain.

It is precisely because the Comintern's role as a contact and source of information was exceptional during the Spanish Civil War, the Chinese hostilities of the thirties, and the Yugoslav resistance during World War II that we chose to single out these cases for separate chapters. We believe that the new material offered concerning them is significant, but we do not argue that these documents give an adequate account of the struggles in these countries or of the Communist role (or the Soviet involvement) in them.

These documents confirm the impression that the Comintern—or at least its Executive Committee (the ECCI)—was a vast bureaucratic apparatus, full of routines, resentments, lassitude, and uncertainties, though outwardly, of course, each member was fully loyal to the Communist cause and the Soviet masters. While it was never a benign organization of well-meaning paper-pushers, the Comintern that emerges from the files is a far cry from the worldwide conspiracy of terrorists it was sometimes believed to be. If indeed some of its activities focused on espionage and subversion, these are not reflected in either the correspondence or the personal records of its key officers and would have been handled through other channels.

The documentary record also confirms the key role of a few personalities—above all Stalin himself, of course, but also Dimitrov. Perhaps less expected is the finding, highlighted by the archives, that Moscow's strategy and tactics were characterized not so much by clarity, cleverness, or consistency as by dilemmas and ambiguities in decision making. Time and again we observe the tensions between conflicting aims and interests—between international Communist audiences and Western establishments, between going it alone and pursuing a policy of alliance, between deferred gratification and cashing in on victories and deals.

The records presented here give the impression that Stalin was something of a sphinx, to whom Dimitrov forwarded a variety of materials from representatives abroad; drafts of Comintern resolutions and instructions, along with other materials for review and comment (or veto); requests for appointments; budgetary allocations; or requests for authorization to proceed with various tasks. In response Stalin typically scribbled a few words in the margin of the document—even in cases of fundamental policy shifts (for instance, in preparation for the Seventh World Congress of the Comintern)—or transmitted his decisions through an underling (Molotov, Zhdanov, or, later, Poskrebyshev) or sent word (as when Dimitrov repeatedly pleaded with him to receive Zhou Enlai in early 1940) that he was too busy: "Decide for yourselves."

True, a rather different Stalin comes across from the notes taken by Dimitrov on the several occasions where Stalin spoke informally to a few trusted associates. This Stalin is far more creative and less circumspect; he more nearly matches the man of other personal accounts, such as Milovan Djilas's. Both Stalins are credible, but the picture that emerges from these documents is plausible, given his many other preoccupations, as well as his relative neglect of the Comintern and its mission as time went on—given also what we know of his general bureaucratic and administrative style. It is possible that this image will receive some correction if we ever gain complete access to the so-called Presidential Archive, which contains files that virtually no scholars have had an opportunity to peruse. But we are confident that the available documentation conveys a generally accurate picture of Stalin and his relationship with Dimitrov, and we doubt that the Presidential Archive holds additional documents crucial to this image.

This book is not a history of the Comintern from 1934 to 1943; but it illustrates both the form and the substance of the Comintern's relation to the Soviet rulers. In addition, it offers unusual insights into Moscow's thinking and decision making on a wide variety of issues, from global strategy to petty disputes. Like the other volumes in the Annals of Communism series, this book offers important sources for new insights into dramatic, controversial, and hitherto obscure events in recent history.

Since this volume went to press, RTsKhIDNI has changed its name to the Russian State Archive of Social and Political History (Rossiisky Gosudarstvenny Arkhiv Sotsialnoi i Politicheskoi Istorii, or RGASPI).

Note on Documents

All the documents in this collection reached us in the Russian language; in some instances they were translations from other languages; where originals could be located in the archives, the Russian was checked against them.

In transliterating from Russian to English we have used a modified version of the standard Library of Congress system in the text and documents. Soft and hard signs have been omitted, and the following changes have been imposed.

In final position:

ii in the LOC system becomes y (Trotsky, not Trotskii)

iia = ia (Izvestia, not Izvestiia)

nyi = ny (Nagorny, not Nagornyi)

In initial position:

E = Ye (Yezhov, not Ezhov)

Ia = Ya (Yaroslavsky, not Iaroslavsky)

Iu = Yu (Yudin, not Iudin)

In citations and translator's notes, we have followed the Library of Congress system. For a small number of familiar names the customary English spelling has been retained (Joseph, not Iosif, Stalin; Leon, not Lev, Trotsky). A list of acronyms and abbreviations is provided to assist the reader.

Wherever possible, foreign place names and personal names (for example, in Spanish or Serbo-Croatian) are reproduced in their original spelling, rather than in transliteration from Russian. We have used standard current (*pinyin*) spelling of Chinese names (with earlier alternative spellings indicated in the name index). Here too familiar spellings have been retained (Chiang Kai-shek, rather than Jiang Jieshi). Since the Chinese names were transliterated from Chinese into Russian and then into English, mistakes are almost certain to have occurred: our apologies for any remaining errors. Enumerated dates in documents follow European style: day, month, year.

Unless otherwise indicated, the documents published below were located in the collections at RTsKhIDNI, whose records are organized by *fond* (collection), *opis'* (inventory), *delo* (file), and *list* (page); source references are accordingly abbreviated f., op., d., and l. The Russian abbreviations "vkhod." and "iskh." found in the identification of some of the documents refer to "incoming" and "outgoing" messages received by the ECCI, usually its coding and decoding section. The page numbering of some documents (such as translated and decrypted telegrams) in the archives is in reverse order, reflecting the order of insertion in the archival files (thus, for example, ll. 75–72).

The abbreviation TsPA (Sofia) stands for Tsentralen partien arkhiv na TsK na BKP, the Central Party Archive of the Central Committee of the Bulgarian Communist Party (more recently, of the Supreme Council of the Bulgarian Socialist Party), in Sofia. The letters "a.e." are the Bulgarian abbreviation for "archival unit" (the equivalent of the Russian *delo*).

Documents, or parts of documents, printed in **boldface italic** were handwritten in the original. <u>Single underlining</u> indicates that the underlining was part of the original typescript. <u>Double underlining</u> indicates that the underlining was done by hand, either at the time the document was written or perhaps by a reader.

Ellipses in the original document are typed as they appear: . . .

Ellipses in brackets indicate editorial omissions: [. . .]

Ellipses in angle brackets indicate illegible words: < . . . >

The annotations are the responsibility of the American editor. The biographical notes identify individuals mentioned in the documents. The most familiar names, such as Hitler, Marx, Stalin, and Roosevelt, have been omitted.

A small number of these documents, or parts thereof, have been previously published or cited in Soviet journals, a Bulgarian collection of Dimitrov's writings, or Palmiro Togliatti's collected works (in Italian).

Acknowledgments

We are eager to express our gratitude for their assistance to the staffs of the archives and libraries we consulted, notably at the Russian Center for the Preservation and Study of Documents of Recent History (Rossiiskii tsentr khraneniia i izucheniia dokumentov noveishei istorii, or RTsKhIDNI) in Moscow. We are also grateful for the help we received at the library of the Hoover Institution at Stanford.

We wish to give special thanks to the directors of the Russian archives as well as to Mansur Mukhamedzhanov, in Moscow, who was kind enough to review and endorse the original selection of documents and annotations. Above all, we owe a debt of gratitude to Elena Nechayeva, Vadim Staklo, and Yuri Tutochkin, who searched through mountains of archival files to locate many of the documents published here and who provided some of the original identifying annotations and commentary. Thanks are also due to Zheng Yuan for assistance with the spelling of Chinese names.

We owe a special debt of gratitude to Vadim Staklo for his triple contribution to this project. After first participating in the screening and selection of documents, he was their conscientious and careful translator from Russian into English. And as the project coordinator at Yale University Press he played an essential role in cheerfully and efficiently shepherding this volume through publication.

The editors wish to thank Jonathan Brent, editorial director of Yale University Press, for asking us to produce this volume. Sincere thanks are due likewise to the Yale University Press staff responsible for the Annals of Communism series, and in particular to manuscript editor Susan Laity for her high standards and thoroughly professional work on the completed manuscript.

Abbreviations and Acronyms

AUCP(b)	All-Union Communist Party (Bolshevik). See VKP(b).
CC	Central Committee of a Communist party
CCP	Chinese Communist Party
CGT	Confédération Générale du Travail, the French labor union federation
CI	Communist International (Comintern), founded by Lenin in 1919, disbanded in 1943
CNT	Confederación Nacional del Trabajo, the Spanish trade union federation, which in the 1930s was under "anarchist" influence
Cominform	Communist Information Bureau, active 1947–56
Comintern	See CI
CP, CPs	Communist Party or parties
CPSU	Communist Party of the Soviet Union, the official name of the party after 1952. See also VKP(b).
CPUSA	Communist Party of the United States of America
CPY	Communist Party of Yugoslavia
ECCI	Executive Committee of the Communist International
GMD (KMT)	Guomindang (Kuomintang), Chinese Nationalists
ICC	International Control Commission
ILS	International Lenin School. Communist school attached to the ECCI for foreign Communists and Soviet Communists who worked with foreign Communists. Active 1925–38.

KIM	Communist Youth International
Komsomol	All-Union Leninist Youth League
KPD	Communist Party of Germany
KPÖ	Communist Party of Austria
KPP	Communist Party of Poland
KUTV	Communist University of the Toilers of the East, established in Moscow in 1921
MOPR	International Red Aid
NKVD	People's Commissariat of Internal Affairs. A successor to the GPU and predecessor of the KGB.
OMI	Department of International Information of the Central Committee of the CPSU
OMS	Department of International Liaison of the ECCI. After 1935, known as the Liaison Service (SS).
PCE	Communist Party of Spain
PCF	Communist Party of France
PCI	Communist Party of Italy
POUM	Partido Obrero de Unificación Marxista, a Leninist opposition group to the PCE during the Spanish Civil War
PSOE	Socialist Party of Workers of Spain
Politburo	Political Bureau, the highest executive organ of a Communist party
Profintern	Red International of Labor Unions, the counterpart to the Comintern's trade union arm
RTsKhIDNI	Russian Center for the Preservation and Study of Documents of Recent History, an archive holding records of the Comintern and the CPSU up to 1953
SED	Socialist Unity Party, the Communist-controlled ruling party of the German Democratic Republic (East Germany)
SFIO	French Socialist Party
TsPA (Sofia)	Bulgarian Central Party Archive, Sofia
UGT	Unión General de Trabajadores, the Spanish trade union federation close to PSOE
VKP(b)	Russian abbreviation of All-Union Communist Party (Bolshevik), the official title of the Soviet Communist party from 1925 to 1952, when it became the CPSU
WFTU	World Federation of Trade Unions

CHAPTER ONE

Introduction

BY 1934 THE SOVIET UNION had undergone a series of traumas that had profoundly transformed the country, the way it lived and the way it was governed. World War I had inflicted widespread devastation. And before that was over, in 1917 the February Revolution ousted the tsarist regime and, amid chaos and suffering, the October Revolution brought Lenin and his followers the Bolsheviks to power and instituted Soviet rule. There ensued three years of civil war, in which some twelve foreign powers intervened. By 1921, when the Reds emerged victorious, the country was on the verge of starvation, the people were exhausted, and the Communists' hopeful illusions of the early years were bitterly disappointed. Lenin felt compelled to launch a new policy of moderation to help the economy recover (the so-called New Economic Policy, or NEP), though never relaxing his party's monopoly of power, a policy marked by "coexistence" with both enemies at home—above all, the peasants who constituted the majority of the population—and the non-Communist world abroad.

Lenin died in 1924, and from the bitter struggle for succession emerged Joseph Stalin, who soon consolidated his grip on the party and tightened its control of the country. In 1929 he launched a massive transformation program that probably affected more people more deeply than any of the previous upheavals—the so-called first Five Year Plan, which called for the rapid industrialization of the country "from above" and the forcible collectivization of agriculture. This entailed the resettlement (and exile) of millions of peasants. By 1934, it seemed, the worst was over, but the siege mentality persisted. And now new crises were in the offing, both at home and abroad.

Although profound suspicions persisted on both sides, in the 1920s the Soviet Union had established diplomatic and trade relations throughout the world. Britain and France were seen as its major capitalist enemies, but the country was too weak to contemplate a major test of strength with anyone, even its smaller neighbors. By 1934 that situation had begun to change, as the implications of the rise of the Nazis in Germany and an aggressive Japan in the East sank in.

One institution whose existence was unique to the Soviet Union was the Communist International: the Third International, or Comintern.[1] Its establishment in March 1919 reflected the Bolsheviks' belief in—and commitment to promote—world revolution. In Bolshevik theory, Russia had merely been the first to see Communists come to power; other countries, especially the major developed nations in the West, were bound to follow. And in this process the Comintern would coordinate, direct, and assist Communist efforts worldwide. The Comintern considered national Communist parties to be sections of the International; these parties were obliged to follow the directives and the discipline of Moscow headquarters. To varying degrees, the national parties, eager to support the one country that had had a successful Communist revolution, went along with this. If there was a heavy dose of self-deception and naïveté in this effort, it soon came to serve as the principal vehicle for all forms of aid and instructions to Communist parties abroad.

It did not take long for the Communists to realize that their hopes

1. The Comintern was the "Third International" because the "First" had been the International Working Men's Association, founded with Karl Marx's support in 1864 and disbanded a dozen years later; the "Second" was the Labor International launched in 1889, which, after some mutations, still survives. In Lenin's view, the Second International had betrayed true proletarian internationalism and been "captured" by moderate social democrats; thus, the Third International was needed to replace it.

for early revolutions had been sadly misplaced. By 1921 it was apparent that all the efforts outside the Soviet state had failed, whereas the Soviet state itself had survived. Inevitably, and with vigorous manipulation from Moscow, the Comintern became an instrument of Soviet foreign policy, at times in bureaucratic rivalry with the Soviet Foreign Office but increasingly "Sovietized," "Bolshevized," and "Stalinized." Still, appearances—vis-à-vis foreign Communist parties as well as foreign states—required that the Comintern be seen as separate from the Soviet government, and Stalin himself (and therefore his underlings) remained mildly suspicious of the organization. Not without reason, he never had great confidence in its ability to score important successes abroad.[2]

Formally, the world congresses were the highest body of the International; in fact, they were never decisive, and (just as with the congresses of the Soviet Communist party) they took place with increasing infrequency. After the Sixth Congress in 1928, the Seventh did not convene until 1935, and it was to prove the last ever held; even the dissolution of the Comintern in 1943 took place without a world congress. In the International's operation the key body was the Executive Committee, or ECCI. Originally the national parties named their own delegates to the ECCI, but as Soviet control tightened, Moscow began proposing the whole slate. The ECCI in turn elected its Presidium and Secretariat. Other administrative units, such as regional secretariats and international liaison and coding sections, were also created by the ECCI. The ECCI Secretariat (un-

2. There are no fully satisfactory histories of the Communist International. For helpful though not always objective or accurate accounts, see, e.g., Julius Braunthal, *History of the International*, vol. 2 (London: Thomas Nelson, 1967); Franz Borkenau, *World Communism* (Ann Arbor: University of Michigan Press, 1962); E. H. Carr, *Twilight of the Comintern* (New York: Pantheon, 1982); Richard Lowenthal, *World Communism* (New York: Oxford University Press, 1964). The quasi-official survey of its history is Institute of Marxism-Leninism at CPSU Central Committee, *Kommunisticheskii Internatsional* (Moscow: Izd. Pol. Lit., 1969). On the organization of the Comintern, see also Günther Nollau, *International Communism and World Revolution* (New York: Praeger, 1961), chap. 4. A reliable documentary collection is Jane Degras, ed., *The Communist International, 1919–1943: Documents*, vol. 3 (London: RIIA, 1965). See also Aldo Agosti, ed., *La Terza Internazionale: storia documentaria*, vol. 3, pt. 2 (Rome: Ed. Riuniti, 1979), pp. 1928–43; Kevin McDermott and Jeremy Agnew, *The Comintern* (New York: St. Martin's Press, 1997); and the careful and well-documented study by Grant Adibekov, Eleona Shakhnazarova, and Kirill Shirinia, *Organizatsionnaia struktura Kominterna, 1919–1943* (Moscow: ROSSPEN, 1997).

til 1935, the Political Secretariat) conducted much of the Comintern's current work. Some of the activities of the International, such as its intelligence functions, are scarcely mentioned in the documents here surveyed.

The first president of the Comintern, who served from 1919 to 1926, was Grigory Zinoviev, a prominent "left" Communist who was widely disliked among his colleagues and later a victim of Stalin's purges. (Chapter 2 will look at the "left" and "right" factions of the Soviet Communist party.) Formally the position was then abolished, but in fact Zinoviev was succeeded from 1926 to 1928 by a leading member of the Political Secretariat, Nikolai Bukharin, at that time a brilliant "rightist"; ultimately, he, too, was a victim of the purges. After his ouster the leadership was left open until 1935, when Georgi Dimitrov, one of the leaders of the Bulgarian Communists, was formally named secretary general of the Executive Committee of the International.

Dimitrov was born in 1882 near Radomir, Bulgaria. His father was an artisan, and when the family moved to Sofia, young Georgi went to work as a typesetter. He joined the Social Democrats in 1902, and when the party split he supported the Tesniaks—in some regards, the Bulgarian equivalent of the Russian Bolsheviks (though Dimitrov later objected to the identification of the Tesniaks with the Bolsheviks). In 1909 he was elected to their Central Committee and began to attend political and trade union conferences.

In 1913 Dimitrov was elected to the Bulgarian parliament from Sofia. In 1918 he was sent to prison for undermining military discipline but was freed in December, after Bulgaria surrendered to the Allies. In 1921 he managed to attend the Third Congress of the Comintern in Moscow (the Tesniaks had reorganized as the Bulgarian Communist Party), as well as the founding congress of the Profintern, the Red International of Labor Unions, also run from Moscow.

In September 1923 Bulgarian Communists launched an ill-conceived and futile insurrection. For his alleged role in the uprising, Dimitrov was sentenced to death in absentia. Having fled the country, he remained abroad until 1945. In the intervening twenty years he worked for the Comintern, first in Vienna, then in Moscow and Berlin. Although he could not return to Bulgaria, he attended Comintern congresses and the plenums of the ECCI as a Bulgarian delegate and rapidly gained visibility. Beginning as an alternate member of the ECCI in 1924, he moved to alternate member of the Presidium and Secretariat (1926), member of the Central Council (1921) and then of the executive of the Profintern (1922), and finally secretary of the Balkan Communist Federation (1926).

In 1929 the Comintern placed Dimitrov at the head of its clandestine but important West European Bureau in Berlin. There, on 9 March 1933, he was arrested for setting fire to the Reichstag—the German parliament building. The newly ascendant Nazis used the fire to portray their enemies, especially the Communists, as dangerous subversives, but their efforts were rather clumsy. The prosecution's case was weak, and Dimitrov's behavior in particular, boldly challenging the case and especially Hermann Göring, then president of the Reichstag, earned him a good deal of publicity, not only in Communist circles but in other Western media as well.[3]

The German court, which was not yet fully under the control of the Nazis, found Dimitrov and his fellow Bulgarian defendants Not Guilty, and in December 1933, Wilhelm Pieck, a leading German Communist, sent a telegram to Osip Pyatnitsky, a prominent member of the Political Secretariat of the ECCI: "It would be politically expedient if the Sov[iet] gov[ernment] in some form informed the German government that it—the Sov[iet] gov[ernment]—is prepared to offer Com[rade] Dimitrov and the other Bulgarian com[rades] the right of asylum in the USSR." Pyatnitsky forwarded this message to Stalin on 29 December.[4] Bulgaria had meanwhile deprived its three defendants of citizenship. On 16 February 1934 the Soviet embassy in Berlin sent a note to the German Foreign Of-

3. This sketch of Dimitrov is based on Joseph Rothschild, *The Communist Party of Bulgaria, 1883–1936* (New York: Columbia University Press, 1959); Branko Lazitch, *Biographical Dictionary of the Comintern* (Stanford: Hoover Institution Press, 1973); Edward H. Carr, *Twilight of the Comintern, 1930–1935* (New York: Pantheon, 1982); Elena Savova, ed., *Georgi Dimitrov: Letopis na zhivota i revoliutsionnata mu deinost* (Sofia: Bulg. Akad. na Naukite [1952]); and F. I. Firsov, "Georgi Dimitrov and the West European Bureau of the Comintern," in *Georgi Dimitrov: An Outstanding Militant of the Comintern* (Sofia: Sofia Press, 1972), pp. 48–78. On the Reichstag Fire trial, see Georgi Dimitrov, defendant, *Leiptsigskii protsess* (Moscow: Politizdat, 1961).

4. RTsKhIDNI, f. 495, op. 19, d. 248, l. 243; also cited in F. I. Firsov, "Stalin i Komintern," *Voprosy istorii*, 1989, no. 9, p. 11.

fice stating that the three had been granted Soviet citizenship. The Foreign Office was requested to assist in their prompt release and early departure for the Soviet Union.[5]

On 27 February Dimitrov and his comrades, Blagoi Popov and Vasil Tanev, arrived in Moscow, where Dimitrov was received by Stalin on 7 April and, after derogatory comments by Stalin regarding the performance of leading Comintern officials—Dmitry Manuilsky, Wilhelm Knorin, and Pyatnitsky—invited to join the leadership of the Comintern.[6] For all intents and purposes he headed the Communist International from then on, though his formal elevation to the post of secretary general did not occur until the Seventh World Congress in August 1935.[7]

5. Ministerstvo inostrannykh del SSSR, *Dokumenty vneshnei politiki SSSR*, vol. 17 (Moscow: Izd. polit. lit., 1971), docs. 59, 60, 61, 64.

6. Dobrin Michev, "Georgi Dimitrov i podgotovkata na Sedmiya kongres na Komunisticheskiya internatsional," *Vekove* (Sofia), 1972, no. 2, p. 34 (citing Dimitrov's diary).

7. Vasil Tanev was killed after parachuting into Bulgaria during World War II to set up a partisan unit. Blagoi Popov was arrested in November 1938, "confessed," recanted, and was sentenced to fifteen years' confinement. In 1940 Dimitrov requested that Popov and twenty-eight other Bulgarian Communists be released from Soviet labor camps but was turned down by Viktor Abakumov of the NKVD. Popov was finally released and "rehabilitated" after Stalin's death and returned to Bulgaria. See Arkadi Vaksberg, *Hôtel Lux* (Paris: Fayard, 1993), pp. 126–131.

CHAPTER TWO

The "United Front," 1934–1939

JULES HUMBERT-DROZ, a leading Swiss Communist and a senior Comintern representative in the Latin world until he was ousted as a Bukharinite, was acquainted with Georgi Dimitrov. Later he would claim that in 1929 Dimitrov had been sent to Berlin to run the West European Bureau in order to get him out of Moscow, where he was seen as a "right deviationist."[1]

Although this undoubtedly overstates the case, it does point to a political context that is essential for an understanding of Dimitrov's career: the factional struggles between left and right in the Soviet Communist Party, in the Bulgarian Communist Party, and in the Comintern.[2] These struggles—waged in different forms at different times by different actors—were well-nigh continual in the Com-

---

1. Jules Humbert-Droz, *Dix ans de lutte antifasciste* (Neuchâtel: La Baconnière, 1972), p. 112; also cited in E. H. Carr, *Twilight of the Comintern, 1930–1935* (New York: Pantheon, 1982), p. 88n.

2. We are using "right" and "left" not in the Soviet sense by which every such designation amounted to an intolerable deviation from the "general line" and hence required condemnation or worse, but rather as a shorthand for a broad political orientation and temperament that were natural and ubiquitous, even if they could not be explicitly acknowledged or sanctioned. In this (rather simplified) dichotomy, "left" implies utopianism, optimism, a stress on transformation, mobilization, cultural revolution, centralization, violence, and voluntarism, while "right" implies pragmatism, pessimism, a search for stability, gradualism, and determinism.

munist world. In Soviet Russia, Joseph Stalin, from his position as general secretary of the party, had successfully bested his rivals as Lenin's successor by deploying these labels as part of his campaign for control. First, he ousted Leon Trotsky as a leftist, with the support of Grigory Zinoviev and Lev Kamenev; then Zinoviev and Kamenev were in turn tarred with the "leftist" brush, with the help of Nikolai Bukharin; finally, Bukharin and his followers on the Bolshevik "right" were purged. The turn against the "right" in the Soviet party coincided with the end of the NEP and the start of what has sometimes been called the Second Revolution—the forcible collectivization of agriculture, the introduction of a central command economy, and the first Five Year Plan of massive industrialization.[3]

The Comintern, complying with signals from the Stalin leadership, underwent a corresponding shift from moderate alliance-building, which had meant refraining (with a few exceptions) from immediate revolutionary activity, to an "ultra-left" policy of going it alone, "direct action," and preparing for armed struggle. This Third Period, as it is sometimes called, which lasted from 1928 to 1934, proved disastrous for the Comintern and virtually all its parties. Although the Comintern correctly foresaw the economic depression in the West—an inevitable crisis of world capitalism, in its view—it erred profoundly in predicting that this crisis would lead to an upsurge of revolutionary sentiment or that the capitalist powers would opt for war as a way out of the depression. The Comintern's characteristic overoptimism proved unfounded: no Communist parties came close to coming to power; and the Comintern's insistence on lumping together all non-Communist forces produced such divisive labels as "social fascism" for social democracy, and demonstrated the CI's chronic inability to read the political scene abroad.

It would be an error to see the shifts—to the far left and later away

3. See, e.g., Ronald G. Suny, *The Soviet Experiment* (Oxford University Press, 1998); Robert C. Tucker, *Stalin in Power . . . 1928–1941* (New York: Norton, 1990) (in spite of serious reservations about his treatment of Soviet-German relations); Robert V. Daniels, ed., *The Stalin Revolution,* 3d ed. (Lexington, Mass.: D.C. Heath, 1990); Moshe Lewin, *Russian Peasants and Soviet Power* (Evanston, Ill.: Northwestern University Press, 1968). On Soviet foreign policy in this period, see Jonathan Haslam, *The Soviet Union and the Struggle for Collective Security in Europe, 1933– 39* (London: Macmillan, 1984).

from it—as purely opportunistic. Different leaders were committed to different positions. Whereas Stalin was able to preside over several such shifts and manipulate them skillfully, others could not or would not show similar agility, and each turn created its scapegoats. At least until Dimitrov took over, there was also some political differentiation within the Moscow bureaucracy, in line with the saying that where you stood depended on where you sat. In the Comintern, the "left" approach—optimistic, action-oriented, ideological, and at times extraparliamentary—had always been more strongly represented than it was in Soviet diplomacy. In the 1920s the difference in viewpoint between the Comintern's Grigory Zinoviev and the foreign commissar, Georgy Chicherin, was occasionally acknowledged even in the Soviet press. And the Comintern headquarters remained a haven for a number of vocal, dedicated, and stubborn advocates of "heroic" leftism.

Dimitrov's takeover of the Comintern leadership at Stalin's initiative both betokened and carried forward the vigorous abandonment of the "ultra-left" line, marking the espousal of a "united-front" strategy. Some of the International's staff balked at what they saw as a betrayal of revolutionary perspectives and opportunities. As will be seen, some (like Béla Kun) disappeared. Others, like Wilhelm Knorin, tried to resist the line pushed by Dimitrov and such allies as Otto Kuusinen and Dmitry Manuilsky for adoption at the Seventh World Congress, while some senior staffers (such as Osip Pyatnitsky and Solomon Lozovsky) found it difficult to adjust to the new regime and were transferred out of the Comintern. One consequence of the internal resistance was evidently the postponement of the congress from 1934 to 1935; another was probably the liquidation of the diehards (along with many others) in the Great Terror that hit the Soviet Union in the following years.

In the Bulgarian Communist Party, Dimitrov and Vasil Kolarov, who were part of the "older" generation of émigré leaders, identified themselves with the more moderate line, as against younger firebrands operating illegally within Bulgaria. The radical fringe, with apparent support from some in the Comintern, staged a silent coup and ousted the Kolarov-Dimitrov leadership in 1931, at a time of revolutionary activism, only to be replaced in turn when Dimitrov came into his own after the Reichstag Fire trial and Moscow shifted away from the far left: no national section could defy with impunity the general orientation laid down by the Comintern.[4]

To be sure, it was not merely the similarity of political orientations that was required for advancement—indeed, for political survival—in a Soviet-type system: utter loyalty was another essential. Here again Stalin could feel comfortable about Dimitrov. As far back as September 1926 Dimitrov had insisted in a letter to Manuilsky that the "liquidation of the Russian [left] opposition" was a precondition for the survival of the Comintern. As he put it,

> The Russian opposition is becoming a serious disease of the entire Comintern. It would be a fatal mistake to permit the growth and further spread of this disease. I personally am doubtful whether it will be enough to fight it only by means of psychotherapy (information, explaining the essence of the opposition, etc.): this is extraordinarily necessary and important, but it is not sufficient. It will be necessary to resort to the methods of party surgery. However difficult, it will be necessary to cut off the rotten [*gnilye*] members of the VKP(b) and other sections of the Comintern in a timely fashion, so that the entire organism does not become infected. . . . If we succeed in this, it will be 90 percent easier to liquidate as well the destructive opposition in the entire Comintern.[5]

At that time Dimitrov proposed that an ECCI delegation attend a forthcoming conference of the Soviet Communist party to provide active support against the Russian opposition. Indeed, at a Central Committee plenum in October 1926, an ECCI delegation, which included Dimitrov, proclaimed its lack of confidence in Zinoviev and demanded his removal as president of the ECCI. Such loyalty could not go unnoticed by the Stalinists.

1 July 1934

The first major task facing Dimitrov after his appointment was to reorganize the Comintern and reorient it politically, a unique strate-

---

4. On the Bulgarian Communist Party, see Joseph Rothschild, *The Communist Party of Bulgaria* (New York: Columbia University Press, 1959), and Nissan Oren, *Bulgarian Communism* (New York: Columbia University Press, 1971). On Dimitrov's career, see also F. I. Firsov in *Novaya i noveishaya istoriya*, 1982, nos. 1–3.

5. TsPA (Sofia), f. 146, op. 2, a.e. 1740, ll. 4–5.

gic and ideological challenge. For the preceding five years the Soviet Union and the Comintern had pursued an ultra-leftist course. Rejecting alliances with democratic socialists and non-Communist labor unions, the Comintern had derisively labeled these groups social fascists, in line with Stalin's earlier contention that socialists and fascists were "not antipodes but twins." Ultimately, claimed the Comintern, all "class enemies"—whose "class interests" were bound to be objectively identical—were sure to unite against the Soviet Union and the Communists in their own lands. Such an attitude had inevitably led to the self-imposed isolation of the Soviet Union and Communist parties everywhere. At the same time, the labor movement had split into separate federations of rival Communist and non-Communist unions.

But with Hitler's rise to power in 1933 and the failure of the Communists to gain political power in the "capitalist" world, even during the worst of the depression, the ultra-leftist line and the Communists' refusal to forge political alliances were widely perceived as disastrous. Nonetheless, many officials, both in the Comintern apparatus and in Communist parties abroad, stubbornly persisted in the go-it-alone policy for ideological or tactical reasons; moreover, they invoked Moscow's (and ultimately Stalin's) support, not only out of conviction but also because of anxiety over their own political standing if the policy were reversed.

Clearly, Dimitrov's appointment implied a reconsideration of the previous policy, especially since the move was accompanied by a similar reversal already under way in Soviet foreign policy.[6] It is likely that in general terms Dimitrov and Stalin, as well as their surrogates, had discussed the change before his appointment. Soon afterward Dimitrov began to lobby for the policy shift, drawing on the experience of foreign Communist parties like the French.[7] In May 1934 the Presidium of the ECCI announced the preliminary

6. Soviet foreign policy, which had been based on cooperation with Germany since the early 1920s, took on an anti-German cast, highlighted by the Soviet entry into the French- and British-sponsored League of Nations, diplomatic recognition by the United States, and movement toward Franco-Soviet and Soviet-Czechoslovak accords. In addition, the Soviets abandoned their earlier support of revising the military and territorial restrictions imposed on Germany by the Versailles Treaty.

7. Soviet scholars have given Dimitrov's earliest expression on behalf of such a shift as 7 April 1934. On that date Dimitrov also met with the Politburo of the Soviet Communist Party. See *Voprosy istorii KPSS*, no. 7, 1965, pp. 83–88; Boris Leibzon

agenda of the forthcoming world congress. It included as a major item a report by Dimitrov on the tasks of the Communist International in the face of the growing fascist menace and the need for "unity of the working class." While preparing this report, Dimitrov sent Stalin the following letter.

It is hardly surprising that Dimitrov felt he needed Stalin's explicit sanction before proceeding. What is noteworthy, considering the importance of the issue, is that Stalin chose to respond by scribbling a few words in the margin of Dimitrov's letter. And his endorsement was not unequivocal. As on other occasions, he suspiciously responded to some of Dimitrov's ideas by asking, "Against whom is this thesis [directed]?" In fact, as is apparent from Stalin's cryptic comments, he was not yet prepared to depart completely from the ultra-left line. The new policy would need to evolve over the following year. Indeed, it may well be, as has been claimed, that Stalin never explicitly endorsed the Seventh Congress line but instead indicated "tacitly his agreement with the congress' decisions rather than their active support."[8]

The Seventh Congress did mark the official termination of the Third Period of Comintern policy and the start of the new antifascist united-front line. But behind-the-scenes resistance to the change had been so great, not simply in some of the national parties but especially in the ECCI headquarters, that Dimitrov and his allies had found it politic to have the congress postponed from September 1934, first to 15 March and then to 15 July 1935.[9] Dimitrov finally delivered the speech, a major document anticipated in this letter, at the congress on 2 August.

---

and Kirill Shirinya, *Povorot v politike Kominterna* (Moscow: Mysl', 1975); and K. K. Shirinya et al., eds., *VII Kongress Kommunisticheskogo Internatsionala i bor'ba protiv fashizma i voiny* (Moscow: Politizdat, 1975). On 29 April, Dimitrov was elected a member of the ECCI Political Secretariat; on 23 May he was made a member of the ECCI Presidium. See also Georgi Dimitrov, *Pisma, 1905-49* (Sofia: Politizdat, 1962), p. 297, and D. Michev, "Georgi Dimitrov i podgotovkata," *Vekove*, 1972, no. 2.

8. Shirinya et al., *VII Kongress*, p. 308; and F. I. Firsov, "Stalin i Komintern," *Voprosy istorii*, 1989, no. 9, p. 13. Stalin commented positively on the Seventh Congress in a note to Molotov. See Lars T. Lih, Oleg V. Naumov, and Oleg V. Khlevniuk, eds., *Stalin's Letters to Molotov, 1925–1936* (New Haven: Yale University Press, 1995), p. 237.

9. RTSKhIDNI, f. 495, op. 1, d. 4a, and op. 18, d. 988. On the Seventh Congress, see also Carr, *Twilight*, chap. 18, and Kermit McKenzie, *Comintern and World Revolution . . . 1928–1943* (New York: Columbia University Press, 1964), chap. 6.

Document 1

Dimitrov to Stalin, 1 July 1934. RTsKhIDNI, f. 495, op. 73, d. 1, ll. 1–3. Original in Russian. Type-written, with handwritten comments by Stalin. The draft outline has been omitted.

1.7.34

*From C. **Dimitrov***

Dear Com. Stalin!

The enclosed draft outline of [my] speech shows how I see the essence of the speech regarding the 2nd point of the agenda of the congress. In addition, I would like to raise in our forthcoming conversation the following questions:

I. On Social Democracy[10]

1. Whether it is correct to refer to social democracy indiscriminately as social fascism. By taking such a position, we have frequently blocked our way to social democratic workers.[11]

2. Whether it is correct to consider social democracy everywhere? and at all ? times the main social base of the bourgeoisie.[12]

3. Whether it is correct to consider all leftist s[ocial] d[emocratic] groups as the major threat under any ? conditions.[13]

4. Whether it is correct to treat all the leading cadres of the s[ocial] d[emocratic] parties and of the reformist trade unions indiscriminately[14] as conscious traitors of the working class. One can expect, after all, that in the course of struggle quite a few[15] of today's leading functionaries of the s[ocial] d[emocratic] parties and of the reformist trade unions will choose the path of revolution along with the s[ocial] d[emocratic] workers. It is in our interest to facilitate this transition for them and thus accelerate the transition of the s[ocial] d[emocratic] workers to our side.

5. Whether it is time to abandon useless discussion about the possibility or the impossibility of winning over the reformist trade unions instead of clearly formulating the task for its members to transform these trade unions into an instrument of the proletarian class struggle.[16]

---

10. This subhead is also underlined by hand.

11. In the margin, handwritten by Stalin:
As to the leadership — yes; but not "indiscriminate."

12. In the margin, handwritten by Stalin:
Of course, not in Persia.

13. In the margin, handwritten by Stalin:
In the major cap[italist] countries — yes.

14. In the margin, handwritten by Stalin:
Objectively — yes; consciously — some [of them].

15. In the margin, handwritten by Stalin:
"Quite a few" — not; some — yes.

16. In the margin, handwritten by Stalin:
It is time.

6. The question of unifying the revolutionary and reformist trade unions without making the recognition of the hegemony of the Communist Party a necessary condition.[17]

II. On the United Front

1. The necessity to modify our united-front tactics in response to the changed conditions. Rather than using them exclusively[18] as a maneuver to expose social democracy without seriously attempting to forge a real workers' unity through struggle, we must turn them into an effective factor in developing the mass struggle against the offensive of fascism.[19]

2. The necessity to reject the idea that the united front can only ? be built from below, and to stop regarding any ? simultaneous appeal to the leadership of a s[ocial] d[emocratic] party as opportunism.[20]

3. The necessity to launch the active initiative by the masses without petty tutelage of the Communist parties in their relations with the organs of the united front. Not to declare the hegemony of the Communist Party but to assure the actual leadership by the Communist Party.[21]

4. The necessity to radically alter our attitude toward s[ocial] d[emocracy] and non-party workers in all our mass work, agitation, and propaganda. It is essential to go beyond the general statements about the treason of social democracy, and to explain to the workers, concretely and patiently, what the social democratic policy of cooperation with the bourgeoisie is leading to and has already led to.[22] [It is essential] not to dump everything on the s[ocial] d[emocratic] leaders but to point out as well the responsibility of the s[ocial] d[emocratic] workers themselves, to make them think about their own responsibility and to look for the right way of struggle, etc.[23]

III. Regarding the Comintern Leadership

It is essential to change the methods of work and leadership in the Comintern, taking into account that it is impossible effectively to oversee from Moscow every detail of the life of all 65 sections of the Comintern, which find themselves in very different conditions (parties in the metropolis and in the

17. In the margin, handwritten by Stalin:
Conditions are necessary.
18. In the margin, handwritten by Stalin:
Against whom is this thesis [directed]?
19. In the margin, handwritten by Stalin:
[We] must.
20. In the margin, handwritten by Stalin:
Nevertheless, the United Front from below is the foundation.
21. In the margin, handwritten by Stalin:
No doubt, but against whom is this thesis [directed]?
22. In the margin, handwritten by Stalin:
Correct.
23. In the margin, handwritten by Stalin:
Yes!

Оʃ ʋ̃ Димитров

1

1.7.34г Дорогой тов.Сталин!

Из прилагаемой черновой схемы доклада Вы увидите,как я представляю себе характер доклада по 2-му пункту порядка дня Конгресса. Кроме того мне хотелось бы в предстоящем разговоре с Вами поставить следующие вопросы:

1. О социал-демократии.

1.Правильной ли является (огульная) квалификация социал-демократии как социал-фашизма.Этой установкой мы часто преграждали себе путь к социал-демократическим рабочим.

2. Правильно ли считать социал-демократию везде и при всяких условиях главной социальной опорой буржуазии.

3.Правильно ли считать все левые с-д группировки (при всяких условиях главной опасностью.

4.Правильной ли является (огульная) трактовка всех руководящих кадров с-д партий и реформистских профсоюзов как (сознательных) предателей рабочего класса.Ведь можно ожидать,что вместе с с-д рабочими в процессе борьбы перейдут на революционный путь и не мало нынешних ответственных функционеров с-д партий и реформистских профсоюзов;в наших интересах всячески облегчить им этот переход и таким образом ускорить и переход с-д рабочих на нашу сторону.

5.Не пора ли бросить бесполезные разговоры о возможности или невозможности завоевания реформистских профсоюзов,вместо того,чтобы ясно ставить среди их членов задачу превращения этих профсоюзов в орудие классовой борьбы пролетариата.

6.Вопрос об об'единении революционных и реформистских профсоюзов

DOCUMENT 1. First page of Dimitrov to Stalin, 1 July 1934

colonies, parties in highly developed industrial countries and in predominantly peasant countries, legal and illegal parties, etc.).

It is necessary to concentrate on the general political guidance of the Communist movement, on assistance to the parties in basic political and tactical questions, on creating a solid Bolshevik leadership in the local Communist parties, and on strengthening the Communist parties with workers while reducing the heavy bureaucratic apparatus of the ECCI.

It is essential to further promote Bolshevik self-criticism. Fear of this [self-criticism] has at times led to failure to clarify important political problems (questions of the current stage of the crisis and of the so-called military-inflationary juncture, the assessment and lessons of the Austrian events, etc.).

It is impossible to change the methods of leadership and work in the Comintern without partially renewing the cadres of Comintern workers.

It is especially essential to secure close ties between the Comintern leadership and the Politburo of the VKP(b).

---

6 and 25 October 1934

In another early letter to Stalin, Dimitrov raises some basic issues concerning the running of the International and the need, as he sees it, to change both the structure and the personnel of its "leading organs." Though a bit cautious, Dimitrov essentially attacks what had been a central operating assumption ever since the adoption in 1920 of the "Twenty-one Conditions" for admission to the Comintern: the sweeping uniformity of the Soviet model that was prescribed for all member parties and Moscow's authority to dictate their conduct. The notion that Communist policies were set in Moscow and applied worldwide was also congruent with the long-held idea that the International was the General Staff of World Revolution.[24] Because of this insistence on a single authority, the Comintern (and the Soviet leadership), often lacking—or ignoring—local insight into local conditions, repeatedly misjudged the situation abroad, be it in

24. This approach was still part of the ECCI's outlook in early 1934. The draft of the "theses" (probably by Béla Kun) for the fifteenth anniversary of the International still refers to "the single worldwide Communist Party that leads the struggle for the establishment of the dictatorship of the proletariat, for the worldwide USSR, for world communism." This party "leads an irreconcilable struggle against social

regard to Poland in 1920, Germany in 1923, or China in 1927; it also erred fundamentally in its appraisal of fascism and the prospect of war.

Dimitrov's stress on the greater autonomy of the national parties to formulate and pursue their own tactics was given voice at the Seventh World Congress; many years later, this change in policy was cited by prominent Communist leaders like Maurice Thorez of France and Palmiro Togliatti of Italy as an important development that ostensibly foreshadowed their parties' quest for greater independence from Moscow. The significance of the changes actually implemented under Dimitrov remains to be examined further, however. In practice, Moscow's control over the parties remained—administratively, psychologically, and in many instances financially—virtually complete and unchallenged. In Document 2, dealing with the reorganization of the Comintern, Dimitrov makes it clear that he is not thinking of instituting a quasi-parliamentary pluralism but instead is seeking to revamp the central organs of the Comintern to remove the deadwood, as well as (he implies) people he is having trouble working with.

Stalin's reply—one of the few instances where we have a handwritten reply by the *vozhd'* (leader)—reflects both an effort to propitiate Dimitrov with assurances of the Politburo's future support and basic agreement with his argument (which they had apparently discussed before). But it also indicates Stalin's desire to defer action: late 1934 was not the moment for such changes, it seems, and the Comintern was not among Stalin's priorities and preoccupations. Nonetheless, the Soviet delegation to the ECCI clearly received instructions on organizational matters and interparty relations which corresponded closely to Dimitrov's proposals in this letter. As for the personnel changes, the Seventh World Congress eventually provided the occasion for some of them; the Soviet purges during the following years no doubt removed more of the Comintern's staff than Dimitrov could have imagined.

---

democracy . . . against the hegemony of the bourgeoisie in both its forms—fascist and 'democratic.'" In the Third Period of the general crisis of capitalism the Comintern "directs its major fire against rightist opportunism" ("15 let K.I. [proyekt tezisov]," 60 pp., RTsKhIDNI, f. 495, op. 18, d. 988, ll. 1, 9, 48).

Document 2

Dimitrov to Stalin, 6 October 1934, and Stalin reply, 25 October 1934. Dimitrov letter: RTsKhIDNI, f. 495, op. 73, d. 1, ll. 4–7. Original in Russian. Typewritten. Stalin letter: RTsKhIDNI, f. 558, op. 1, d. 3162, ll. 1–2. Original in Russian. Handwritten.

To Com. I. V. STALIN

Esteemed Comrade Stalin,

Having familiarized myself better with the situation in the Comintern, I came to the conclusion that the changes which are taking place in the international workers' movement and the tasks before the Comintern, especially regarding the struggle to unify the working class against fascism and the threat of war, require the urgent revision of and change in the work methods of the Comintern's leading organs.

After an exchange of opinions with the leading comrades in the Comintern, I became convinced that such a change is impossible without intervention by and assistance from you and the Politburo of the CC VKP(b). This is all the more essential as the solution to these problems is complicated by a certain conservatism and bureaucratic routine embedded in the Comintern leadership, as well as by unhealthy relations among the comrades who directly participate in the Comintern leadership.

Without prejudging where and how these issues will be raised and resolved, I consider it essential to put before you those concepts which, in my opinion, should govern the revision of the work methods of the Comintern's leading organs.

In drafting these concepts, I based my ideas on the two following notions:

1. The impossibility of effectively controlling from Moscow all the Comintern sections, which find themselves in very diverse conditions (legal and illegal parties, parties in the metropolis and in the colonies, parties in highly developed industrial countries and those in predominantly agrarian countries, etc.).

2. The necessity of strengthening the general ideological-political leadership of the Communist movement by the Comintern as the world party of the proletariat while at the same time systematically developing the autonomy and initiative of its sections and assisting in the creation of local Bolshevik leadership. Our major weakness is precisely this lack of firm, secure, and independent local leadership.

In my opinion, the work methods of the leading Comintern organs have to be reconsidered roughly on the basis of the following suggestions:

1. Shift the emphasis of the Comintern leadership's work to resolving major questions of policy and tactics, while concentrating [our] major effort on strengthening the leadership of the sections, so that they can solve their political, tactical, and organizational problems independently, on the basis of the Comintern's general guidelines, and so that the everyday administration [of the sections] can systematically shift to the local [leadership]. In current prac-

tice the leading organs of the Comintern are charged with resolving all of the sections' problems—which results on the one hand in the impossibility of concentrating on the major issues and on the other in the Comintern sections' habitually waiting for decisions from Moscow without developing initiatives of their own and without assuming responsibility for the leadership of their parties.

2. The Comintern must implement its political leadership of the individual sections on the basis of a thorough, discrete study of the specific conditions and peculiarities of the Communist movement in each country, using the methods of explanation, persuasion, and friendly advice and trying to avoid substituting the leadership of the Comintern organs (in composing and publishing documents on behalf of the parties, petty tutelage, etc.) for an individual party's leadership.

As a rule, every major political decision regarding individual countries must be adopted by the Comintern leadership in agreement with the leadership of that section. In case there are objections from the section's leadership, the question has to be reexamined with the participation of the direct representatives of that party's C[entral] C[ommittee].

As a rule, organizational questions must be solved independently by the Comintern's sections. The Comintern leadership must serve as an instance of appeal in cases where the organizational questions become the cause for dissent in the leadership of a given section. The Comintern leadership must take the initiative to resolve these questions in cases where, owing to the threat of factional struggle or where sections are illegal, the Comintern's intervention is absolutely necessary.

3. The Comintern leadership must pay special attention to those parties that are doing illegal work, to help them with its experience in illegal work, to assist them in creating an illegal apparatus and in undertaking a number of practical measures against provocation, as well as to secure the replacement of leading comrades lost [to our ranks] with workers trained in advance.

4. Contributing to promoting initiative and responsibility of the sections, the Comintern leadership must, in particular:

a) assist in creating and strengthening truly Bolshevik local leadership, to promote the growth and education of party cadres;

b) provide effective support to the parties in the matter of agitation and propaganda, and in their ideological struggle with political opponents;

c) work systematically with the leading foreign comrades, to help them in their political growth and in their promotion to leading positions in the Comintern.

5. While utilizing the experience of the VKP(b)'s work, and popularizing it among the Communist parties, it is nevertheless necessary to avoid the mechanical transfer of the VKP(b)'s work methods to the Communist parties in

Товарищу Димитрову.

Письмо Ваше получил. С ответом, как видите, запоздал, за что приношу извинение. Я пребывал в отпуску, не сижу на одном месте, а брожу по разным углам ввиду чего и мог получить Ваше письмо лишь с некоторым опозданием...

Я целиком согласен с Вами на счет пересмотра методов работы органов КИ, реорганизации последних и изменения их личного состава. Я уже говорил Вам как-то об этом во время беседы с Вами в ЦК ВКП/б/.

Теперь дело в том, чтобы придать помощникам Вашего

письма конкретно: види
наметить новые формы ор-
ганов КИ, наметить их
личный состав и предельный
момент, к которому сле-
довало бы приурочить прак-
тическое осуществление
этого дела.

Надеюсь, — скоро уви-
димся и поговорим обо всем
этом подробно.

Не сомневаюсь, что
Политбюро ЦК ВКП(б)
поддержит вас.

Привет!

И. Сталин.

25/X - 34.

the capitalist countries, [to parties] that are working under completely different conditions and are at quite a different level of development.

Distilling the experience of the world Communist movement and using it in its work, the Comintern leadership must, at the same time, carefully consider the variety of conditions and the unevenness of development of the Communist movement in different countries, avoiding a wholesale approach and substituting general statements and stereotyped formulations for concrete Marxist analysis and a serious study of a given question.

6. Taking into consideration the vital importance of solid Bolshevik cadres in organizing and directing the struggle of the masses, the Comintern leadership must base its policy of educating cadres on helping to promote workers who have authentic ties to the masses, who have proved, by their work with the masses, their devotion to the cause of the working class—[promoting] those [cadres] who have been tested and forged in the struggle, those firmly conducting the party line and capable of independently finding their way in [any] situation, and [capable of] taking responsibility for the necessary decisions.

After reviewing and changing the methods of work of the Comintern's leading organs, it will be necessary to reorganize these organs accordingly and to make appropriate changes in their compositon.

With communist greetings,

GD

6.10.34.

To Comrade Dimitrov

I have received your letter. As you can see, I am late in replying, and I apologize for that. Here on vacation I do not sit in one place but move from one location to another. As a result, I received your letter after some delay . . .

I entirely agree with you regarding the review of the methods of work of the CI organs, their reorganization and the changes in their composition. I have already mentioned this to you during our meeting at the CC VKP(b).

Now the question is to concretize the ideas [outlined] in your letter, to draft new forms for the CI organs, to draft their composition, and to determine the appropriate time for implementing this.

I hope to see you soon and to discuss it all in detail.

I have no doubt that the Politburo of the CC VKP(b) will support you. Greetings!

I. Stalin.

25/X/34.

27 January 1936

We have no evidence that Stalin and Dimitrov exchanged any written communications at the time of the Seventh World Congress or in its immediate aftermath, although it is virtually certain that they conferred personally, by telephone, and through their deputies. Indeed, we know that Stalin instructed the Politburo to approve a list of key personnel changes he had in mind.[25]

By January 1936 Dimitrov wished to raise several major questions with Stalin stemming from the congress' decisions, as well as discuss the implications of Italy's recent invasion of Ethiopia. Dimitrov singled out two international organizations for attack, the Profintern (Red International of Labor Unions) and MOPR (International Red Aid); both had been assailed at the Seventh World Congress, and in characteristic terminology, the congress now declared them bureaucratic and "sectarian" (the standard adjective for impermissible leftism). Dimitrov uses the strongest arguments he has to turn Stalin against these bodies, declaring the Profintern counterproductive at a time when the aim was to merge Communist with non-Communist unions abroad. As for MOPR, he charged its leadership with lack of vigilance—a dangerous allegation in the days of the terror. In the end, he gained Stalin's support for the reorganization or purge of the two groups, although each lasted for another year or two.[26]

25. Stalin "proposed" the names of the Russian members of the ECCI, the ECCI Presidium, and the Secretariat of the ECCI (RTsKhIDNI, f. 558, op. 2, d. 6158, ll. 1–2). On 10 August, before the congress' vote, the Politburo approved his selections, including the appointment of Dimitrov as general secretary and the transfer of Pyatnitsky to work outside the International (RTsKhIDNI, f. 17, op. 162, d. 18, l. 110).

26. In spring 1936 the question arose of how to handle efforts to organize a world peace congress, promoted by a broad coalition and sponsored largely by British and French pacifists. At Dimitrov's suggestion, after canvassing the CPSU Politburo, the Central Committee decided to hand the problem over to the Soviet labor union federation, which had been active in international front organizations, and instructed Nikolai Shvernik, its secretary, to join the organizing committee. The congress eventually took place in Brussels in September 1936, with substantial (though clandestine) Soviet financing; see RTsKhIDNI, f. 495, op. 73, d. 15, ll. 21ff. This was one of several international enterprises in which Communists sought to gain a significant foothold worldwide camouflaged by a coalition of organizations.

On the Communist Youth International (KIM), see Richard Cornell, *Revolutionary Vanguard* (Toronto: University of Toronto Press, 1982).

Document 3

Dimitrov to Stalin, 27 January 1936. RTsKhIDNI, f. 495, op. 73, d. 48, ll. 3–5. Original in Russian. Typewritten.

Copy.

To Com. STALIN

Dear Comrade Stalin!

We have a number of questions on which we need your advice and direction, mostly related to the practical implementation of the decisions of the Seventh Comintern Congress.

First, the question about trade union unity.

After the merging of the reformist and Red unions in France and Spain, the question of international trade union unity and, in particular, of our attitude toward the Amsterdam international organization is becoming very timely. A number of the Soviet trade unions (educators, transport workers, miners) have received offers from the secretariats of the corresponding internationals that are members of the Amsterdam organization to join these professional internationals. In the English trade unions, as well as in the united French trade unions, there is a growing mood among the masses in favor of a rapprochement with the Soviet trade unions. Pollitt from England and Thorez [and] Frachon from France insist on [giving] a positive answer to the offer to include the Soviet unions of educators, miners, and transport workers in the corresponding internationals. We think that accepting this offer would significantly promote the cause of international trade union unity, accelerate radicalization in the ranks of the mass unions in the capitalist countries, make the Soviet trade unions a magnet for all the left elements of the reformist trade union movement, help our comrades in the capitalist countries to strengthen their positions in the mass trade unions, and, in some countries where the Communist parties are illegal, provide an opportunity for semilegal activities of Communists in the trade unions. This prompts a question: What to do with the Profintern, how to reorganize it, and on what to concentrate its activities so that it might justify its existence in the future? In its present form, the Profintern not only fails to contribute to the creation of international trade union unity but in some sense is even a hindrance to it. It is also important to consider that after the trade union merger in France and Spain, the Profintern has lost its independent trade union base in the capitalist countries.

The second question is about MOPR. In its present form, in capitalist countries MOPR is a sectarian organization, sometimes just an apparatus for agitation and distribution of help from [Moscow] center. The number of MOPR members there is usually smaller than the number of members of the Communist parties. In effect, MOPR duplicates the Communist Party in its policies and practical work. At the same time, the hatred of fascism found in the largest sectors of the population of capitalist countries and the growth of the united-front movement open broad possibilities for building a large, legal mass organization in most capitalist countries, rather than remaining underground, as now. However, the current MOPR leadership, used to sectarian methods of work, gives no assurance that it would be up to this task. Besides, [we hear] complaints from all the Communist parties against the present leadership of MOPR, accusing MOPR of a bureaucratic approach. MOPR leadership also fails to use the necessary vigilance, which results in the penetration of the USSR by agents of the class enemy disguised as political émigrés. We consider it necessary to introduce changes in the MOPR leadership, first of all to put at its head a secretariat composed of foreign comrades like Tom Bell (England), Dolores (Spain), Miner (USA) and a suitable representative of the VKP(b). This secretariat would be charged with reviewing MOPR's work methods and with preparing an international congress (to be held abroad) of all antifascist organizations ready to extend political and material support to the struggle against fascism and to the victims of this struggle. This congress should result in the creation of a new world organization headquartered abroad. MOPR will become a component of this mass organization.

The third question concerns the <u>use of sanctions</u> by the League of Nations, on which the Second International is speculating. Should we resolutely support applying and extending sanctions against Italy (oil sanctions)? Should we not [also] move against Germany, Austria, Switzerland, and Belgium, through which Italy makes all the purchases it needs? How to accord our attitude toward the sanctions by the League of Nations with the so-called proletarian sanctions, i.e., sanctions initiated by the working class itself (delaying transports for Italy, etc.)? Would it not be beneficial, for the sake of proletarian sanctions, to propose a meeting of the representatives of the Soviet trade unions and the representatives of the Amsterdam international of trade unions? Should we extend a new offer to the Second International to mobilize the masses [in support of] real application of sanctions against Italy, and use this proposal [as a tool] against the double-dealing policies of the Second International on this question?

I beg you to receive me and Com. Manuilsky in the immediate future regarding the questions raised in this letter.

With fraternal greetings,

G. Dimitrov.

Moscow,
27/I/36.

28 November 1937

The Great Terror reached its peak in 1937. Among its victims were not only many of the most prominent leaders of the Bolshevik party and the Red Army but also a substantial number of Soviet and foreign officials associated with the Communist International.[27] Usually, the arrest and subsequent liquidation of the victims were based on their individual "cases." But Moscow could also condemn an entire organization; in one of the most dramatic of such instances, the Comintern ordered the dissolution of the Communist Party of Poland in 1937

It is still not clear why the Polish Communists were singled out for such treatment. Although other foreign parties were heavily hit by purges, none suffered as brutally as the Poles: at least thirty of thirty-seven members of the Central Committee were purged. Speculation among observers abroad centered on Stalin's suspicions of Trotskyist sympathies among Polish party members, on the prevalence of Jews in the leadership, and on Poland's geopolitical importance to the Soviet Union. But these arguments could equally apply to Communist parties in other countries. The idea that the dissolution was meant as a hint to Nazi Germany that Stalin might be seeking an accommodation seems totally wide of the mark. It is noteworthy, however, that the purge was carried out before the party was dissolved—which shifted responsibility from the Soviet government (and particularly, the NKVD) to the Comintern.

The closest thing to a contemporary explanation was an article published in 1938 in the journal *Communist International* that speaks of widespread infiltration of the party by Polish police.[28] The

27. On the purges in the Comintern, see the volume on the Communist International and the repression of the 1930s edited by William J. Chase forthcoming in this series. See also Branko Lazitch, "Stalin's Massacre of the Foreign Communist Leaders," and comments by Boris Souvarine in Milorad Drachkovitch and Branko Lazitch, eds., *The Comintern: Historical Highlights* (New York: Praeger, 1966); Evgeniya Ginzburg, *Journey into the Whirlwind* (New York: Harcourt, Brace, 1967); Alfred Burmeister [pseud.], *Dissolution and Aftermath of the Comintern* (New York: Research Program on the USSR, 1955); Walter Krivitsky, *In Stalin's Secret Service* (New York: Harper, 1940); Arkadi Vaksberg, *Hôtel Lux* (Paris: Fayard, 1993); Margarete Buber-Neumann, *Under Two Dictators* (New York: Dodd, Mead, 1949); and Suzanne Leonhard, *Gestohlenes Leben* (Frankfurt: Nikolaische Verlagsanstalt, 1968).

28. I. A. Święcicki [pseud.], "Provokatory za rabotoi," *Kommunisticheskii In-*

draft resolution for the dissolution of the Polish Communist Party printed below, which Dimitrov sent to Stalin, supports this allegation. But though there had probably been instances of such penetration, the evidence to support the charges included in the resolution was as fictitious as that relating to other victims of the purges. Indeed, the idea that the intelligence service of the Polish "fascists" engineered party divisions, infiltrated the party, took over its leadership, and promoted "Trotskyist-Bukharinist" agents to run it was ridiculous. No doubt many on the staff of the ECCI did not believe the charges but in the political atmosphere of the time would not risk questioning or objecting to them.

After Stalin's death, when Nikita Khrushchev delivered his so-called Secret Speech to the Twentieth Congress of the Soviet party, a hand-picked group of international Communist leaders publicly acknowledged the total baselessness of the charges.[29]

ternatsional, 1938, no. 1; [English translation as Y. Sventsitski, "Provocateurs at Work," *Communist International,* 1938, no. 2, pp. 193–196. The Comintern resolution dissolving the Polish party was published some fifty years later in Jarema Maciszewski, ed., *Tragedia Komunistycznej Partii Polski* (Warsaw: Książka i Wiedza, 1989), pp. 219–222.

Other national parties were also heavily hit; one article later claimed that there were individual victims in at least twenty-six Communist parties. Tito later asserted that in 1938 when he was in Moscow, "we were discussing whether to dissolve the Yugoslav Communist Party or not" (Dedijer, *Tito Speaks* [London: Weidenfeld and Nicolson, 1953], p. 391).

On the fate of the Polish party and the role of the Comintern (and Stalin's comment, cited above), see F. I. Firsov and I. S. Yazhborovskaya, "Komintern i Kommunisticheskaya partiya Pol'shi," *Voprosy istorii KPSS,* 1988, no. 12, pp. 40–55; and their "Miedzynarodòwka Komunistyczna a Kom. Partia Polski," in Maciszewski, *Tragedia,* pp. 9–79. The article reveals that Mikhail Trilisser ("Moskvin"), a high NKVD official appointed to the ECCI at Stalin's urging, was responsible for supervising the Polish and Baltic parties for the ECCI.

29. See *Trybuna Ludu* (Warsaw), 19 February 1956; translated in *Pravda,* 21 February 1956.

Document 4

Dimitrov to Stalin, 28 November 1937, with enclosed draft resolution of the ECCI. RTsKhIDNI, f. 495, op. 74, d. 402, ll. 2–6. Original in Russian. Typewritten with handwritten comments by Stalin.

Top secret.[30]

Dear Comrade Stalin!

We are thinking of passing the attached resolution on the dissolution of the Polish Communist Party in the ECCI Presidium, and then publishing it.

After publishing this resolution, we would send an open letter to the Polish Communists that would reveal in greater detail the enemy's decomposing activities within the ranks of the Communist Party and the Polish workers' movement.

In reestablishing the CP of Poland, it has been suggested that a special organizational commission be formed. We plan to select some of the members of this commission from the most distinguished and tested fighters from the International Brigades in Spain.

We beg you, Comrade Stalin, to give your advice and directives:

1. Regarding this issue, whether this announcement will be expedient before the investigation of the former Polish party leaders under arrest is completed, or should we wait longer?

2. Regarding the contents and the character of the resolution on the dissolution of the CP of Poland itself.

With fraternal greetings,

G. Dimitrov

No. 132/ld

28 November 1937

T[op] Secret.

RESOLUTION OF THE EXECUTIVE COMMITTEE
OF THE COMMUNIST INTERNATIONAL

Polish fascism, unable to cope with the growing mass revolutionary movement by means of overt terror alone, has made espionage, sabotage, and provocation the major tool of its struggle against the workers' movement, against all antifascist, democratic forces, [having] poisoned the entire political and social life in Poland with this foul system. For many years, it has been planting its spies and agents among all the workers' and peasants' democratic organi-

---

30. Handwritten in the margin:

N1433/2 XII 37

Across the letter, Stalin wrote:

The dissolution is about two years late. It is necessary to dissolve [the party], but in my opinion, [this] should not be published in the press.

This resolution was first published in *Voprosy istorii KPSS*, 1988, no. 12, p. 52.

zations. However, the Pilsudchiks[31] made a special effort to infiltrate the Communist movement, which represents the greatest threat for Polish fascism.

The Executive Committee of the Communist International has established, on the basis of irrefutable documentary evidence, that for a number of years enemies, agents of Polish fascism, have been operating within the leadership structures of the Polish Communist Party. By organizing splits, often fictitious, within the workers', national-democratic, and petty-bourgeois organizations, the Pilsudchiks poured their spies and provocateurs into the Communist Party, disguised as oppositional elements coming over to the ranks of the Communist movement (the PPS group headed by Sochacki-Bratkowski, the Poalei-Zion group headed by Henrykowski and Lampe, the Ukrainian s[ocial] d[emocratic] group, the UVO group of Wasyłkiw-Turianski, Korczyk's group of Belorussian SRs, the "Wyzwolenie" group of Wojewódzki).[32] By arranging the arrests so as to remove the most loyal elements from the Communist ranks, the Polish defenziwa [counterintelligence] gradually advanced its agents into leading positions in the Communist Party. At the same time, in order to give its agents provocateurs and spies authority among the workers [and] members of the Communist Party after staging mock trials, the fascists would often subject their own agents to imprisonment so that later they could be liberated, at the earliest convenience, by organizing "escapes" or by "exchanges" for spies and saboteurs caught red-handed in the USSR. With the help of their agents in the leading organs of the party, the Pilsudchiks promoted their people (for example, Żarski, Sochacki, Dombał) to the Communist faction of the Sejm [parliament] during the elections to the Sejm, instructed them to deliver provocative speeches, which the fascists used to attack the Soviet Union and for the bloody repression of the workers' and peasants' movement.

The gang of spies and provocateurs entrenched in the leadership of the Polish Communist Party, having planted, in turn, agents in the periphery of the party organization, systematically betrayed the best sons of the working class to the class enemy. By organizing failures, [they were] destroying, year after year, party organizations in the Polish heartland, as well as in Western Belorussia and Western Ukraine. [This gang] systematically perverted the party's political line so as to weaken the influence of communism among the masses, to make the party increasingly alien and hostile to the Communist International. For its work of disintegration, Polish fascism widely used the Trotskyist-Bukharinist reprobates, [who] either were already, or were willingly becoming, agents of the Polish defenziwa, by virtue of having a common political outlook with fascism. The

31. *Pilsudchiks:* a derisive name used to describe the Polish government under Marshal Piłsudski, and a generic term for his followers. Józef Piłsudski was a leader of the right wing of the Polish Socialist Party. In 1918 he was war minister, and between 1918 and 1922 head of state. After May 1926 he was again war minister, then prime minister, and later inspector general of Poland's armed forces—Trans.

32. Various Polish, Jewish, Ukrainian, and Belorussian groups.

Дорогой товарищ Сталин!

Мы думаем провести через Президиум ИККИ прилагаемое здесь постановление о роспуске Коммунистической партии Польши и потом его опубликовать.

После опубликования этого постановления, следовало бы обратиться с открытым письмом к польским коммунистам, в котором более подробно вскрыть разлагающую работу врага в рядах Компартии и рабочего движения Польши.

По восстановлению КП Польши предвидится создание специальной организационной комиссии. Часть людей для этой комиссии мы хотим подобрать из наиболее отличившихся и проверенных бойцов, сражающихся в Интернациональных бригадах в Испании.

Очень просим, товарищ Сталин, Вашего совета и указания:

1. По вопросу, целесообразно ли делать это выступление до окончания следствия в отношении арестованных бывших руководителей польской партии, или нужно еще подождать.

2. По содержанию и характеру самого постановления о роспуске КП Польши.

С товарищеским приветом

№: 132/18

28 ноября 1937 г.

DOCUMENT 4. First page of Dimitrov to Stalin, 28 November 1937

Polish defenziwa kindled the factional struggle in the party, through its agents both in the Kostrzewa-Warski group and in the Lenski-Henrykowski group, and used both factions to disorganize the party and its work among the masses, and to separate the workers from the Communist Party.

However, the most ignoble role that this espionage agency played was following the directives of the fascist intelligence in relation to the USSR. Playing on the nationalist prejudices of the most backward masses among the Polish people, it sought to create obstacles to the rapprochement of the peoples of Poland and the peoples of the USSR, and in the interests of the fascist warmongers, to wreck the cause of peace that is selflessly defended by the great country of the Soviets. At the same time, this network of class enemies, disguised as political émigrés, was transferred by Polish fascism to the USSR so as to conduct espionage, sabotage, and wrecking activities.

All attempts to purge the agents of Polish fascism from the ranks of the Communist movement, while retaining the current organization of the Polish Communist Party, proved futile, since the central party organs were in the hands of spies and provocateurs who used the difficult situation of the underground party to remain in its leadership.

Based on all this and in order to give honest Polish Communists a chance to rebuild the party, once it is purged of all agents of Polish fascism, the Executive Committee of the Communist International, in accordance with the statutes and the decisions of the congresses of the Communist International, resolves:

1. To dissolve the Polish Communist Party because of its saturation with spies and provocateurs.

2. To recommend that all honest Communists, until the re-creation of the Polish Communist Party, shift the emphasis of their work to those mass organizations where there are workers and toilers, while fighting to establish the unity of the workers' movement and to create in Poland a popular antifascist front.

At the same time, the ECCI warns the Communists and the Polish workers against any attempt by Polish fascism and its Trotskyist-Bukharinist espionage network to create a new organization of espionage and provocation, under the guise of a pseudo-Communist Party of Poland, to corrupt the Communist movement.

The Communist International knows that thousands of Polish workers sacrifice themselves and their lives to serving and protecting the vital interests of the toiling masses; it knows that the heroic Polish proletariat had, in its glorious revolutionary past, many remarkable moments of struggle against the tsarist and Austro-Hungarian monarchies, against Polish fascism. It knows about the heroic deeds of the Dombrowski battalions sent by the Polish proletariat to defend the Spanish people. It is convinced that the Polish proletariat will have [again] a Communist party, purged of the foul agents of the class enemy, which will indeed lead the struggle of the Polish toiling masses for their liberation.

Stalin returned this document to Dimitrov on 2 December, with a handwritten message scribbled across the cover letter: "The dissolution is about two years late. It is necessary to dissolve [the party], but in my opinion, [this] should not be published in the press." For reasons that are not apparent from the record, the resolution was not formally approved by canvassing the members of the ECCI Presidium until 16 August 1938.[33] Previously, to show its loyalty and as a preemptive self-defense, the ECCI Presidium on 3 February 1937 had discussed and adopted a lengthy document which, as Dimitrov wrote Stalin in transmitting the text for his comments before its publication, was intended to expose and pillory the so-called anti-Soviet Trotskyist center, whose alleged members had been convicted in a major show trial in January 1937. (Dimitrov, Kuusinen, and Dmitry Manuilsky were instructed to edit the text.)[34] Stalin discussed this document with Dimitrov on 11 February. According to Dimitrov's diary, Stalin was dismissive, even remarking ominously that "all of you in the Comintern are serving [na ruku] the enemy"[35] At Stalin's request, a letter whose contents were in line with Stalin's directives was substituted for the resolution and sent to all member organizations. Dimitrov sent Stalin the

33. On the reestablishment of the Polish Communist Party during the war, see below, Chapter 9.

34. RTsKhIDNI, f. 495, op. 73, d. 48, l. 65, and op. 2, d. 244, ll. 138–146. One incident that called for especial vigilance and a particularly vigorous response on the part of the ECCI staff involved a veteran Hungarian Communist, Zoltan Török, who had worked in the ECCI Cadre Section (Personnel Department). Török, suspected of close ties to Béla Kun, who was being eased out, was dismissed on orders of his superviser Manuilsky. Török responded by sending Stalin a broad denunciation of the ECCI, implying that it had been penetrated by former Trotskyists and hinting at various other offenses. Dimitrov instructed Manuilsky to investigate and produce a report, which in turn made a number of charges against Török. In self-defense Manuilsky insisted that the Cadre Section had been active and vigilant in identifying class enemies, having turned over to the NKVD information on some three thousand people suspected of espionage, "provocation," or "diversionary" activities. "A number of the biggest cases concerning the Polish, Romanian, Hungarian, and other parties most infected by provocation and alien anti-party elements were raised by the Cadre Section in a proper and timely fashion. In the Central Committees of a number of parties with the help of the Cadre Section, alien elements, agents of the class enemy, were identified." In the end, the material on Török was turned over to the NKVD, and in 1938 Török was arrested. (He was released ten years later.) The Cadre Section, and with it the ECCI, thus weathered one more set of charges at a particularly trying time. See RTsKhIDNI, f. 546, op. 1, d. 331, l. 90; and f. 495, op. 73, d. 48, l. 55; f. 495, op. 10a, d. 391, ll. 44–50; f. 495, op. 199, d. 2386, ll. 102–104.

35. TsPA (Sofia), f. 146, op. 2, a.e. 3.

new text on 17 February 1937.[36] The ECCI drafters unhesitatingly repeated the fabricated charges; in addition, they accused themselves of having underestimated the danger of Trotskyism, in effect calling for purges comparable to those going on in the Soviet Union to be undertaken in all foreign Communist parties. Stalin was still dissatisfied.[37]

26 January 1938

The fundamental issue in Communist strategy and tactics—the definition and order of importance of allies and enemies—bedeviled the policymakers and analysts throughout the life of the Comintern (and for that matter, before and afterward as well). Characteristically, the periods of radical, "left" communism were marked by a go-it-alone policy; in substance, the CPSU proclaimed a plague on all their rivals' and enemies' houses, professing to see a fundamental identity among them. This orientation resulted in the splitting of the labor movement (in some specialists' judgment, this contributed decisively to Hitler's takeover of power in 1933). By contrast, in periods of "rightist" strategy (not so designated by the Communists themselves), Communists strove for "united fronts," "popular fronts," or later "national fronts" against particular enemies— notably, fascism, as in France or Austria, or an aggressive Japan, in the case of China.

The Dimitrov years in the Comintern were identified with a return from the ultra-left course of the depression years to a search for a united front, within each country, and for European alliances against Nazi Germany. As Dimitrov expressed it at the Seventh World Congress: "The first thing that must be done, the thing with

---

36. RTsKhIDNI, f. 495, op. 73, d. 48, l. 66, and op. 2, d. 245, ll. 53–72.

37. RTsKhIDNI, f. 495, op. 73, d. 48, ll. 86–94. One of the Comintern's targets was Willi Münzenberg, a German exile operating out of Paris and long a committed Communist of exceptional skill. Münzenberg had organized a variety of front organizations and publications, but he was becoming increasingly alienated from the party by Soviet and Comintern behavior during the years of the purge. After the Comintern made repeated requests that he return to Moscow, he broke with Moscow; he was killed in 1940 under mysterious circumstances. See Babette Gross, *Willi Münzenberg* (Stuttgart: DVA, 1967); Helmut Gruber, "Willi Münzenberg, Propagandist for and Against the Comintern," *International Review of Social History,* 1965, vol. 10, no. 2, pp. 188–210.

which to begin, is to form a united front, to establish unity of action of the workers in every factory, in every district, in every region, in every country, all over the world. Unity of action of the proletariat on a national and international scale is the mighty weapon which renders the working class capable not only of successful defense but also of successful counterattack against fascism, against the class enemy."[38]

But in fact this is where the problem began: What sort of "united front" were Communists to pursue? With whom? Who would make decisions within it? What organizational and financial autonomy would each participant maintain? What if the partners had basic disagreements? In practice, within the general framework of Comintern policy, the situation developed differently in different countries. Meanwhile, the united-front policy aroused considerable resistance among the Comintern staff and was indirectly responsible for the ouster (and at times, purge) of a number of veteran staffers.

One example of the difficulty of the united-front policy was the situation in France, where the Communists faced the challenge of creating one with the Socialists while at the same time resisting joining a coalition government led by Socialist Léon Blum. The problem became real when the united-front coalition won the parliamentary elections in May 1936.

Although he had earlier held rigidly to the "social-fascist" line of denouncing non-Communist leftists, Maurice Thorez, head of the Communist Party of France (though not the entire PCF leadership), favored having Communists join the cabinet, but on 12 May, Dimitrov sent him a cable: "Under present circumstances in France . . . the Communists' participation in the cabinet is not a matter of principle but one of expediency. We believe it to be the correct position of the party not to participate in the government but to support it against the right for the sake of implementing the program of the popular

38. Seventh Congress of the Communist International, *Abridged Stenographic Report of Proceedings* (Moscow: Foreign Languages Publishing House, 1939), p. 142. There is no verbatim transcript of the Seventh Congress, but we have no reason to question the authenticity of this statement. On French politics, cf. Carr, *Twilight;* Irwin Wall, *French Communism in the Era of Stalin* (Westport, Conn.: Greenwood, 1983); Philippe Robrieux, *Histoire intérieure du Parti communiste,* vol. 1: *1920–1945* (Paris: Fayard, 1980); Ronald Tiersky, *French Communism, 1920-1972* (New York: Columbia University Press, 1974).

front."[39] One may assume (by analogy with other such cases) that Dimitrov had first secured Stalin's consent to this message. During the succeeding months, with Stalin's approval, he advised Thorez more than once not to push criticism of French policy at home and abroad to the point of precipitating a government crisis.[40]

The situation changed somewhat on 10 January 1938, when Blum's successor as premier, Camille Chautemps, was forced to resign. According to Thorez's report to Dimitrov, below, this was the result of British pressure; ostensibly England wished to get rid of the anti-Nazi elements, so as to seek an accord with the Germans. There is no independent evidence to support Thorez's version of the French government crisis. This raises some questions (as did some of the reporting from Spain and elsewhere) about the impact of misleading perceptions on Soviet policymakers and top-level analysts of "information" distributed by the Comintern.

Document 5

Dimitrov to Stalin, 26 January 1938. RTsKhIDNI, f. 495, op. 74, d. 517, l. 1. Original in Russian. Typewritten.

To Comrade Stalin

Com. DECAUX, a member of the CC CP of France, is here and is planning to return [to France] tomorrow evening.

Comrade Thorez informs [us] that the latest government crisis was generated under direct influence from the English conservatives aiming at destroying the popular front and creating a government in France which would in no way depend on the Communists. They consider this a necessary condition for

---

39. RTsKhIDNI, f. 495, op. 184, iskh. 1936, d. 43, l. 97. The same question had arisen even earlier, in October 1935, when Thorez had declared that the PCF was prepared to take responsibility for the formation of an antifascist popular-front government. In Dimitrov's absence Manuilsky was instructed to send Thorez a coded cable indicating that the ECCI Secretariat was "alarmed" by the mood in the PCF in favor of Communist participation in a popular-front cabinet: "The situation is not ripe" for such a development (RTsKhIDNI, f. 495, op. 18, d. 1023, l. 144; and op. 184, iskh. 1935, d. 44, l. 37). Dimitrov, on leave in Kislovodsk, wired Manuilsky "full support" of the line taken with regard to the PCF (RTsKhIDNI, f. 495, op. 18, vkhod. 1935, d. 20, l. 14).

40. RTsKhIDNI, f. 495, op. 74, d. 510, ll. 63, 65. See also Victor Loupan and Pierre Lorrain, *L'Argent de Moscou* (Paris: Plon, 1994).

satisfactorily adjusting relations with Germany. Chautemps, Bonnet, and Delbos, along with the English, will seek agreement with Hitler. Our party considers it essential to pursue flexible tactics with regard to the Chautemps government: on the one hand, to press the government by means of mass movements in the spirit of the popular-front program in order to prevent the destruction of the popular front, and on the other, to refuse to give a vote of No Confidence in the government in the parliament.

The party has to direct its main attention to launching a mass movement to safeguard the popular front and carry out its program. During the crisis, more than 80,000 telegrams from Communists, Socialists, and radical and other organizations and meetings were received from all over the country.

If you consider it necessary to give Com. Thorez any special directives (which can be done personally through the comrade who is leaving for France), please inform us about them.

With fraternal greetings,

G D

26 January 1938.
No. 156/ld.

---

19 March 1938

On 11 March the Secretariat of the ECCI decided to recommend that the PCF refrain from joining the cabinet but that it lend its full support to what was still nominally a popular-front government. On 19 March Dimitrov and Manuilsky forwarded a message to Stalin that was received from Thorez "after we gave the French Communist Party instructions not to participate in the Blum government"—a frank statement of Moscow's directing role. Thorez appears rather unhappy with the instructions he has received from Moscow, that once again the Communists are not to participate in the new French coalition government.

Thorez was explicit: "Rejecting such participation will either undermine the national concentration of forces or else this concentration will occur without us and against us." He pointed to the need to mobilize French sentiment and resources in the face of Hitler's menace. After consulting with Stalin, on 20 March, Dimitrov sent the following cable to Thorez, in code:

The Secretariat [of the ECCI] is against the participation of the Communists in a government of national unity. Under present conditions such participation will inescapably compromise the party. If the question should arise, we recommend that you assume something like the following position: the Communists do not object to the plan for national unity and the formation of a government on that basis. But our understanding of the tasks of the popular front differs from that of other parties. According to the understanding of our party, such a government must arrest the fascists, smash their organizations as traitors to the nation, seriously improve the conditions of workers, peasants, and intelligentsia, not drag in the tail behind reactionary elements [and] English Conservatives, and conduct its own national antifascist policy. Inasmuch as this understanding does not coincide with the other parties' understanding of the tasks of such a government, the participation of Communists in the government [would] provoke a split in its ranks and a breakup of national unity. Therefore the Communists refuse to participate in such a government but will support it, provided this government will not infringe the existing rights of the toiling masses and provided it offers effective help to Republican Spain, will actively strengthen national defense, and will pursue a consistent policy against foreign fascist aggression.

The Secretariat believes that only a state of war against fascist aggression could change such a position of the Communists, who in case of war would enter a government of national unity in order to strengthen the forces of international democracy against fascism.

On 23 March, Thorez cabled that he had received Moscow's instructions and would act accordingly.[41]

Document 6

Dimitrov and Manuilsky to Stalin, 19 March 1938, with enclosure. RTsKhIDNI, f. 495, op. 74, d. 517, ll. 3, 4. Original in Russian. Typewritten.

TO COMRADE I. V. STALIN
Dear Comrade Stalin,
We are sending you a telegram that we have just received from Com. Thorez. This telegram was sent after we gave the French Communist Party instructions

41. RTsKhIDNI, f. 495, op. 18, d. 1237, l. 26, and f. 495, op. 74, d.517, ll. 5–6 (cable to Thorez); RTsKhIDNI, f. 495, op. 184, vkhod. 1938, d. 13, l. 67 (Thorez's reply).

not to participate in the Blum government, which [the party] followed. We ask for your advice and directives.

With fraternal greeting,

(G. Dimitrov)
(D. Manuilsky)

19 March 1938.

Telegram from Com. Thorez of 18 March 1938.

"Political circles in France are hurriedly preparing the formation of a government of national unity composed of the representatives of all the parties, except for the small pro-Hitler groups. Without a doubt, the Communist Party will be invited to participate in the government. This proposal will be made in the next few days; if the international situation deteriorates further, the question about reorganization of the government will emerge much earlier. We consider cooperation with the parties that are not members of the popular front inescapable, since the continuation in power of only parties of the popular front is associated with the policies of sabotage of the economic and political actions of the government by the bourgeoisie, and with undermining its measures to defend the country. We clearly realize the danger of Communists participating in the government, but rejecting such participation will either undermine the national concentration of forces, or else this concentration will occur without us and against us. It is important to take into consideration that if this concentration collapses, the country will face the Hitlerian danger ununited, insufficiently armed, and at risk of defeat in case of war. On the other hand, accepting the offer to create a government of national concentration will reinforce resistance to Hitler and facilitate the struggle of the united front. We are waiting for [your] answer. If no answer is given, we will consider it an endorsement of the policy of participation of communists in the government. If you look upon [the policy] negatively, instruct us as to which tactics we should pursue. In this case, could we not send you a delegation to discuss [this] question together."

---

20 April 1939

French Communists asked Moscow for "advice" on the proper attitude toward the French government on one other occasion. By then, April 1939, the world situation had significantly changed. War loomed. In March, Hitler had violated the Munich agreement of September 1938 and seized the unoccupied portion of Czechoslovakia as well as Lithuanian Memel/Klaipeda. Poland was the next likely target. In London sentiment for a firm guarantee to Poland had greatly increased. Meanwhile, for all intents and purposes, the Spanish Civil War was over, and large numbers of Republican refugees were pouring into France. In the preceding year—with the failure of international cooperation in Spain and the Munich agreement, which symbolized the Western attempt to appease Hitler—Soviet foreign policy and propaganda had become sharply critical of the Western powers. The French Communist Party had a legitimate question of policy: Should it still argue on behalf of "collective security," the Soviet slogan of the mid-thirties? Moscow had begun to distance itself from its Western "allies," and the first (highly secret) German-Soviet feelers that were to lead to the nonaggression pact began in April 1939. Maxim Litvinov was about to be dropped as Soviet foreign minister.

As Dimitrov and Manuilsky comment, the PCF line is complex if not contradictory, in that the Communists voted against the centrist Daladier-Bonnet government in parliament but did not openly attack it "outside," out of fear that if it were to fall, its successor would be far worse from the Communist point of view. But now the PCF was prepared to shift to an open attack on the government as one of "national treason," which had undermined resistance to aggression and divided the French people.

When Dimitrov raised the policy question in a personal conversation on 26 April, Stalin, in a curious case of equivocation, declined to decide, referring to his busy agenda: "Decide these questions by yourselves."[42] Accordingly, on 4 May 1939 the ECCI Secretariat felt free to reverse course and adopt a resolution closely corresponding to the argument presented by the PCF, which was communicated to the French comrades.[43]

---

42. TsPA (Sofia), f. 146, op. 2, a.e. 5.
43. RTsKhIDNI, f. 495, op. 18, d. 1278, ll. 75–78.

Document 7

Dimitrov and Manuilsky to Stalin, 20 April 1939. RTsKhIDNI, f. 495, op. 74, d. 517, ll. 34–40. Original in Russian. Typewritten.

Sent on 20/IV
in package No. 105.

<. . .>

TO COMRADE STALIN

Dear Comrade Stalin,

The Politburo of the French Communist Party is asking for our advice regarding the following questions:

a) Which policy should the party pursue toward the Daladier-Bonnet government: should [the party] decisively aim at its overthrow, or [should it] tolerate it for the time being, since at present it is not clear what kind of government would replace it?

b) What should be the party's attitude toward the "new course" in the foreign policy of England proclaimed by [Prime Minister Neville] Chamberlain? What position should it take in respect to the plans of Daladier and Bonnet, who declare that they want to establish closer cooperation between France and the USSR, inasmuch as these plans conceal the aspirations of the French reaction to involve the USSR in possible military conflicts? Should the party, in the present international situation, serve as leader on behalf of collective security [and] a strengthening of the Franco-Soviet pact, or would it be better if the party did not place itself in the vanguard on these issues?

c) Should [the party] in France aim at creating a government which bases itself in the popular front or, given that there is not much chance to create such a government in France in the near future and given that in all the parties, including the rightist ones, there is a growing opposition to the capitulationist policy of Daladier-Bonnet, should the party aim at [creating] a government broader than the popular-front concentration of social forces?

d) Taking into consideration that the French reaction managed to carry out the Munich capitulation, to destroy the popular front, to launch an offensive against the social gains of the toilers under the deceptive pretext of "safeguarding the peace," the French comrades think that they should appropriate the slogan of protecting the "peace" from the reactionaries, without fearing that this slogan might encourage pacifist illusions in the masses. They ask [our] advice regarding how best to connect this slogan to the policy of repelling the aggressors and thus to contribute to the liberation of the masses from pacifist illusions.

e) What should be the position of the party regarding the arming of France?

These are the questions raised by the French comrades. It is important to observe that the party does not have a definite and clear position on all these questions. In the parliament, the Communists vote against the government of Daladier-Bonnet, but outside the parliament, they do not conduct a broad or decisive campaign for its overthrow. This contradiction stems from the Communists' fears that the Daladier government could be replaced by a more reactionary government. They fear that a direct attack on the Daladier government will be used by Daladier and the reactionaries to denounce the Communist Party and make it illegal. French comrades have too much faith in Daladier's rhetorical statements about the readiness of the French government to protect the inviolability of France. They do not seem to notice that these "statements" are, in large measure, a maneuver intended to check the growth of the anti-Munich opposition in the country. They also seem to be pressured by the "national unity" moods that have engulfed broad sectors of the French population in the face of the threat of aggression from abroad.

Having discussed with the representatives of the CC of the French Communist Party the questions raised by them, we give the following joint appraisal of the situation in France.

In France, a <u>new situation</u> is being created. The policy of Daladier-Bonnet has failed. The hope that the Munich agreement would bring lasting peace is collapsing in the eyes of the masses. In the light of Hitler's seizure of Czechoslovakia [and] Klaipeda, of the growing pressure on Poland and Romania, of the advance of German fascism into the Balkans, of the occupation of Albania by Italy, it becomes clearer to the masses that the opponents of Munich were right. Under the influence of these events, the masses come to recognize—from the perspective of French security—the criminality of the Daladier-Bonnet policy toward the Spanish Republic. Therefore, the opposition to the policy of capitulation of the Daladier-Bonnet [government and] to the "Munchenites" is growing in the Socialist Party, in the General Confederation of Labor, in the Radical Party, among the army cadres, in the intelligentsia, [and among] the Catholic masses and the clergy.

These shifts in French public opinion create a fertile ground for the Communist Party to overcome its temporary isolation. As opposed to a few months ago, it is much harder now for Daladier to drive underground the party that consistently and tirelessly fought against Munich. At present, the decisive dividing line is not over issues of the socioeconomic program of the popular front but rather over resistance to external aggression. Communists now have to define their attitude toward any government, depending, in the first place, on whether that government pursues a capitulationist policy or a policy of resistance to external aggression.

Given the changes in the situation in France, we think that the party should take a hard stance against the government of Daladier-Bonnet that aims at its overthrow. The party should tirelessly criticize the duality of the "new" foreign policy course of Chamberlain-Daladier-Bonnet. The essence of this course of Chamberlain-Daladier is to strive to utilize the USSR in their imperialist interests against Germany and Italy while on the other hand seeking a compromise with the aggressors at the expense of the USSR. The party has to demonstrate to the masses that the so-called new course is intended to lull public opinion, but that it is in fact a continuation, in a disguised form, of the old capitulationist policy.

To the double-dealing, hypocritical policy of Daladier-Bonnet the party has to juxtapose a policy of organizing economic, political, and, if necessary, military resistance to the aggressors, a policy of true collective security, a policy of strengthening the Franco-Soviet pact as conditions for [achieving] real guarantees of peace and security for France. This is the way to save France from disaster. Only such a policy will be a truly national policy in accordance with France's national interests. This is the only way to protect peace that is not a pacifist deception. Promoting such a defense of peace, the Communists will demonstrate that they are the real fighters for the cause of peace, as opposed to Daladier and Bonnet, who in fact are leading the war party in France and who have actually led France to the brink of war. The party has to show that the policy of collective security and the Franco-Soviet pact serve above all the interests of France, since it is France that is facing the threat of direct attack, and because the capitulationist policy of Daladier-Bonnet has weakened the defensive capability of the country.

The party has to explain to the masses that protecting and widening the economic gains and the democratic rights and freedoms of workers is a condition for [maintaining] the defensive capacity of the country and the defense of peace. A people that is defending its social gains will struggle determinedly against the external fascist aggression which is threatening these gains. Therefore, anyone encroaching on the gains and democratic liberties of the workers undermines the defensive capability of the country, facilitates the aggressors' attack on France, puts its security in jeopardy, acts against preserving the peace.

The party has to show to the masses that to defend the peace, to guarantee the security of France, it is necessary, first of all, <u>to remove the government of Daladier-Bonnet as a government of national treason, as the government that destroyed France's system of alliances which had been</u> a certain barrier to the aggressors, [the government] that has opened the approaches for the aggressors for an attack on France (Spain), [the government] that has pushed, by its treacherous policy, small peoples into the sphere of influence of the fascist aggressors, [the government] that split the French people in the face of external aggression. In order to get the country out of the dead end into which it was led by Daladier and Bonnet and to secure peace, a <u>new policy and new people</u> are required.

We believe that in the present situation it is inappropriate to aim at creating a popular-front government: first, because at present there is little possibility to rebuild the popular front; second, because creating such a government under present conditions might hinder the unification of the majority of the French people to repel external aggression.

Therefore we think that the party, under present conditions, ought to aim at creating the government with a broader [social] base than a popular-front government. While continuing its struggle to rebuild and widen the popular front, [the party] must launch a slogan of [creating] a government of national defense. This government must pursue a firm and consistent policy of collective security. It must achieve a united front of large and small states interested in preserving peace. It must pursue a free, independent foreign policy which corresponds to the interests of the French people, rather than following in the wake of the English conservatives. This independent foreign policy does not rule out, but rather presupposes, close contacts between France and England. A government of national defense has to be ready to adopt, and pursue the adoption by other governments of, decisive economic and political measures against the aggressors. Not only must it not retreat before the aggressors, but it should strive to clear them from the already occupied territories (Czechoslovakia, Klaipeda, etc.). Basing itself on the national interests of France, [this government] must support in every possible way the struggle of the Spanish Republicans against the creature of Italian and German fascism, [Francisco] Franco. It should purge the army and the country of German and Italian fascist agents, [and] traitors like Flandin, Doriot, La Roque,[44] and others. It must preserve and strengthen Republican freedoms and the social gains of the toilers.

At present, the party supports an increase in armaments in France under the following conditions: maintenance of socioeconomic legislation, securing the material interests of the workers, and increasing the military-industrial output; first, by fully utilizing the existing industrial equipment and introducing new equipment, by employing the unemployed, and only as a last resort by prolonging the working day.

However, we think that the party should also stress the inability of the Daladier-Bonnet government to increase and secure the defensive capacity of France, and to insist on creating a government which will create political conditions under which the working class would be interested in increasing the armament production. This government should provide certain guarantees that these arms will not be used against the toilers.

Dear Comrade Stalin, we are asking you to let us know whether our opinion on the above questions is correct. We will adopt the final decision only after receiving your instructions.

With fraternal greetings,

(G. DIMITROV)
(D. MANUILSKY)

20 April 1939

---

44. French political figures who had assumed more favorable positions toward Nazi Germany.

CHAPTER THREE

The Spanish Civil War

THE SPANISH CIVIL WAR broke out on 17 July 1936, with the revolt of General Francisco Franco and a substantial part of the Spanish army against the popular-front government that had been formed as a result of the parliamentary elections in February. The country had been uneasily split between these forces, while a number of interest groups struggled for power. The civil war rapidly became a major contest, with Italy and Germany supporting the Franco forces and thousands of volunteers from many countries offering their services to the Republic.

Spain was a difficult issue for Moscow to come to terms with, and for several years it occupied a substantial share of Dimitrov's exchanges with Stalin. The Comintern had a number of important advisers and observers in Spain, mostly clandestine or pseudonymous. In time, Soviet military commanders came to play a major part on the Republican side. Soviet diplomats provided a separate and important conduit for information. (So did the NKVD, which was increasingly out of the control of any government organization.) The Republican leadership welcomed Soviet aid (virtually the only foreign assistance it received) but often was outraged by Soviet behavior; this was true even of the Spanish Communists as well as the other elements of the popular front.[1]

1. On the Spanish Civil War, see the authoritative volume by Hugh Thomas, *The*

The Communists were an important component of the popular front but had carefully stayed out of the government. Initially they enjoyed relatively little support, even among the workers, but the rapidly spreading confusion offered the potential for great political gains. In their correspondence, the Spanish Communist Party (PCE) and the Comintern virtually ignored the many other facets of Soviet aid and involvement in the Spanish Civil War.

23 July 1936

On 23 July 1936 the ECCI Secretariat met to discuss the Spanish situation and, after hearing a report by Ernö Gerö, a Comintern officer dealing with Spain, agreed on the instructions to the Spanish Communists that were enclosed with Dimitrov's note to Stalin, below. Stalin scribbled, "Correct. St," on the note and returned it to Dimitrov, whereupon it was sent to Madrid on 24 July.

The Comintern policy outlined here shows a clear agenda in favor of a popular front against the primary enemy—in this case, the "fascist rebels." Obviously unhappy about an earlier message from (or about) the PCE, the Comintern warns against efforts to move prematurely in demanding a Soviet-style regime, and against sentimentality, romantic revolutionary visions, or an exaggeration of the Communist forces. At the same time, the Comintern sticks to the standard Communist line of refraining from participation in united-front governments except under extraordinary circumstances. This was to be a continuing topic of disagreement, consultation, and instruction. But the notion of tactical gradualism and the support of a broad Republican regime fits the Stalinist instinct for careful "dosage" and foreshadows Soviet postwar policy in Eastern Europe as well.

Spanish Civil War (New York: Harper, 1972), as well as Pierre Broué and Emile Temime, *The Revolution and the Civil War in Spain* (Cambridge: MIT Press, 1972). On the Soviet and Comintern role, see David Cattell, *Soviet Diplomacy and the Spanish Civil War* (Berkeley: University of California Press, 1957). See also Jesus Hernandez, *La Grande Trahison* (Paris: Fasquelle, 1950); Valentin Gonzalez and Julian Gorkin, *El Campesino: Life and Death in Soviet Russia* (New York: Putnam, 1953); Castro Delgado, *J'ai perdu la foi à Moscou* (Paris: Gallimard, 1950); Francisco Largo Caballero, *Mis Ricuerdos* (1954), repr. as *Escritos de la Republica* (Madrid: Pablo Iglecias, 1985); and James W. Costada, ed., *Historical Dictionary of the Spanish Civil War, 1936–1939* (Westport, Conn.: Greenwood, 1982).

Document 8

Dimitrov to Stalin, 23 July 1936, with enclosure. RTsKhIDNI, f. 495, op. 74, d. 201, ll. 2, 3. Original in Russian. Handwritten note to Stalin and typewritten telegram to "Luis" (a pseudonym for Vittorio Codovilla, a Comintern representative in Spain) and José Diaz, the general secretary of the PCE, with handwritten comment by Stalin.

From C. Dimitrov²
Dear Com. Stalin,
This evening, we sent the enclosed directive to the Spanish C.C. I beg you to let us know any comments or new directives that you might consider necessary to give us.
With fraternal greetings,
G. Dimitrov.
23. VII. 36.

[To] Diaz, Luis. Madrid.
Your information is insufficient, not concrete enough, and sentimental. Once again, we ask you [to provide] serious factual information. We strongly recommend [you]: 1) To concentrate everything on the most important task of the moment, i.e., on the prompt suppression and the definitive liquidation of the fascist rebellion, rather than being carried away by plans to be realized after victory; 2) To avoid any activities which might undermine the unity of the popular front in the struggle against the rebels; 3) To warn against any tendency to exaggerate our own forces and the forces of the popular front, *and* to underestimate the difficulties and new dangers; 4) Not to run ahead, not to depart from the positions [in favor] of a democratic regime, and not to go beyond the *struggle for* a genuine democratic republic; 5) As long as it is possible to avoid the direct participation of Communists in the government, it is expedient not to enter the government, since it is easier thereby to retain the unity of the popular front. To participate in the government only in extraordinary circumstances, if it is absolutely necessary to defeat the rebellion; 6) Today, when it is essential to unite all the forces of the popular militia as well as those of the military units loyal to the Republic in order to defeat the rebellion, [we] consider it inappropriate to raise the question of replacing the regular army with the popular militia, in particular because in the current battles, a new Republican army is being forged which, along with the popular militia, will support the Republican regime against external and internal enemies. In every possible way recruit loyal Republican officers to the side of the people, and strive to get the rebel units to go over to the side of the popular front. It is essential that the government declare an amnesty *for those* who

2. In the top left corner, handwritten by Stalin:
<u>Correct.</u> St[alin].

46

DOCUMENT 8. Cover letter of Dimitrov to Stalin, 23 July 1936

immediately abandon the ranks of the rebels and go over to the side of the people.

SECRETARIAT

2/MK
24.7.36.

---

23 March 1937

It wasn't long before the Spanish Civil War became a major concern of the Comintern's. Moscow correctly saw that the conflict had the potential to be both a considerable danger and a great opportunity. Dimitrov generally kept Stalin informed of his contacts in Spain and secured his consent to instructions sent to the PCE and to the Comintern representatives in Spain (though not all contacts are recorded in writing). On 28 August 1936 Dimitrov took part in the Politburo meeting that authorized the organization of the International Brigades for Spain. These groups of volunteer soldiers drawn from around the world represent the Soviet Union's most ambitious and dramatic effort at mobilizing international support for the Republican cause under de facto Communist auspices.[3]

Three days later, the ECCI Secretariat received a coded cable from José Diaz and "Luis" reporting that Francisco Largo Caballero, the leader of the Spanish Socialist Workers' Party (PSOE), was insisting on a change of government, of which he would be the head. "It is desirable in the future to give the government the character of a national government for the salvation of the country, and our [PCE] participation will be required. You know our orientation. We are insisting on it. But if our position gives occasion for the disruption of the national front, we will agree to take part in the government as ministers without portfolio. Please reply immediately."[4]

As Stalin was out of town, Manuilsky promptly informed Politburo member Lazar Kaganovich about the cable, stressing that "Ca-

3. On the International Brigades, see, e.g., Vincent Brome, *The International Brigades* (London: Heinemann, 1975), and Arthur H. Landis, *The Abraham Lincoln Brigade* (New York: Citadel Press, 1967), as well as Broué and Temime, *Revolution and the Civil War.*

4. RTsKhIDNI, f. 495, op. 184, vkhod. 1936, d. 20.

ballero insists on the participation of our party in this government."[5] After first securing Stalin's approval by telephone, Dimitrov sent Diaz a message on 2 September specifying in some detail the kind of government Moscow wanted established:

> We recommend the reorganization of the Giral government into a government of national defense that would continue to be headed by Giral and in which the Republicans would have a majority. It would be expedient to include in such a government, in addition to representatives of Catalonia and the Basques, two Socialists—e.g., [Indalecio] Prieto and Caballero—and two Communists. This must be a government committed to the defense of the democratic republic that would subordinate everything to the basic task of suppressing the revolt. Let [Jacques] Duclos prevail on Caballero, stressing that a cabinet headed by Caballero would propel England to the side of the rebels [Franco] and would increase the danger of German and Italian intervention. We propose that Duclos stay temporarily [in] Madrid.
>
> The Secretariat[6]

On 4 September the PCE replied, over the signatures of Diaz, "Luis," and Duclos: "In spite of our efforts it was impossible to avoid the creation of a Caballero government. We secured the participation of Giral as minister without portfolio. . . . We behaved so as to end the crisis of the present government. Everyone insisted strongly on the participation of the Communists in the new government; this was impossible to avoid without creating a very dangerous situation. We are taking the necessary measures to organize the work of our ministers."[7] Crossing out the signatures, Dimitrov forwarded the message to Stalin and other Soviet leaders.[8]

It is significant that Moscow chose to become involved in the Spanish Civil War, though perhaps not surprising, given the intervention of Germany and Italy on the other side, as well as the growing power and prospects of the PCE. It is no less important that although the Comintern was liberal in dispensing advice— even on internal Spanish politics—and Moscow was quick to assail the passivity of the Western democracies, Soviet involvement

5. RTsKhIDNI, f. 495, op. 10a, d. 385, l. 39.
6. RTsKhIDNI, f. 495, op. 184, iskh. 1937, Osobye, d. 15, l. 68.
7. RTsKhIDNI, f. 495, op. 184, vkhod. 1936, d. 20.
8. RTsKhIDNI, f. 495, op. 184, iskh. 1937, Osobye, d. 15, l. 70.

remained strictly limited insofar as troops, arms, and credits were concerned.

On 21 December, Stalin, Molotov, and Voroshilov addressed a letter to Largo Caballero, now head of the Spanish government, re-iterating the theme of support for the democratic Republic and the popular front.[9] But a broad Soviet strategy for Spain was not yet apparent. The Kremlin had other preoccupations at this time, including the mounting purge trials.

Spain was the subject of discussion at a meeting with Stalin on 13 March 1937 (with the participation of Voroshilov, Molotov, and Kaganovich, along with three Comintern figures, Dimitrov, André Marty, and "Ercoli" [Palmiro Togliatti]). Here Stalin noted that Largo Caballero was useful as the head of the government but that an effort should be made to get him to resign as minister of war. Rather unexpectedly, Stalin remarked that if foreign—German and Italian—forces were withdrawn from Spain, he would favor disbanding the International Brigades. He also spoke in favor of a unification of the PSOE and the PCE.[10] This was to remain a major theme in PCE efforts over the next year or two. The ECCI Secretariat accordingly advised Diaz to seek a merger between the PCE and the PSOE and to begin conversations with Largo Caballero about it; but despite protracted negotiations, the two parties merged only in Catalonia.

In the meantime, Dimitrov urged Stalin to meet with him and Marty, who was scheduled to return to Spain on 16 March. Stalin received them along with "Ercoli" at his dacha.[11] The following week Dimitrov sent Stalin a lengthy report from "Stepanov" (one of the pseudonyms of Stojan Mineff, a long-term Bulgarian official of the Comintern apparatus), who had been dispatched to the PCE some two months earlier. An excerpt from his report follows. Whatever its bias, it highlights the continued tensions between the Communists and their opponents on the Republican side.

9. V. V. Pertsov, ed., *Voina i revolyutsiya v Ispanii 1936–1939*, vol. 1 (Moscow: Progress, 1968), pp. 419–421.

10. TsPA (Sofia), f. 146, op. 2, a.e. 3.

11. Ibid.

Document 9

Dimitrov to Stalin, 23 March 1937, with enclosure. Letter: RTsKhIDNI, f. 495, op. 74, d. 201, l. 15; enclosure: RTsKhIDNI, f. 495, op. 74, d. 204, ll. 22–32. Original in Russian. Typewritten. Enclosure originally handwritten in French; Dimitrov sent Stalin a Russian typescript.

Dear Comrade Stalin!

I am sending you a copy of the report by our Comrade Stepanov, who has been with the CC of the Communist Party of Spain for two months already. During the past few years, Com. Stepanov dealt directly with Spanish affairs in the Comintern.

The report has no date. It was evidently written in early March.

With fraternal greeting,

_GD_

23 March 1937

* * *

[. . .]

The ability of the government to govern is very limited. Everybody realizes the unusual weakness of the government. Everyone, the broad popular masses, feels the need for a strong government, a government capable of ruling. The popular masses and all the newspapers daily repeat the slogan "All power to the government." Never and nowhere before in history has there been a similar strange situation when the people are unanimous in demanding that the government govern, that it be strong, that all power be in the hands of the government. Nevertheless, the government is very weak, in particular as a result of the practical political line it has adopted. A unified government political line to follow and implement is lacking. There is no unified government perspective, no unified government will. The practical policy of the government is [pure] empiricism, in fact, a rather diversified one. But the fundamental source of weakness of the government is that it lacks the means to rule, it lacks a state apparatus. After 18 July 1936 the remnants of the old state apparatus turned into an active force against the people, against the Republic. Most of the state apparatus's functions were transferred to the trade unions, UGT, CNT, to different committees, councils, local party organizations, and sometimes (although it has become less frequent) to gangsters and the "uncontrollables." Industry, trade, transportation, housing are still in the hands of the trade unions. The economy is extremely decentralized. Control of economic life does not belong even to the two trade union centers but to thousands of trade unions affiliated with them. Little by little, slowly, and only as a result of the struggles on the fronts (as well as of the bitter experience of the many defeats suffered by the Republican army), militias, battalions, [and] regiments organized by different trade union organizations and political parties are disappearing, although traces [of them] can still be found. Today the Republican army is a sector of the government apparatus: the most powerful and best

La situation est extrêmement grave. Il faut épurer l'armée
des officiers traîtres et des officiers incapables et les remplacer
par des officiers fidèles, dévoués et capables, qui existent
déjà. Mais Caballero fait le contraire. Les traîtres, il les
protège, aux incapables il fait des éloges, les fidèles et capables
sont déplacés ou empêchés d'être maximalement utilisés.
Pour avoir dénoncé Asensio et Cabrera, Caballero est
devenu fou de rage contre le parti communiste. Il
ne ... avec opiniâtreté farouche aux demandes de faire
la lumière sur les responsabilités de la catastrophe de
Málaga. Le service militaire obligatoire décrété sous
la pression des masses, est saboté par le même mi-
nistre de la guerre. La mobilisation de l'industrie de
guerre marche trop lentement. Au lieu d'entendre les
avertissements du parti communiste des avertissements
du front, des pétitions des officiers du front, des
avertissements des républicains, des clameurs avertissants
de la presse courageuse et sincère, il se fâche et fulmine
contre tous ceux qui osent faire la critique, qui osent
montrer de l'initiative. En réponse aux avertissements des
communistes, Caballero fait le chantage avec la crise gou-
vernementale. À chaque occasion il provoque les
ministres communistes, se permet et dit des choses inad-
missibles -s'attendant que les ministres communistes
vont perdre leur sang-froid et démissionner. Il
maltraite aussi les ministres républicains. Il maltraite
aussi Del Vayo. Par des insultes et provocations il pense
arriver à provoquer les ministres qui osent exprimer et
défendre leur opinion, à donner leur démission. Il
mène une campagne, de par ses hommes, pour
obliger la presse et les organisations et tous les
partis à accepter inconditionnellement ses ordres
personnels. Exige serment de fidélité personnelle

DOCUMENT 9. A page of the French original of "Stepanov's" report and its
Russian translation enclosed in Dimitrov to Stalin, 23 March 1937. The last
paragraph of the Russian matches the first paragraph of the French.

читаете газет? Читайте газеты,пожалуйста и вы будете знать все
что вас интересует". Каждый раз, когда на обсуждение ставится
серьезный вопрос, председатель совета министров разрешает его
таким образом: "Мое мнение такое. Я разделяю его и так как я
его разделяю, оно правильно. И ,так как оно правильно, его нуж
но принять". Вот метод,который применяется ко всем министрам и
министерствам, исключая министерства войны. Вопросы из области
министерства войны, как правило, не обсуждаются в совете мини-
стров.Если министр осмеливается поднять подобный вопрос или
требовать об'яснения или дать предложение, председатель напоми
нает ему: "Не вмешивайтесь в такие дела, которые не касаются
вас".В лучшем случае отвечают ему,что вопрос будет обсужден в
военном совете. Если же министр настаивает, как это делают два
коммунистических министра как представители партии, то председ
тель вспыхивает, заявляя: "Здесь нет представителей партии, вы
министры такой-то отрасли и больше ничего.Я не хочу знать ни о
каких партиях".

        Положение исключительно серьезное.. Нужно очистить армию
от офицеров-предателей и неспособных офицеров и заменить их
преданными, верными и способными офицерами, которые уже имеют
но Кабальеро действует наоборот. Предателям он протекирует,
неспособных он хвалит, верных и способных он заменяет или не
дает возможности их использовать максимально. Компартия разоб
лачила Асенцио и Кабреро-и Кабальеро взбесился против партии.
Он тоже упрямо сопротивляется, компартия требует расследова
ответственность за катастрофу в Малаге. Принудительная военна
служба, декретированная под нажимом масс, саботируется тем же
самым министерством войны.

organized. However, this instrument of the state apparatus, the army, is tied up at the fronts. The government cannot use it to control the rear.

In the rear there is a permanent official government—to be exact, three official governments: Valencia, Catalonia, and Viscaya. Around these three governments are a number of more or less autonomous governments, large and small, demonstrating their power. All this is created by the weakness of the [central] government. However, all this could be changed significantly and rather quickly, especially now, when the popular masses themselves demand energetic government actions, if only the government could act as needed and had the will to act in a proper way. We have reached the point when the masses, with the exception of the soldiers on the front, have outgrown the government and the trade union leaders in their political maturity, especially after the fall of Malaga.

The government consists of 18 ministers. The Military Council consists of five. However, the government does not rule, and the Military Council does not direct the war effort, and when it finally makes decisions, it does not control their implementation; it has neither the means nor the will to enforce them. In most cases, each minister administers in his area at his own risk and by his own initiative. There is no practical policy pursued by the government as a whole. Studying problems and legislative drafts in different areas by the council of ministers is, for the most part, a mere formality. Once the Ministry of Finances attempted to present a series of measures for discussion, as well as a project for bringing some order to finances and beefing up the peseta. The chairman of the council [of ministers] rudely interrupted him [the finance minister] and said: "Your responsibility as finance minister is to secure payments. When you run out of money, you tell [us]. Everything else is none of your business." On 13 February, Minister Giral (a former chairman of the council and currently a minister without portfolio), expressing the opinion of the president of the Republic, asked most politely that the chairman of the council and the war minister provide him with some information about what was going on at the front. The answer: "What? You do not read newspapers? Be so kind as to read the newspapers, and you will know everything that interests you." Each time a serious issue is presented for discussion, the chairman of the council resolves it in the following manner: "This is my opinion. I hold it and, since I hold it, it is correct. And, since it is correct, it is to be adopted." This method is applied to each minister and ministry, except for the War Ministry. As a rule, questions regarding the War Ministry are not discussed by the Council of Ministers. If a minister dares to raise such a question or to demand explanations or to make a proposal, the chairman reminds him: "Do not interfere with issues that are none of your business." At best, he is told that the question will be discussed at the Military Council. If the minister insists, as the two Communist ministers do as party representatives, the chairman explodes and declares: "There are no party representatives here.

You are branch ministers and nothing more. I do not want to know about any party."

The situation is extremely serious. It is essential to purge the army of officers-traitors and inept officers, and to replace them with loyal, devoted, and capable officers, who do exist. However, Caballero acts in the opposite way. He protects traitors, praises the incapable, removes loyal and capable [officers] or does not permit making the best use of them. The Communist Party exposed Acencio and Cabrero, and Caballero became mad at the party. He stubbornly resists the demand to investigate responsibility for the Malaga disaster.[12] Forced military recruitment, decreed under the pressure from the masses, is being sabotaged by the minister of war himself.

Mobilization of the defense industry proceeds very slowly. Rather than listening to the warnings by the Communist Party, to the warnings from the front, to Republicans, to frontline soldiers, to the voice of the courageous and sincere press, he gets angry and attacks all those who dare to criticize, who dare to display any initiative.

In response to the warnings by Communists, Caballero threatens a ministerial crisis. He uses every occasion to provoke the Communist ministers, he permits himself to say impermissible things, expecting the Communist ministers to lose self-control and resign. He treats the Republican ministers in a similar way. He treats del Vayo similarly. By offenses and provocation he thinks to push those ministers to resign who dare to express and defend their opinion. He conducts a campaign through his people to make the press, organizations, and all the parties unconditionally follow his personal orders. He demands [that people] take an oath of loyalty to him personally. At the same time, he and his closest trustees make an effort to reach an agreement with the CNT, to sign a pact with the UGT and CNT in order to form a UGT-CNT government bloc, and to exclude the Communists and push the Republicans aside. The UGT and CNT press is conducting a systematic campaign in this regard. However, such behavior by Caballero provokes strong dissatisfaction among the military, and incites and breeds anxiety and dissatisfaction among the soldiers at the front. The best, most sincere and active elements in the UGT leadership are also beginning to protest. On the other hand, not everyone in the UGT is ready to support Caballero's petty political intrigues in regard to the CNT. In the CNT there is also a deep current against these dirty intrigues. Republicans, initially hesitant and terrorized by the blackmail and the specter of a bloc between the CNT and the UGT, now declare their solidarity with the Communist Party. Caballero makes desperate attempts to isolate the Communists. Why this anti-Communist rage of Caballero? There are many reasons for that, especially because the influence and authority of the Communist Party are growing,

12. Unknown officials. The "Malaga disaster" refers to a Republican defeat.

—because the front trusts the Communists alone;

—because Communists, in their campaign against the officers and traitors, who are direct collaborators of Caballero, have put Caballero in a position where he had to say: "If I am not a traitor, then I am a fool."

—because the young people cooperate with Communists,

—because Republicans express their preference for the Communist Party,

—because the course of events proves that the Communists are right, and that he, Caballero, is wrong.

The crisis is also becoming more acute as a result of the decision on control and, in particular, as a result of pressure by one foreign state. Which government provides support or promises support to Caballero? To what extent does the intervention of that foreign government contribute to the government crisis, or favor or inspire Caballero's strange behavior? There is no doubt that Caballero gets support, or hopes to get support, from that foreign state. No doubt, he is connected. What kind of engagement is that? At whose expense and against what? There are some indications pointing at England as being this foreign state. A series of coincidences and facts would remain unexplained unless one considers the hand of England. A series of strange events took place (what a strange coincidence!) after the recent visit, in late January, by English naval vessels, after the meeting of Caballero and Prieto with the English admiral and British councilor. Prieto said something to the English guests [that since has become] well known: "If your visit had not been a protocol visit, it would be possible to offer you a deal: take Cartagena, take something else, but help us repel the fascists, Germans and Italians."

However, from late January (a mere coincidence!) there started a careful but systematic campaign against the International Brigades, against the Soviets, against Communists, against political commissars at the fronts. In the first days of February, Caballero approached Azaña and suggested to expel Del Vayo in order to organize the UGT and CNT ministry without Communists or Republicans. To this Azaña replied that he preferred to resign immediately as president of the Republic rather than to accept such a deal.

The suggestion to expel Del Vayo acquires special importance if one takes into consideration a cynical remark made by Prieto at the recent meeting of the Council of Ministers after Del Vayo reported on the decision of the Nonintervention Committee. He said: "All that you say and suggest I already heard verbatim earlier today from the Soviet representative. We would like to know your personal opinion and your proposal to the ministry of Spain." After that, Prieto proceeded with insinuations against the USSR, implying that, as it were, the USSR has abandoned Spain and shows no interest in it any more because it has failed to achieve its goals. From the first days of February (this is another coincidence!) a loud campaign started in connection with the assistance from Mexico and Mexican solidarity. The underlying idea was this: first to equate the solidarity of the USSR and Mexico, and then to contrast the "impartial"

Mexican assistance and the "partisan" assistance from the USSR. After that came an invitation to the Republican government to attend the coronation of the English king. After that a systematic and growing flirtation started between the Spanish Socialists and Trotskyists (POUM). One can sense a dirty general campaign taking shape, [initiated by] Socialists from other countries along with Trotskyists and the Gestapo against the Comintern, against the USSR, against the Spanish Communist Party. At the same time, a huge campaign [is being conducted] to advertise food supplies to the Spanish workers by the Second International and the Amsterdam [International]. Also, censors eliminate from the articles in "Frente Rojo" every attack on the Trotskyists, in particular, arguments that demonstrate the counterrevolutionary activities, the fascist sabotage by these people in Spain. After that, there came an offer from the UGT (presided over by Caballero) to this international conference, from which Communists are excluded and which, according to the plans of the UGT leaders, is supposed to have a certain anti-Communist cachet. After that there was a pure pretense, an impossible devilish pretense of England's direct assistance to Republican Spain in agreement with Germany. (I do not go into details; let the carrier of this [report] tell you [about it].)

Taking into consideration all these coincidences, one comes to the conclusion that England is beginning to play a very active role in the domestic policy of Republican Spain. Therefore, we are beginning to think that the energetic and growing campaign which Caballero and his closest friends have initiated against Communists is partially inspired and supported by England and, probably, by Deterding from Royal Dutch.[13]

Are Caballero and England haggling about Cartagena or other territory and other economic concessions? Is that all? Is there an agreement to sacrifice the Communist Party, to destroy the Communist Party? However, to destroy the Communist Party would mean to destroy the front, since 130,000 Communists are at the front, or their work is directly or indirectly connected to the front. Communists are the brain, soul, and muscle of the army. To destroy the Communist Party, the party which peasants trust almost fanatically, <. . .> The Communist Party represents a great political, worker-peasant, and military force. It incites fear and respect. Moreover, the party already possesses enough experience and flexibility not to let itself be provoked, not to isolate itself from the masses. It is capable of exposing the anti-Communist campaign, of disrupting the enemy's plans. But it is essential that there be no unpleasant surprises at the front. It is essential that there be no more disasters like Malaga. This is why the party is of such importance to the front, to the army. [This is why the party] pays its major attention to them, and makes heroic efforts to se-

13. Sir Henri W. H. Deterding was the director-general of the Royal Dutch Petroleum Company, a "capitalist" company that ostensibly had behind-the-scenes influence on the British side.

cure and facilitate the victory of the Republic over fascism. The front knows the party, its people, its work, its position, its suggestions. The front trusts the party. [The front] trusts the party more than the government itself, and this enrages Caballero and the Socialist leaders and some of the anarchists. This is a fact. It is a result of the consistent work of the popular front and of the Republican party "Izquierda Respublicana," and of the Republican union. These [organizations] recognize, openly and sincerely, that the Communist Party is the strongest party, that it is the most loyal and energetic fighter in the popular front at the front as well as in the rear.

Such is the situation. The situation is difficult, critical. The most diverse, the most contradictory events are flashing and changing with lightning speed. The situation here is changing three times a day. Who is the traitor? The trade union and Socialist politicians who are doing and will continue to do a lot of harm.

The general conclusion: in order to win the war, in order to prevent new failures at the front, the front requires rapid radical changes, meaning a purge of headquarters, reorganization of the defense industry, securing of transportation at the front, securing of food supplies to the front, arranging the organization and training of the reserve troops, [and] implementation of forced recruitment. Our party will do everything possible to achieve all this, since it is vital. It will do everything possible to get it done by the government of Caballero. However, if Caballero and his friends continue to resist [these changes], a new disaster may happen. In order to avoid it, it is essential to speed up the reorganization of the [Council of] Ministers, with a new Ministry of War, a ministry without Caballero. This is a matter of ten days. In this connection, public opinion at the front is being prepared. In this sense, negotiations are being conducted with Republicans, with anarcho-syndicalists, with the UGT, with Socialists, [and] with Azaña. [These negotiations] are conducted so as to strengthen the popular front, on the basis of a positive program, the concrete program of the popular front addressing burning, immediate tasks, which must be solved immediately. The party is convinced it will not be late. The party is a great force. In only 22 provinces, it has 250 thousand members, out of whom 135 thousand are at the front. Young people follow the party: about 250 thousand members. In addition, the United Socialist Party of Catalonia has 45 thousand members. The peasants follow [the party], and are fanatically devoted to it. With the help of the Republicans. Taking into consideration that the UGT masses in their majority support the positions of the Communist Party.[14] The situation is extremely hard and complicated, but we are convinced that the Communist Party will be able to overcome all these difficulties and that the cause of the popular front will triumph, that the cause of the popular front will end up victorious.

Cordial greetings, B.

---

14. The original is very choppy at this point.—Trans.

16 September 1937

In his reports to Moscow, "Stepanov" repeatedly denounced Largo Caballero, in effect urging that he be replaced. On 14 April, Dimitrov wrote to Stalin that the PCE leadership shared this view, and, although he urged the Spanish Communists to strengthen rather than undermine the popular front, he was concerned about the efforts of anti-Communists to oust friendly officers in the government and army (where the PCE occupied a number of key positions). Perhaps in order to mobilize Moscow against Largo Caballero, "Stepanov" and the PCE leadership reported that Largo Caballero, surrounded by anarchists and anti-Communist trade-unionists, was seeking to disrupt the popular front.[15] In the prevailing political chaos, the Communists scored a major success: in May 1937 Largo Caballero was forced to resign and was replaced by Juan Negrín.

Although the Franco forces had failed to achieve the quick military victory they had hoped for—they were stopped before they reached Madrid—the military situation of the Republican side was deteriorating as well. Disorganization, incompetence, inexperience, and petty rivalries were a large part of the story. Comintern observers on the spot were reporting the situation to Moscow, but whether they were accurate in assigning reasons for the problems is questionable. The Spanish Communists were looking to the Comintern for guidance on a number of key issues. They sent a delegation to Moscow with a broad outline of strategy and tactics for which they solicited advice and help. Rather than articulating a clear policy, Moscow proved hesitant and unclear on its own role and what advice to give the PCE.

In September 1937 Comintern and Soviet policy in Spain was at the center of attention of Moscow decision makers. On 4 September two representatives of the PCE (Pedro Checa and "Luis," who had left Spain to be the Moscow delegate of the PCE) arrived from Spain. They delivered detailed reports to the CC, and "Ercoli" in-

---

15. Dimitrov to Stalin, 14 April 1937, and enclosed report from "Stepanov," in RTsKhIDNI, f. 495, op. 74, d. 201, l. 21 (enclosure in op. 10a, d. 223, ll. 1–35); and Dimitrov to Stalin, 17 April 1937, and enclosed resolution of PCE Central Committee, 27 March 1937, in op. 74, d. 201, l. 24, and op. 12, d. 92, ll. 153–158.

dependently sent lengthy, candid, and well-informed messages from Spain, which, once they were translated, Dimitrov promptly forwarded to Stalin.[16]

The fall of Bilbao and Santander turned over the Basque region to the Franco forces, in effect giving them control of the north coast. The Italians were providing considerable troops in the southeast as well as heavy artillery and airplanes. The creation and deployment of the International Brigades, however dramatic and important symbolically, hardly offset these developments: most of the personnel were more dedicated than skilled, and their organization left much to be desired. Meanwhile, the Spanish leaders, increasingly dependent on Soviet support, dared not oppose the overt and covert activities of the NKVD, whose agents embarked on a campaign of purges and kidnapping (this was the height of the terror in the Soviet Union) whose victims included Communists, anarcho-syndicalists, members of POUM (who were equated with "Trotskyists"), and left Socialists—as well as Soviet diplomats, journalists, and military men. Many of the mysterious disappearances remain unexplained.

Reports from Spain by Comintern representatives ("Pedro" [Gerö], "Stepanov," and "Ercoli") typically dealt with major national topics, but they also discussed feuds and intrigues within the PCE as well as relations of Spanish Communists with other members of the popular front. A basic dilemma was whether the Communists ought to press for a greater share of power—some wished to take over the government—or whether too much interference by the PCE would both split the popular front and antagonize the foreign supporters of the Republic. This was particularly notable in the

---

16. Dimitrov to Stalin, 4 September 1937, RTsKhIDNI, f. 495, op. 74, d. 201, l. 25; Dimitrov to Stalin, 7 September 1937, l. 26; Dimitrov to Stalin, 8 September 1937, and enclosed memorandum from PCE representatives, l. 29, and op. 18, d. 1224, ll. 134–141; Dimitrov to Stalin, 11 September 1937, with enclosed reports by "Ercoli," 29 and 30 August 1937, and report by "Pedro" (Ernö Gerö), 16 August 1937, f. 495, op. 74, d. 201, l. 31; op. 10a, d. 219, ll. 44–60, 24–33; op. 18, d. 1224, ll. 83–105; op. 10a, d. 222, ll. 14–21. The first part of the "Ercoli" report was published in Palmiro Togliatti, *Opere,* ed. Franco Andreucci and Paolo Spriano, vol. 4: *1935–44* (Rome: Ed. Riuniti, 1979), pt. 1, pp. 258–272. The ECCI Secretariat discussed the draft instructions to the PCE on 15 September, and the ECCI Presidium adopted them on 20 September.

reports of "Ercoli," who from July 1937 on was a secret observer in Spain.[17]

No less troubling for the ECCI was "Ercoli's" report on the mood in the International Brigades. By mid-1937 morale was sagging. Fresh replacements had been reduced to a trickle, the largely incompetent officers' corps had been responsible for a number of serious errors, and some volunteers were eager to return home.

On the basis of these reports, the Comintern and its PCE agents drafted the statement printed below. After consulting with Stalin, the ECCI Secretariat on 15 September adopted the document, entitled "The Most Important Tasks of the PCE." Once more Dimitrov sent the text to Stalin, who evidently indicated his approval, for on 20 September the ECCI Presidium adopted it. At Stalin's request, it included an unusual clause: a call for new elections to the Cortes (the Spanish parliament), which had, the document claimed, become "unrepresentative." Comintern observers in Spain like "Ercoli" had believed that it was pointless to talk of new elections while the country was in a state of crisis, but in their wisdom after their meeting with Stalin, Dimitrov and his associates called for them anyway. Other points in the document similarly reflected Moscow's inability to comprehend the situation in Spain, as well as Stalin's apparent assumption that the Spanish situation was somehow comparable to the phase of "war communism" in the Russian Civil War.[18] Although the PCE, and especially the Soviet advisers and agents, were indeed playing a larger role in Spain than previously, Soviet officials seemed to assume, erroneously, that Communist authority and control in Spain were strong enough to nationalize major enterprises and banks, and militarize the defense industry at the height of a civil war.

17. See especially his reports of 29 and 30 August 1937, in RTsKhIDNI, f. 495, op. 74, d. 201, ll. 24–33, 44–60; partly published in Italian translation in Togliatti, *Opere,* vol. 4, pt. 1, pp. 309–324.

18. That phase had been characterized by widespread nationalization and militarization.

Document 10

Dimitrov to Stalin, 16 September 1937, with enclosure. Letter: RTsKhIDNI, f. 495, op. 74, d. 201, l. 33; enclosure: f. 495, op. 2, d. 357, ll. 92–105. Original in Russian. Typewritten.

Dear Comrade Stalin!

I am sending you a document on the most important tasks of the party; it was worked out together with the Spanish comrades after the discussion with you. To save time, we have sent Com. Checa with this document back [to Spain], and have kept Com. Luis here for a couple of days in order to discuss and settle a number of specific questions regarding the International Brigades, the new recruitment of volunteers, the international campaign, the struggle against Trotskyism, etc.

Since a CC plenum will be called immediately after Com. Checa's arrival in Valencia, we urge you to give us your thoughts about and corrections of this document, if any, so that we can promptly forward them to the CC of the Spanish party.

p. p. With fraternal greetings,

(G. Dimitrov)

16 *September* 1937.

No. 108/lD.

Final text[19]

THE MOST IMPORTANT TASKS OF THE PCE

A) Regarding the political situation.

1. Taking into account that the current parliament was elected at a time when a reactionary government was in power; that most of the deputies have disappeared (some joined the enemy, others were killed by the fascists); that the current parliament does not reflect the changes in the balance of class forces which have occurred in the country during the civil war; that the Spanish fascists, relying for support on the occupying German and Italian troops to oppress the popular masses in Spain, have antagonized all the people of Spain who are now fighting for their national independence; and that the policy of the popular-front government has won over a very large section of the masses as supporters of a new type of democratic republic, the Communist Party considers it essential to propose holding new elections to the Cortes. This nationwide plebiscite will demonstrate to the whole world that, at a time when the bourgeois-democratic states allow German and Italian fascism to attack the Spanish people with impunity, and while the British conservative government moves toward recognizing General Franco as a [legitimate] combatant, the absolute majority of the Spanish people support the popular-front government, support democracy, oppose fascism, unconditionally vote for working for victory over fascism, and oppose whatever compromises with fascism

19. A stamp.

that are sponsored, as is well known, by the English conservatives. The Cortes elections will also bring into the open the bankrupt politicians who, by systematically opposing the popular-front government, assume the role of accomplices of fascism. The elections will demonstrate that these politicians and the oppositional alliances created by them, who rejoice at the smallest failures of the Republican troops and are using these failures against the popular-front government, and who are protecting the POUM spies, have no roots in the country and are being indignantly repudiated by the majority of the Spanish people. The new elections will further mobilize the masses to struggle against fascism, raise their enthusiasm, fortify the popular bloc of antifascist forces, strengthen and increase the authority of the popular-front government, and create conditions for bringing the war to a victorious end even more quickly.

In order to conduct new elections on a democratic basis, it is essential that the Cortes, at the suggestion of the government, move to dissolve itself, to call for new elections, and to vote in a new electoral law, which should establish universal, equal, direct, and secret suffrage and proportional representation, reduce the age limit for voters, give the military the right to vote, etc.

If, for some reason, it is not possible to ensure that the Cortes will decide to hold new elections, it is necessary to strive [to get] the president of the Republic, basing himself on the clearly expressed will of the popular-front parties, to decree the dissolution of the Cortes and schedule new elections.

The elections are to be held in the spirit of <u>strengthening the popular front and mobilizing the popular masses for the victory over the insurgents and the German and Italian interventionists, in the spirit of struggle for the national independence of the Spanish people.</u> In order for this task to succeed, <u>the Communist and Socialist parties</u> have to join <u>in a single bloc</u>, leading all other antifascist parties and organizations. It is therefore necessary that the Communists and Socialists agree beforehand on the necessity for the [new] elections, on the way to hold them, as well as on the principal points of the electoral platform, which should summarize the major demands of the masses <u>in organizing the victory over fascism and, consequently, in consolidating the gains of the popular revolution</u>. By proposing new elections, the Communists and Socialists [should] approach the elections with a common program and a common candidate list, which also has to represent non-party members, in particular, peasants and soldiers.

So that the elections accurately reflect the political mood of the masses, it is necessary, in putting together the common popular-front electoral list, for the number of candidates from each party or organization to reflect the real power of each of these organizations. Supporting this principle, the Communist Party will nevertheless be ready to make some concessions in order to secure a unified popular-front list. At the same time, it will insist that, in order to test the actual influence of the parties and organizations participating in the elections, [the various groups] be allowed to place their names and emblems on the electoral bulletins distributed by them.

However, if, despite all the efforts of the Communist Party, it is not possible to reach agreement on a common popular-front list, it will be absolutely essental to achieve common electoral action among the Socialists, Communists, and the United Socialist Youth. In that case, the Communist Party must make all the necessary concessions for agreement on the common list. If the government does not agree to our proposal to call new elections, the Communist Party should go to the people and explain its position on this issue, a position determined by the interests of international as well as internal strengthening of the people's republic and its prompt victory over the coalition of enemy forces.

Taking into account that as a result of a decree by the former interior minister Galarza, elections to the municipal and provincial councils have not been held; [taking into account] that nomination to these [councils] contradicted the popular-front interests, since a significant majority [of seats] in these councils was given to the representatives of the UGT and the CNT and an insignificant minority [of seats] to the political parties; taking into account the complexity and importance of the tasks facing the municipal councils (supplies, public transportation, housing, sanitation, etc.) and [the idea] that all the forces of the popular front should cooperate in resolving these problems, the Communist Party should demand, in accordance with the Republican constitution, that elections to the provincial and municipal councils be held. While participating in these elections in a bloc with the Socialists, the Communist Party should also insist that a unified list of all the popular-front antifascist parties be created; with a united program of demands, allowing for special conditions in each locality.

2. In order to strengthen the authority of the government, the Communist-Socialist bloc will strive to have the government organize the election campaign by naming an electoral junta, consisting of the representatives of all the organizations and parties —members of the antifascist front, presided over by a member of the government.

Aiming at strengthening the authority of the government, the Communists and Socialists will also seek:

a) To replace the current minister of the interior with a solid, energetic, and honest Socialist or Communist capable of bringing order to the rear and to cleanse it of spies and traitors; to prepare the elections [to be held] under conditions that would prevent any provocation on the part of the enemy.

b) To create a special Ministry of Armament, which should restructure all the industry in accordance with the needs of the national defense; to put at the head of this ministry a capable energetic person, Communist or Socialist, who would be able to provide all kinds of weapons to the army.

c) To replace Irujo, the current minister of justice, who is connected with profascist elements and is an agent of conservative circles in England, with a representative of the Basque nationalists, who would be ready to struggle against Franco to the end.

If the UGT and the CNT wish to loyally participate in promoting the policy of the popular front, it will be desirable to invite one representative from each of these organizations into the government.

3. The new difficulties which the Spanish Republic is experiencing at this moment are seen by the fact that the Spanish people have to struggle not only against domestic insurgents but also against the armed intervention of the fascist countries, Germany, Italy, and Portugal, which are supported by the conservative government in England and by the reactionary forces in France. The fascist states are using a naval blockade against the Spanish Republic, aiming at depriving the Spanish people of food, oil, and coal, and dooming it to starvation. [They hope] that the prolonged war will frighten the unstable, vacillating elements. All this requires that the parties and organizations of the popular front, Communists and Socialists especially, pursue a firm and consistent policy toward all the oppositional groups, which are becoming mouthpieces of fascism in Republican Spain and mouthpieces of an inclination to capitulation to the fascist aggressors, a leaning that is being masked by radical rhetoric.

Just like all the other truly antifascist parties and organizations in the popular front, Communists and Socialists should strengthen their campaign among the masses, explaining that despite all the difficulties, the Spanish people, supported by the international proletariat and all the democratic forces of the world, will win provided they promptly realize the measures specified in the popular-front program, namely:

a) Accelerated reorganization of the army and its transformation into a united army, subordinate to a unified command under the leadership of a single commander-in-chief. Preparation of reserves numbering hundreds of thousands of soldiers. Checking the construction of fortifications at all fronts and strengthening them adequately. This will permit the temporary recall of some forces from all the fronts in order to retrain and reeducate them, so that in the future they can be used as shock troops of the unified army, engaged on all the fronts. Activization of the Republican fleet, making it an active, combat-ready force.

b) Acceleration of the reorganization of the military industry in such a way that Spain will be able to produce, as soon as possible, all the armaments necessary for the successful prosecution of the war (airplanes, cannons, guns, machine guns, ammunition, etc.). It is necessary to put an end to the continuing plundering of arms and ammunition by introducing the principle of individual and collective responsibility. In addition, it is necessary to create repair shops near the fronts to fix and check all the damaged weapons.

c) The merchant fleet must be put under the Ministry of National Defense.

Document 10 *continued*

It is necessary to create a government secretariat of the civil fleet. All its technical personnel should be militarized.

d) To create consumer and trade cooperatives throughout the country, in order to combat speculation and the high cost of living, and to improve the organization of distribution of food and items of basic necessity. To introduce food rationing for the entire population, on the principle that soldiers at the fronts and those civilians in the rear who work for victory at the front should be the first to receive supplies.

e) It is essential to seriously cleanse the rear of deserters and those elements who are trying to avoid conscription, of Trotskyist agents of fascism, of Fifth Column bandits, of spies who disorganize industry and try to sow panic in the population by using the [existing] difficulties to demoralize the masses in order to create favorable conditions for capitulation to the fascism.

f) To conduct a fierce struggle against all tendencies leading to capitulation to the enemy, no matter where they originate. To struggle against all the "Vergara kisses," openly exposing the authors of these dishonest offers as enemies of the people.*

4. Despite the great difficulties in establishing united action with the CNT, it is essential that Communists and Socialists make maximum efforts to approach this organization and conclude a pact for united action. For this purpose, it is necessary:

a) To conduct work inside the CNT organizations, trying to isolate "uncontrollable" and Trotskyist-fascist elements in these organizations.

b) To conduct fraternal discussions with the anarchists in the press, at meetings, and at the open meetings, avoiding unnecessary friction.

c) To rebuild ties between the CC PCE and the CNT in order to achieve cooperation in the political, economic, and military spheres, on the national as well as the local level.

d) To pursue a consistent policy of trade union unity, trying to complement the nonaggression pact with the UGT and the CNT leadership with a program of cooperation of both organizations in the cause of creating conditions for the victory over fascism.

Communists should likewise participate in the work of the communications committees of both organizations, to initiate the creation of such committees in order to make them useful to the unity of action between the CNT and the UGT, and thus to create conditions for trade union unity.

Taking into account the schismatic work [conducted] by the group of Largo Caballero in the leadership of the General Workers Union, Socialists and Com-

---

*Vergara: a place in Spain where a peace was signed between the Carlists and the Liberals. The Carlists used the time of negotiations and exchange of solemn promises of friendship to rearm themselves and later to massacre the Liberals (Trans.) [i.e., the Russian translator of the original document].

munists, after protesting against this policy, should strengthen common actions inside the General Workers Union to protect its unity, with the aim of persuading the member organizations of the UGT to denounce the schismatic elements. Socialists and Communists should demand that the National Council of the General Workers Union hold a meeting, with representatives from all the trade union federations, including those which have been expelled. It is essential that the criminal schismatic work be stopped; that a leadership that will express the will of the mass of the UGT members and secure participation of these organizations in the popular front be organized.

5. The CC CP of Spain should establish closer cooperation with the United Socialist Party of Catalonia, helping it to rectify some of its leftist mistakes, which found expression in:

a) its mistaken assumption that the anarchists had lost their influence in Catalonia, and, as a result, there was no need to involve them in the popular front; that a government could be created in Catalonia consisting [only] of the United Socialist Party of Catalonia and of the representatives of the petty bourgeoisie, without participation of the anarchists;

b) its wrongful assumption that Catalonia has already passed through the period of bourgeois-democratic revolution and has entered the phase of proletarian revolution.

The CC of the Communist Party of Spain should learn from the experience of the military failures in Viscaya, and pay special attention to the Aragon front, helping the United Socialist Party of Catalonia to fortify this front, to reorganize the industry to satisfy the needs of defense, and to establish firm revolutionary order, so that the United Socialist Party of Catalonia can follow in general the same political and tactical line as the Communist Party of Spain.

6. While continuing the campaign to create a united workers party in Spain, Communists should not force the merging of the Communist Party with the Socialist Party. In regard to the Socialist Party, Communists should keep in mind that in order to fortify and expand the popular front, the most important and basic [factor] is the united action of both parties in the government, in all the organs of power, in the trade unions, in the army, in directing the industry, as well as common action during the parliamentary and municipal elections. If the leaders of the Socialist Party are not ready for an immediate merger, Communists should not by their actions create the impression that they plan to absorb the Socialist Party: they must demonstrate that it is necessary, in the interests of the common cause, to continue [the policy of] united action to secure victory by the people against fascism.

If the leadership of the Socialist Party delays the merger of the two parties, and if, as a result, certain local organizations of the Socialist Party want to join the Communist Party individually, it will be necessary to persuade them that at the present it will be much better for the cause if they continue working within the Socialist Party, strengthening the unity of action, thus preparing the merger of the two parties into one workers' party.

In case of merger of the Communist and Socialist parties, Communists can propose that the [new] party be called "United Socialist and Communist Party."

As to the international affiliation, the united party could maintain connections with both Internationals in order, as is indicated in the program of action adopted by both parties, to struggle for the unification of both Internationals.

7. The party has to do everything possible to galvanize the organs of the popular front, and to create them in places where they do not yet exist. It is essential to plant firmly into the consciousness of the antifascist masses [the understanding] that the policy of the popular front is not a transitional policy but the only <u>correct and lasting policy</u> which provides the possibility to unite all the forces <u>to gain victory over fascism</u> and thereafter to build a new Spain together. For this purpose, it is essential that the Communist Party take the initiative to expand the common actions of the popular front (meetings, discussions, declarations in the press, etc.). Despite all the hardships, the party should persistently, firmly, and consistently, pursue the policy of the popular front, fighting the tendencies to narrow it and taking all the necessary measures to strengthen and expand it and to achieve cooperation of all of the trade union organizations with the popular-front government.

B. <u>Regarding the economic situation.</u>

8. Taking into account that since the outbreak of the revolt, large and medium-size enterprises in the territory controlled by Republican troops were abandoned by their owners and in fact passed into the hands of the workers; [taking into account] that the management of these enterprises by individual trade unions or by the workers was chaotic, without any plan; [taking into account] this disintegration of the economy, which fulfills anarcho-syndicalist theories about the leading role of trade unions in the leadership of the economy, parties and organizations of the popular front should immediately take [appropriate] measures <u>to normalize production and to regulate the whole economy by organs of state power</u> in close collaboration <u>with the trade unions</u>. This is all the more essential since the successful waging of the war requires mobilization of all of the country's economic resources, and their most rational utilization for the needs of the national defense. Therefore, the government should <u>nationalize all the large industrial [and] commercial enterprises</u>, turning them to serve the needs of the people. Exceptions can be granted only to individuals who have demonstrated their loyalty to the people's Republic, as well as to foreigners. The latter should be compensated for the nationalized enterprises or should be permitted to run them as private enterprises as long as they are obeying the laws of the Republic.

The government should lead and direct these enterprises through the Council for Economic Management, which is to be created by the government.

This economic council consists of one representative each from: the Ministry of Finance, Ministry of Industry, Ministry of Agriculture, Ministry of Trade, Ministry of Communications; the cooperatives, the peasant organizations, the trade unions, and the Generalitat of Catalonia. (A council of the same kind should be created in Catalonia; the Catalan council should work in close contact with the National Council of Spain.)

The economic council should work out production plans for industry and agriculture, ensure the work of the factories, plants, commercial enterprises, agricultural collectives, cooperatives, etc., in order to maximize the output of these enterprises and to achieve price reductions. [The council] should deal with the supply of raw materials to industry and of seeds and fertilizers to agriculture. It should establish limits on the selling prices of manufactured goods and agricultural products. In order for this policy of firm prices to be successful, it is essential that the ministers of agriculture and industry always have at their disposal stocks of goods and agricultural products so that when needed, they could be thrown into the market to lower the prices. The economic council should regulate the distribution of goods on the basis of the productive capacity, and the demand of the country. It should work out a plan of exports and imports, and see to its implementation.

9. The nationalized enterprises should be put under control of a technical director, named by the Ministry of Industry or by the ministry to which a given enterprise is subordinate. When naming a director, the opinion of the workers about the candidate being promoted to the director's position should be taken into account. In all the enterprises, nationalized and private, there should be a control committee elected at the general meeting of all the employees and workers of the enterprise. This committee, responsible to the employees of the enterprise, should regularly report to them, and could be removed and replaced by a newly elected committee. The number of members of the control committee should be determined by the size of the enterprise. The control committee should set itself the following tasks:

a) Control over production, in close cooperation with the technical leadership of the enterprise, in order to improve the quality of production and increase the productivity of the enterprise;

b) control over the incoming and outgoing materials in order to struggle against the plundering of money and raw materials;

c) protection of the living and working conditions of workers: discipline, protection of labor, hygiene, etc.

10. The entire war industry should not only be nationalized but militarized as well. All the employees of the war enterprises should be considered conscripted. Directing the war industry and fending off intervention by the trade union organizations, the Ministry of Armament should at the same time secure close cooperation with these organizations for the sake of the maximal increase of production of all types of weapons, mercilessly punishing any sabotage or indolence as complicity with the enemy.

11. The party should strengthen the campaign to create agricultural cooperatives and trade and production cooperatives, providing assistance to the already existing cooperatives, [which were] created on the voluntary basis. The party should also help reorganize the forcibly created cooperatives, giving their members the right to leave the collective at their discretion. It is essential to struggle to develop democratic methods in the already existing collectives (elections to the governing bodies, financial accountability, etc.). The party should protect the prices established by the government, for agricultural products as well as manufactured goods, struggling against speculators and the "new rich" as enemies of the people.

12. In view of the fact that it is impossible to direct the national economy without nationalizing banks and integrating them into the common economic system, it is important to nationalize all the banks in the country, and to reorganize them in accordance with the new economic structure of the country. For this purpose, it is essential that the following banks function: Banco de España (emission bank), Industrial Bank, National Agricultural Bank, Bank for Foreign Trade, Mortgage Bank.

C. <u>Regarding the international situation</u>.

13. It is essential to intensify:

a) A <u>political campaign</u> in all of the capitalist countries, demanding that the governments:

<u>Stop supporting Franco in the war against the Spanish people</u>.

It is especially important to mobilize the public opinion of the democratic circles in France, England, and the United States against providing assistance to Franco. It is essential to achieve common action of all the workers' organizations (the Socialist International, the Amsterdam trade union federation, the Communist International, etc.) in defense of the Spanish people. It is necessary to press the international trade union centers of longshoremen and transport workers to mobilize their members to cease loading and transporting arms to Franco. Such an action would be especially important in Germany, Italy, and Portugal. It is essential that individual trade unions in Spain (sailors, transport workers, longshoremen, metal workers, miners) appeal to the trade unions of other countries for real action against General Franco and the German and Italian interventionists. Speeches by deputies elected by the workers in the parliaments and municipal governments are essential, as well as the organization of mass meetings and demonstrations in support of the heroic struggle of the Spanish people.

b) Parallel to this political campaign, it is important to intensify a campaign to provide <u>material support</u> to the Spanish people (food, coal, clothes, medical supplies, etc.), giving a broader social base of support to the committees of support already existing in different countries, creating them, on a broad basis, wherever they do not yet exist. It is especially important to help the population of Asturias with food [supplies], as well as to help evacuate the civil population (women, children, the elderly), organizing their admission and placement with the support of workers' and democratic organizations.

c) Settle the issue of the International Brigades, seeing to their prompt reinforcement and growth through an influx of new volunteers, securing for the volunteers and their families the same rights that the Republic has given the Spanish fighters.

"Ercoli" did not hesitate to tell Dimitrov, in however diplomatic a form, that he strongly dissented from the behavior and methods of the other Comintern advisers to the PCE, notably Gerö and Codovilla. He demanded that "our 'advisers' stop considering themselves the 'bosses' of the party, that they in fact stop looking upon the Spanish comrades as incapable of doing anything, and that they [refrain from] replacing them under the pretext of doing things better and faster, etc."[20]

16 June 1938

One of the sources of tension between the Spanish government and the PCE was the decree of Defense Minister Prieto forbidding partisan political activity by officers of the Republican army: this meant the abolition of the institution of political commissars, a virtual Communist stronghold in the army.

In early 1938 the Republican military situation worsened still further. Morale was low, as were supplies of arms, and foreign support was weak. On 17 February, Stalin and Molotov summoned Dimitrov and Manuilsky for a discussion in which Stalin, somewhat unexpectedly, urged the Communists to pull out of the Spanish government. "The Spanish Communists must leave the government," Stalin said (as Dimitrov recorded it). "They have two second-rate positions in it. If they leave, this will help the disintegration of Franco's front, and to some extent it will help the international position of the Spanish Republic. Quitting must not be demonstrative, not as a consequence of unhappiness with the government, but in

20. RTsKhIDNI, f. 495, op. 74, d. 212, l. 56b.

order to ease the tasks of the government. [The members should explain their resignation by saying that] since the [anarcho]-syndicalists are not in it, the Communists consider it inappropriate to be in the cabinet. Support the government but don't enter it—such must be our position at this given stage."[21] Dimitrov transmitted Stalin's instructions through PCE leader Manuel Delicado and the general secretary of the Catalonian United Socialist Party, Juan Comorera, who happened to be in Moscow at the time. Somewhat to Dimitrov's embarrassment, before this message was received in Spain, a report arrived from "Ercoli" urging a greater Communist role—if necessary, Communists should take the lead in forming a new government.[22] Dimitrov rather sheepishly forwarded "Ercoli's" message to Stalin, and a few days later "Ercoli" inquired whether pulling out of the government was a tactical recommendation or a new, principled position. Meanwhile, the PCE leadership discussed the Comintern message, and on 30 March, "Ercoli" reported: "Your advice and directives have been discussed and accepted by the administration [that is, the PCE leadership]."[23]

As "Ercoli's" fuller report later in April indicated, the Comintern guidance had caused considerable confusion in the PCE Central Committee, but Moscow's view prevailed, and "Ercoli" managed to put a positive spin on it—it freed the Communists' hands—although, as document 11 shows, he continued to beg for Soviet help in Spain.[24] In fact, the Spanish government was reorganized, and one Communist remained in it.

21. TsPA (Sofia), f. 146, op. 2, a.e. 3.
22. RTsKhIDNI, f. 495, op. 74, d. 216, l. 4; op. 184, vkhod. 1938, Osobye, d. 3, l. 31.
23. RTsKhIDNI, f. 495, op. 184, vkhod. 1938, Osobye, d. 3, l. 39.
24. RTsKhIDNI, f. 495, op. 74, d. 212, l. 165; also published in Togliatti, *Opere*, vol. 4, pt. 1, pp. 258–272.

Document 11

Dimitrov to Stalin, 16 June 1938, with enclosure. RTsKhIDNI, f. 495, op. 74, d. 216, ll. 14, 15. Original in Russian. Typewritten.

Copy.

TO COMRADE I. V. STALIN

[We] received the enclosed telegram from Com. Ercoli today. I am sending a copy of this telegram to Com. Voroshilov.

_p. p._ With fraternal greeting, **_G. Dimitrov._**

16 *June* 1938
No. 223/ld

15 June 1938
To Dimitrov
From Ercoli.

I beg you urgently to raise with the appropriate organs the question of providing more extensive and effective assistance to Republican Spain. This assistance is essential to increase the combat capacity of the army and, in particular, to strengthen and improve the command. We think that this is the key to the whole situation. As a result of the army's reorganization, the Communist commanding staff plays a vital role at almost every front, but it is inept at commanding military units. Sometimes the disarray is even greater than it was previously, despite the fact that the situation with arms [supplies] has improved. Negrín himself now has more opportunities to influence the course of operations planned by the general staff. Negrín insists that we help him more [by providing] people who know military science. The party is doing everything possible to help Negrín. However, the ability of the Communist Party to send [such people to work in] the general staff is very limited. Therefore, help in this matter is needed from another source that you know about. We all are urgently asking for this help.

Barc[elona] 15.6.38.

---

20 June 1938

Another "Ercoli" telegram reports an impending government crisis in what remains of Republican Spain and urges prompt Soviet help.

Document 12

Dimitrov to Stalin, 20 June 1938, with enclosure. RTsKhIDNI, f. 495, op. 74, d. 216, ll. 11, 16. Original in Russian. Typewritten.

Copy

To Comrade I. V. STALIN

We are sending you a telegram from Com. Ercoli, which we have just received. We are also sending a copy of this telegram to Com. Molotov.

_p. p._ With fraternal greeting,

G. Dimitrov

20 June 1938

No. 225/ld

A copy of the telegram sent has been left in C. Dimitrov's [office].

TO [COMRADE] DIMITROV.

The fall of Castellón coincides with the revival of the backstage intrigues against the Negrín government on the part of some Socialist leaders who are in favor of ending the war. These intrigues create a rather difficult situation for the government. The opponents of the government used measures to reestablish unity within the Socialist Party in their campaign against the Negrín government. In the reorganization of the Executive Committee of the Socialist Party, they promoted for chairman the candidacy of Besteiro (an extreme right Socialist), who declared recently that the policy of the popular front had caused the war in Spain. Caballero and his supporters have also been made members of the reorganized Executive Committee. The first act of the new Executive Committee will be expressing no confidence in Negrín in order to create a government crisis, and to give Azaña a chance to create a government of his choice [composed] of those favoring an armistice and capitulators. This maneuver is being prepared by Prieto and Azaña and is supported by Gonzalez Peña, who is chairman of the Socialist Party and who, until recently, cooperated with the Communists. This maneuver creates a difficult situation for our party. The anarchist National Confederation of Labor is against a change of government. Its general secretary told us that they were ready to fight together with the Communists against the supporters of capitulation. The leadership of the General Labor Union, too, is still supporting Negrín, but may vacillate under pressure from the rightist leaders of the Socialist Party. Leftist Republicans are the driving force of this intrigue; similarly the Catalans are against Negrín. Separatist elements, inspired by the enemy, have become active. Under these conditions, the government crisis and the creation of a new government composed of known capitulators would create an impossible situation for the army. Today the CC will decide on the measures to be taken. We will inform you about the decision of the CC.

Ercoli.

Barcelona, 19.VI.38.

22 June 1938

Two days later Dimitrov sent Stalin the latest message from "Ercoli," which commented among other things on the possibility of proclaiming martial law in Republican Spain.

Document 13

Dimitrov to Stalin, 22 June 1938, with enclosure. RTsKhIDNI, f. 495, op. 74, d. 216, ll. 21, 22. Original in Russian. Typewritten.

TO COMRADE I. V. STALIN

We have received the enclosed telegram from Com. Ercoli.

Regarding the possible proclamation of martial law, we think that our friends should not oppose [it] on condition that the necessary freedom for political work and agitation is assured, in order to intensify the struggle against fascism and its agents in Republican Spain.

We are asking for your advice.

With fraternal greeting,
(G. Dimitrov)

22 June 1938

A copy is being sent to C. Molotov.

Telegram from Ercoli.

The decision of the CC in regard to the scheming maneuvers of Besteiro, Caballero, and Prieto is as follows:

To paralyze these maneuvers by mobilizing all organs of the popular front, both local and national, by mobilizing the popular masses and the army. This measure has already yielded significant results. At the same time, the party has to serve as an intermediary between Negrín and the leadership of the Socialist Party, striving for their reconciliation and for the settlement of the questions in dispute between the Spanish government and the Catalan government. At the same time the party must not oppose the reunification of the Socialist Party but should seek in every possible way to renew and strengthen the agreement between the Communist and Socialist parties for accomplishing common tasks in defense of the Republic. [It is necessary] to establish even closer contact between the General Workers Union and the National (anarchist) Labor Confederation. [It is important] to intensify the work of the party [in] the trade unions, and [in] the United Socialist Youth in order to satisfy the urgent needs of the working and peasant masses, in particular on questions of supplies to the population, on questions of unemployment, of refugees, etc., and thus to eliminate grounds for discontent and alarm among the masses. Besides, Negrín will probably raise the question of declaring martial law in the country. On this question, there are vacillations in the CC. In my opinion, we should not oppose this measure, but it is essential to demand certain guarantees regarding the freedom of agitation. Please tell us your opinion on this question.

28 August 1938

On 28 August 1938 the ECCI Secretariat adopted a resolution on "Practical Steps" to increase the food supply to Republican Spain, including an appeal to the various foreign Communist parties to organize a campaign to gain credits, international loans, and other economic aid. The letter printed below details the need for food and reports what the Comintern is doing. It also conveys the latest request from the PCE for Soviet help.

But by this time it was too late: even if Moscow had decided to provide massive assistance, the collapse of the Republicans had gone too far. The Soviet leadership did not in fact choose to contribute such aid. There remains the intriguing question of whether the Soviet Union could—or by its own criteria should—have helped more. Like most states, it was bound to put its own domestic interests first; Spain seemed far away, and its relevance to the national interest (not a concept Moscow used widely anyway) was obscure. With the prospect of war closer to home looming, and with severe shortages inside the Soviet Union, a "Russia first" approach was bound to have its proponents. Moreover, a greater Soviet assistance program would surely have embroiled the Soviet Union in international complications at a time when it was eager to avoid them. Certainly, the Soviet Union did far more than, say, France and Britain to support the Spanish Republic. In the eyes of many of its friends and followers, however, its conduct in Spain, even aside from the tensions generated by the behavior of its personnel, raised serious questions about the depth of its internationalist commitments.

Document 14

Dimitrov and Manuilsky to Stalin and Molotov, 28 August 1938. RTsKhIDNI, f. 495, op. 74, d. 216, ll. 25–28. Original in Russian. Typewritten. This copy was in Molotov's file.

COPY!
To Comrade Molotov
To Comrade Stalin

Memorandum.

The food situation in the Spanish Republic is extremely difficult. There are shortages of bread, meat, fish, vegetables, sugar, and milk. The populace in the cities, especially Madrid, have been close to starving for several months. Cases of workers fainting at their workplaces due to exhaustion have become frequent. Lately, the lack of food has become acute in the army. Each new day increases the sick rate among the civilian population because of systematic malnutrition, as well as in the army of the central region. The winter will be especially hard.

According to Spanish government calculations, in order to avoid hunger in the country and secure supplies for the army, the Spanish Republic needs to import monthly, in addition to the existing internal resources of food:

Wheat	85,000 tons
Barley	10,500 tons
Vegetables	25,000 tons
(mostly peas and lentils)	
Fish—cod	7,500 tons
Canned fish	700 tons
Frozen meat	7,000 tons
Canned meat	3,000 tons
Pork	500 tons
Ham	200 tons
Lard	200 tons
Cheese	200 tons
Sugar	13,000 tons
Eggs	20,000 cartons
Condensed milk	200,000 cartons
Powdered milk	200 tons
Coffee	1,000 tons
Cocoa	750 tons.

According to the Spanish government calculations, which were passed to us by C. Uribe, a member of the Political Bureau of the Spanish Communist Party and the military council who has come [here], the cost of all these products equals £2,448,825 or 14,458,107 golden rubles.

Besides that, the Spanish popular army is in urgent need of warm clothes [and] shoes to prepare itself for the winter military campaign.

At the proposal of the Politburo of the Spanish Communist Party, the Comintern is mobilizing all its sections to intensify efforts to raise resources and food for the Spanish people, with the help of the Committees of Help to Republican Spain which exist in different countries, and [with the help of] the Central International Committee in Paris. For this purpose it is planned, besides intensified raising of money and food, to impose a levy on all members of Communist parties in capitalist countries, [to impose] a similar levy on trade union members, to have the Central Committee for Assistance to Spain issue a special international loan, to conduct a campaign for extending a food loan to the Spanish government by the governments of France, England, the USA, and the social-democratic governments of the Scandinavian countries, etc.

At the same time, the Politburo of the Spanish Communist Party asks us to raise the following questions with the Politburo of the CC VKP(b):

First, would it not be possible for the Soviet trade unions to participate in the international campaign of food assistance to Spain? The funds raised could be used to purchase food in the USSR, and this food could be sent, on behalf of the VTsSPS[25] to the Spanish government or to the Spanish trade unions.

Second, C. Uribe, following the instructions of Negrín and in agreement with the Politburo of the Spanish Communist Party, has raised a question of whether the Soviet government could supply part of the food needed by the Spanish Republic on favorable credit terms.

We are asking for your directives regarding the questions raised by the Politburo of the Spanish Communist Party.

28.8.38.

       G. D.

       D. M.

P. S. We have already sent this note to C. Stalin.

---

4 December 1938

The ECCI now discussed the withdrawal of the International Brigades from Spain, and on 29 August, Dimitrov and Manuilsky sent Stalin and Voroshilov a letter to this effect; this letter has not been located in the archives. The question of their withdrawal had

25. Russian abbreviation of *Vsesoiuznyi tsentral'nyi sovet professional'nykh soiuzov* (The All-Union Central Council of Trade Unions).—Trans.

come up in the London nonintervention committee and was tied to the withdrawal of Italian and German forces on the Franco side, but Soviet consent to the dissolution of the brigades would not have come if the prospects had been any better. Dimitrov recorded in his diary a telephone conversation with Voroshilov on 1 September, in which he promised to provide the weapons and agreed to the liquidation of the International Brigades.[26] Word was passed to Spain, and on 21 September, Negrín announced to the League of Nations that all foreign volunteers were being withdrawn. The move was not reciprocated by the Franco side.

Many members of the International Brigades made their own way out of Spain, primarily into France, where large numbers were interned. The Comintern mounted a campaign against their extradition to Germany, Italy, or Franco Spain, and Dimitrov asked Stalin to allow them to enter the Soviet Union. In February 1939 the Politburo authorized the return of three hundred "volunteers" dispatched from the Soviet Union (mostly foreign Communists, rather than Soviet citizens).[27] In fact, the fate of most remaining brigade members in France was still unresolved when World War II broke out.

Document 15

Dimitrov to Stalin and others, 4 December 1938, with enclosure. RTsKhIDNI, f. 495, op. 74, d. 216, ll. 29, 31, 41–44. Original in Russian. Typewritten.

Copy.
To Comrade I. V. STALIN
Com. V. M. MOLOTOV
Com. L. M. KAGANOVICH
Com. K. K. VOROSHILOV
Com. N. I. YEZHOV
Com. A. I. MIKOYAN
Com. A. A. ANDREEV
We are sending to you a report "On the Current Situation and Tasks in Spain" by the ECCI staff worker who has been working in the CC CP of Spain for more than a year.

26. TsPA (Sofia), f. 146, op. 2, a.e.4.
27. RTsKhIDNI, f. 17, op. 162, d. 24, l. 104; and f. 495, op. 184, iskh. 1939, d. 14, l. 91.

The conclusions drawn in the report coincide in general with the point of view of the Politburo of the CC CP of Spain.

G Dim

(G. DIMITROV).

4.12.38.

3288 (2) ac

19.XI.38.

Top secret.

ON THE CURRENT SITUATION AND TASKS IN SPAIN.

I. General assessment of the situation. Immediate prospects.

One must expect that the Spanish Republic will be subject, in the very near future, to a very serious test, by all indications the most serious test since the beginning of the war for independence. After the enemy liquidated the "pocket" on the Ebro, it freed large human and material resources. During the past month, the enemy has already systematically probed different sectors of the front, in particular, the Madrid and the Levantine fronts.

According to reliable sources, Italy is sending a new expeditionary corps to Spain. Already by early November, 12,000 troops with appropriate equipment had assembled in the port of Spezia, ready to be deployed.

It is obvious that the military offensive, which should be expected in the very near future, will be combined with the international diplomatic offensive (recognizing Franco as a warring party; a trip by Chamberlain and Halifax to Paris planned for 23 November to prepare a pact to strangle the Spanish Republic), and the offensive in the home policy (intensification of the activity of the capitulators and of the enemies of unity, enemies of the popular front, of the government, of the Communist Party, i.e., the Trotskyists, Caballerists, adventurers from the *Iberian Anarchist Federation* (FAI), etc.).

[. . .]

Some conclusions.

In order to further strengthen the unity, it is necessary to step up the struggle against the enemies of unity, [against] POUM, [against] the Caballerists, [against] the adventurers from the *Iberian Anarchist Federation* (FAI), [against] the capitulators, and tie this struggle with the struggle for a tighter unity between the *Communist Party* and the Soc[ialist] Party, for the unity of youth [organizations], for galvanizing the popular front, and, most of all, for creating a united trade union center as a vital goal of the war itself. In order to achieve this goal, it will be necessary to raise specific questions not only regarding the further improvement of the party's work in the *General Confederation of Trade Unions* (UGT) and in the factories but also about the work in the *National Confederation of Labor* (CNT), so as to have some prominent leaders of the CNT (from among [its] most honest elements) join the Communist Party and the United Socialist Party of Catalonia, utilizing such cases to launch a major political campaign.

V. Some problems of the CP of Spain and of the United Socialist Party of Catalonia.

The new tactical orientation, worked out in August–September (the line toward unification of all Spaniards in the struggle against the interventionists, along with raising the policy of resistance to a higher level), has found <. . .> time. Therefore only 3 out of 7 members of the P[olitical] B[ureau] are capable of carrying out their leadership duties. In addition to that, the situation requires distributing members of the leadership between the Catalonian and non-Catalonian zones in order to place the general leadership in Barcelona (*the Politburo*), and in the non-Catalonian zone, in Madrid, a sufficiently strong and authoritative delegation of the CC, since the party is in fact located there, and more than two-thirds of the population and three-quarters of the army are there, too. This requires the strengthening of the *Politburo.* Spanish comrades (Com. Diaz) foresee co-optation into the *Politburo* of the following comrades: Girola (member of the CC), Manco (member of the CC), Dieguez (secretary of the Madrid regional [party] committee, member of the CC), Palau (secretary of the Valencia regional [party] committee, nonmember of the CC), *and Comorera (member of the CC, gen[eral] sec[retary] of the United Soc[ialist] Party of Catalonia).* It is also planned to recall Com. Carton from the army to conduct work in the P[olitical] B[ureau].

Convocation of a congress of the United Socialist Party of Catalonia is planned for the second half of January. Here the question about the leadership is even more acute than in the CP of S*pain*, since the current leadership is incapable of securing the situation. Besides, there is a danger of factional struggle among factionalist elements. This [conflict] emerged as a result of the recent struggle over the question of relations between the Republican [government] and the Catalan autonomous government. The party currently counts more than 75 thousand members (of whom 35 thousand are in the army). The party is growing especially in Barcelona (800–1,000 new members in Barcelona each month, 70 percent of them workers, 30 percent women, of whom 15 percent are from the CNT) and in the army. The party has a sound basis, and its majority desires friendly cooperation with the Communist Party and consider themselves Communist. However, there are still a number of hostile, Caballerist, and nationalist elements.

In order to secure the united leadership of the CP of Spain and the United Socialist Party of Catalonia, a united secretariat has been created. [This secretariat] is not yet working smoothly, but there has been improvement in the last weeks. It would be expedient, if the situation in the country permits it, before the PCE conference and the congress of the United Soc[ialist] Party of Catalonia take place, to invite Com. *Comorera* together with a member of the Politburo of the PCE to discuss all the questions and finally settle relations between the two parties.

It would also be necessary to send Com. G*uillot* or M <. . .> *l* to Spain in or-

Document 15 *continued*

der to study the situation with the youth movement, together with the Polit-buro and the leadership of the united Socialist Youth, and to take appropriate measures to assure the unity of the united Socialist Youth and to make the an-tifascist alliance of the youth more active.

VI. <u>The international campaign and activities to help the Spanish Republic</u>.

In Republican Spain the opinion that the international proletariat does not actually help the Spanish people, and that one should not expect any real sup-port from it, is widespread. On the other hand, it is necessary to acknowledge that the assistance that has been provided [to Spain] is insufficient.

In face of the imminent danger, it may be essential to take all [necessary] measures to step up the international assistance, not simply in the form of sending food supplies (which is very important since there are already very strong symptoms of hunger in the country) but mostly through mass activities to prevent a new escalation of the intervention, [to prevent] the recognition of Franco as a warring party, and [to prevent] the realization of the Hitler-Mussolini-Chamberlain-Daladier plans to strangle the Spanish Republic.

After the fall of Catalonia, the outcome of the civil war was no longer in doubt. To the end, Pedro and others pressed Moscow to provide more help, but now both the Soviet authorities—in this case, again Voroshilov—and the Comintern (under orders) de-murred. At the end, some of the Communists toyed with attempt-ing a complete seizure of power and imposition of iron discipline in what remained of Republican Spain, but Moscow once more opted against it.

In any event, it was too late. On 6 March 1939 a coup in Madrid led to a cease-fire with the Franco forces. The PCE blamed the col-lapse on everyone but the Communists and, at least on the surface, reaffirmed its total fealty to Stalin and the USSR.[28]

28. TsPA (Sofia), f. 146, op. 2, a.e. 4; RTsKhIDNI, f. 495, op. 74, d. 216, l. 55; d. 220, ll. 33, 65, 66, 72; op. 184, iskh. 1939, d. 12, l. 19; Togliatti, *Opere*, vol. 4, pt. 1, pp. 325–332.

CHAPTER FOUR

Chinese Communism and the Sino-Japanese War

CHINA represented one of the most difficult foreign policy problems for Moscow. The Soviet Union maintained wary relations with the Nationalist Chinese regime of Chiang Kai-shek, though periodically the Soviet media scathingly assailed the Chinese government for its policies toward the Communists and toward Japan. The Comintern, of course, devoted its efforts to the Chinese Communists—a party with its own traditions, its own modus operandi, a remarkable record of military and political struggle, and a greater degree of distance from Moscow, not only geographically but also in attitude and autonomy, than virtually any other section of the Comintern. As Japanese expansionist ambitions became more pronounced, the Soviet Union was eager to use the Chinese as a potential shield and an ally, both to deflect the Japanese from attacking the Soviet Far East and, if it came to a fight, to create a solid front opposing them. At the same time, Moscow naturally favored a more powerful role for the Chinese Communists, but its information about their prospects was often questionable, contradictory, and (as it had been during the various crises of 1927) profoundly biased or inadequate.[1]

1. The terms "soviets" and "Red Army" in Chinese Communist and Comintern

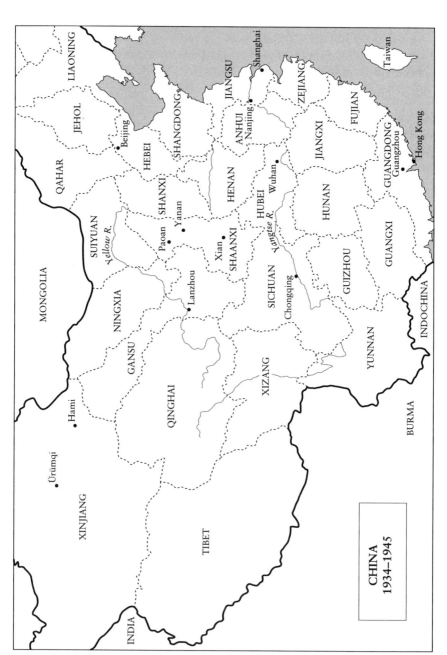

China, 1934–1945

14 April 1936

In 1936 Dimitrov sent Stalin a basic outline of the situation in China and the tasks the Comintern wanted the CCP to undertake that had been prepared in March by Pavel Mif, a prominent young Comintern specialist on the Far East, with the assistance of Wang Ming, an important Chinese representative to the ECCI. Wang was to prove more independent than many Comintern representatives—at times he promoted policies that were at variance with those of Dimitrov and of the CCP leadership under Mao Zedong. Dimitrov as usual asks for Stalin's advice and guidance.

This is one of the first major documents on China prepared after the Seventh World Congress. Essentially, the Comintern applied to the Chinese situation its general strategy of a "united front" that was adopted the previous year. In this instance, it implies that Chinese Communists should form a coalition with the Nationalists against the Japanese. But, unlike its translation into political guidelines in Western Europe, here the document rather extravagantly foresees the possible collapse of the Guomindang—the Chinese Nationalists—and the emergence of the People's Liberation Army and Chinese soviets as the central organs of the united front.

There is a strong, entirely circumstantial likelihood that Stalin never approved this document and therefore it was not sent to the CCP as a Comintern directive. If so, it is not clear why.

Document 16

Dimitrov to Stalin, 14 April 1936, with enclosure. Letter: RTsKhIDNI, f. 495, op. 74, d. 294, l.1; enclosure: f. 514, op. 1, d. 847, ll. 32–46. Original in Russian. Typewritten.

Copy
Top secret.
Dear Comrade Stalin,
    The enclosed document, "The Situation in China and the Tasks of the CP of China," has been worked out by Com. Mif, together with Com. Wang Ming and

parlance refer not to institutions of the Soviet Union but to their equivalents in Communist-held China—an area once referred to as the Chinese Soviet Republic.

Document 16 *continued*

other Chinese comrades, <u>after a detailed discussion of the question</u> of the tactics of the CP of China under the present circumstances.

<u>Due to the special importance of this document, I beg you to give us appropriate advice and guidance.</u>

p. p. With fraternal greeting,
(Dimitrov)

14 April 1936.
No. 330.

4/MKh.
<u>Top secret.</u>

THE SITUATION IN CHINA AND THE TASKS OF THE CPC.
(Draft.)

1. China is at a historical turning point. In large areas of China, popular masses have already been reduced to the position of colonial slaves. Other regions of China, as well as China as a whole, are facing the imminent danger of complete colonial enthrallment. China is going through the greatest national crisis. "A people which, at such moments of greatest crisis, is incapable of cutting the knot by revolutionary means—such a people is doomed" (Marx).

The Japanese imperialists have made a stake in the fate of China. Under these circumstances, organizing the struggle of the entire people against the Japanese occupiers has become the <u>central</u> task for the Chinese Communists, a task to which all others must be subordinated. A correct and consistent implementation of the <u>united-front tactics</u> by the Communist Party of China has acquired paramount importance, since the creation of a united popular anti-imperialist front against the Japanese oppressors is a necessary and most important condition of the liberation of the Chinese people.

2. In China exceptionally favorable conditions have emerged for promoting the new CCP tactics and for creating a united popular front. <u>The unrestrained aggression</u> of the Japanese imperialists has generated a powerful increase in the anti-imperialist struggle by the Chinese masses. An <u>ongoing disintegration</u> of the economy, augmented by the aggressive acts of the Japanese imperialists, dooms millions of toilers to wretched vegetating and to death from starvation. The unheard-of disasters which have befallen the Chinese people cause the cup of popular indignation to overflow. Among broader masses there is a growing understanding that it is necessary to unite all the forces of the Chinese people into a decisive armed resistance to the Japanese occupiers.

3. This is being demonstrated by recent events in China. The student movement has gained a broad scope. Workers' strikes at Japanese enterprises have become more frequent. Peasant disturbances in the occupied zones have become more frequent. The tide of street demonstrations and other actions by

the Chinese masses against the Japanese imperialists and their Chinese servitors is growing. The petty urban bourgeoisie, the progressive bourgeois intelligentsia, and the patriotic segment of the national bourgeoisie are joining the national liberation movement. The rising movement is exerting an ever growing influence upon the military units, including a significant portion of junior and middle-level officers and even part of the high command. This movement reflects a <u>tremendous attraction</u> of the broadest masses of the Chinese people to the united popular, anti-imperialist front.

The new power of the Chinese Communist Party permits it to serve as an initiator and organizer of the popular anti-imperialist front. The successes of the soviet movement, the existence of the armed support of the national revolution in the form of the Chinese Red Army as it has been tested in many battles, facilitates the soviets' and the Red Army's becoming the center of unification of all the Chinese people to struggle for the salvation of their motherland.

4. The creation of the united popular anti-imperialist front is also facilitated by the ongoing process of disintegration of the ruling Guomindang and by the emergence of a number of political groups and organizations of anti-imperialist character. Growing numbers of the Chinese population, including the Guomindang rank and file, are disillusioned by the policy of capitulation pursued by the Guomindang leadership. It is not impossible that not only individuals in the Guomindang but entire groups adhering to it and some of its organizations may, in the very near future, take the course of complete rupture with the policy of the Guomindang leadership and join the powerful popular front of the struggle for national liberation.

Without doubt, the sharp aggravation of antagonisms between the major imperialist powers, due to the continuing aggression of Japanese imperialism, will be a favorable factor. The united front of the imperialist powers, which used to serve as one of the major impediments to the national revolution, is now beginning to crumble.

5. All these circumstances can lead to such a turn of events in China that unexpected and unique combinations will be created in the kinds of struggle and the balances of the struggling forces, somewhat reminiscent of the situation in February 1917 in Russia, which Lenin described: "If the revolution won out so quickly and so—seemingly, at first glance—'radically,' it is only because, due to an extremely original historical situation, <u>completely different</u> currents, <u>completely diverse</u> class interests, <u>completely adverse</u> political and social aspirations <u>merged</u>, and merged in a remarkably 'friendly' way" (Lenin, "Letters from Afar").

The CCP is facing a very serious task: to utilize correctly and fully all direct and indirect reserves, to draw into the general popular struggle all the national-patriotic elements. Japanese imperialism is the bitterest enemy of the entire Chinese people. To fight this common enemy, all forces should be mobilized. Everyone who expresses readiness to struggle against Japanese imperialism should be drawn into the popular front, irrespective of political convictions, class and party affiliation, religious beliefs, etc., including temporary, unsteady, and unreliable allies. Considering the current situation, the Communist Party of China should utilize the historically unique opportunities to create a popular anti-imperialist front and to organize a successful struggle for the national and social liberation of the Chinese people.

6. Despite all these favorable conditions, it would be a mistake to believe that the implementation of united-front tactics is an easy task that does not require the maximal efforts of all forces of the party, its flexible maneuverability and broadest initiative. The Chinese Communists must rid themselves of such wrongful illusions. They must have a clear understanding of all the difficulties they are facing on this road. They have to consider a number of factors that hinder the powerful anti-imperialist upsurge and the unification of the entire Chinese people. These factors include: a) lack of state unity, the feudal-militarist division of China; b) the experience of the 1925–27 revolution and, in particular, the fear of an independent mass movement on the part of the national bourgeoisie; c) uneven distribution of the forces of the Communist Party of China and, in particular, the party's weakness in the major centers of the Guomindang territory and the occupied zones; d) the party's leftist-sectarian mistakes [committed] in both the White and soviet regions, which have not yet been overcome and which to this day obstruct and hinder the CCP's struggle to create a united popular anti-imperialist front. Despite the obstacles to overcoming all the difficulties, the Communist Party of China must at any cost bring about the united popular anti-imperialist front against Japanese imperialism and its Chinese servitors.

7. The struggle for salvation of the motherland, for the independence of the country, for national and social liberation of the masses has to be the starting point and the main content of the popular anti-imperialist front in China. At the same time, the CCP has to propagandize, in word and deed, the notion that the anti-imperialist front will be the stronger and more powerful the sooner and more thoroughly the proletariat, the peasantry, and the urban poor are involved in the struggle. The better the party arranges for the protection of the vital needs and the direct economic and political interests of the toiling masses, the sooner it can rally the widest masses of toilers around the proletarian core, and attract the vacillating patriotic elements to the powerful anti-imperialist front. The popular front can be created and develop only on the basis of common concrete actions and activities. Therefore the CCP should take the most active part in every movement aimed against the Japanese occupiers, regardless of who organizes it, seeking to add to the organizational strength of the united front being forged in the struggle.

The Japanese imperialists are gathering the national traitors under the banner of a "united front to struggle against the Communists." The CCP should explain to the masses that China has the following alternative: either decisive resistance to the Japanese imperialists and the salvation of the motherland or the Chinese will be turned into slaves without any rights. While exposing the maneuvers of the Japanese imperialists and their Chinese agents, the CCP must call for a powerful united front of all the people to struggle against the deadly enemy of all the Chinese people—Japanese imperialism.

8. The main weakness of the liberation movement today is the division, discord, and disconnection of various anti-imperialist actions. The central task is to unify the organizations and forces that are conducting, or are capable of conducting, the anti-imperialist struggle, to centralize the leadership, to overcome the disunity of the movement. This is a guarantee of the success of the struggle against the Japanese imperialists, since the impact of the push of the masses will then be quite different from what it is now. Therefore, the Communist Party of China should take the initiative and, disregarding the difficulties, start negotiations with all the parties (the Nationalist Party, the Guomindang organizations, the national-revolutionary league), with all the mass organizations (trade unions, student unions, Association for the Salvation of the Motherland, the Lawyers' Union, the Journalists' Union, etc.), with all the groups in China and in emigration, and with individual political and military figures for the organization of common actions and the centralization of leadership in the anti-Japanese struggle. Specifying the conditions of agreement with each of these organizations, the CCP should seek the unification of all the forces, including the military forces, and the creation of a united army and a united government of national defense, according to the conditions and the platform outlined in the manifesto of the CC CCP of 1/8/35. The CCP should declare, openly and clearly, that it [joins forces] with all those, including Guomindang members, who support the united anti-imperialist popular front and that it is against those, including Guomindang members, who struggle against the united front.

While maintaining its complete independence, and without rejecting for an instant the propaganda of its program and the goals of struggle, the Communist Party should at the same time loyally comply with all the conditions of the agreements signed and accomplish, flawlessly and consistently, all the tasks of the united popular anti-imperialist front. At the same time, the party should expose and conduct a relentless struggle against those organizations and individuals who oppose the united front from the outside or, while participating in it, attempt to destroy it from within by their vacillation and sabotage.

9. Another weakness of the liberation movement has to do with the fact that the large army of the Chinese militarists—this huge armed force—has not yet been involved en masse in the anti-Japanese struggle and is still being used by reactionary militarists against the popular interest, often participating in the suppression of the national-liberation movement. This question should be the main concern of all the advocates of a united popular anti-imperialist front.

Document 16 *continued*

At the same time, the Communist Party itself should radically improve its work with the army of the Chinese militarists. It is essential to win over not only the mass of soldiers but also the commanding officers to the anti-Japanese popular front, under the slogans of ceasing the civil strife and of military resistance to the Japanese occupiers. It is necessary to avoid premature splits and revolts in the military units. It is important to fortify in all possible ways revolutionary sentiments in the army, sending workers and revolutionary students to the military units for this purpose. At the same time, it is necessary to step up the struggle to [improve] the living conditions of the soldiers, [to fight their] brutal treatment, to improve the [quality of] food and clothing, to increase and regularize the payment of salaries, etc.

10. The Chinese Communists should clearly realize that the success of the united popular front depends, first of all, on the <u>strengthening</u> of the Communist Party itself. The more the strength [of the Communist Party] is recognized, the more willingly and quickly others will negotiate and sign agreements with it. This is why further strengthening the soviet regions and increasing the military might of the Red Army remains one of the most important tasks of the Communist Party of China. However, if in the past, the soviet regions were for the most part a territorial base of the agrarian revolution, nowadays they must be, first and foremost, the most reliable base of the anti-imperialist struggle, the leading force and the strongest bulwark of the united popular anti-imperialist front. Through consistent implementation of the programs of the united government of national defense, the CCP should thus provide an example for anyone who considers himself an advocate of the united popular front. This does not mean, however, that the CCP should limit itself to these programs in the soviet regions. Taking into consideration the moods and demands of the masses, the party can implement measures which go beyond the program of the united government. However, the CCP must take into account the interests of the organization of the liberation struggle in all of China.

11. In accordance with this new policy, certain changes should be introduced into the <u>constitution</u> of the Chinese soviets. There should be democracy not only for the workers but for everybody else who participates, in one way or another, in the armed struggle against the Japanese imperialists and for the salvation of the motherland. While extending civil rights to nontoiling elements, it is necessary to secure certain privileges in the electoral system for the workers, as previously. Freedom of speech, assembly, and press should be given to all non-Communist parties, groups, and social and mass organizations that are struggling not against the soviet power but against the imperialists and their servitors. It is necessary to let truly national-revolutionary parties and groups that are honestly struggling—along with the soviets and the Communist Party—against Japanese imperialism and for the salvation of the motherland participate in the soviet organs. It is essential to draw not only bourgeois specialists but also other bourgeois elements into the work of the correspond-

ing soviet organs in order to utilize their experience, connections, and resources in the interests of national revolution (for example, certain merchants and industrialists in the trade and industrial sections of the soviets, etc.).

12. In the interests of the anti-imperialist front of all the people, it is essential to reform and reorganize the <u>Red Army</u> into the popular army of salvation of China. This should result in broadening the army [and] attracting not only broader masses of workers but also students, professionals, and other strata of petty bourgeois youth who participate in the struggle for liberation. It is necessary to accelerate the training of the commanding officers and to specify the grades and ranks of the army commanders. It is important to display more initiative in concluding military agreements and uniting with other military units that are ready to struggle against the Japanese occupiers. While implementing these actions, the CCP must undertake measures to strengthen [its] military-political leadership and to improve its work among both the rank-and-file soldiers and the officers of the revolutionary army.

13. In accordance with the new situation, it is also necessary to adjust the <u>agrarian</u> policy of the Chinese soviets. While pursuing the line of liquidating the remnants of feudalism, in the interests of building the widest possible popular anti-Japanese front, it is essential at the same time to introduce the following changes in the agrarian policy: first, the lands belonging to craftsmen, artisans, teachers, small merchants, and certain workers who acquired it earlier with their savings should not be confiscated even though [these men] do not work it themselves. In response to the demands of the peasants, either they should be permitted to rent it out (of course, not under conditions of bondage), or the government must reimburse them for the value if it is redistributed. Second, the land and the so-called excessive stock belonging to the kulaks should not be confiscated. In case the leveling redistribution of land [takes place] at the demand of the major peasant masses, the kulak plots should be added to the common land, and the kulaks should receive plots on the same basis as the others. Third, the lands of military landowners who actually participate in the armed struggle against Japanese imperialism and for the salvation of the motherland should not be confiscated. Fourth, regarding merchants who are also large landowners, you must limit yourselves to confiscating their lands, leaving their trade enterprises intact.

14. <u>The policy on trade, industry, and labor questions</u>. In order to secure supplies for the Red Army and to improve the material conditions of the masses, it is important first, to give the utmost encouragement to the development of trade and industry [by] private capital, in addition to developing, in every way possible, mass cooperatives and state enterprises; second, for the soviets to review the directives that hinder and limit free trade and the growth of industry; third, to change the attitude toward the chambers of commerce, in particular, not to dissolve them but to use them to develop trade and industry in the soviet regions as well as to develop trade relations between soviet and non-

soviet regions; fourth, to review the tax policy so as to give more space to the development of private trade and industry, etc.

Aiming at the maximal improvement of the material-legal and cultural conditions of workers and farm laborers, it is essential at the same time to avoid any excessive demands that are impossible to meet or that would lead, in the soviet regions under present conditions, to aggravating the economic collapse and unemployment. Second, it is necessary to abstain for now·from organizing the so-called workers' control over production, for which at present conditions are not yet ripe in the territory of Soviet China.

15. The Communist Party must aspire to a more consistent observation of revolutionary law in the soviet regions. Things that the imperialists and their servitors are using in their struggle against the CCP and the soviet movement in China must be eradicated. The use of torture, executions without trial, etc., must not be permitted under any circumstances. Repression and punitive measures (arrests and demands for ransom) against missionaries and other foreign nationals must be discontinued. [These people] must be permitted to continue their work on condition that they observe soviet laws.

The soviets must aim their struggle against the major enemy of the Red Army and the people, first of all, against Japanese imperialism and its servitors. Not only must the soviets establish friendly relations with everyone who conducts and wants to conduct the struggle against the Japanese imperialism, but they must normalize relations with those who for whatever reason do not conduct an armed struggle against the Red Army. The policy and all the activity of the CCP in the soviet regions must be subordinated to the interests of the national-revolutionary war against Japanese imperialism, for the integrity, independence, and revolutionary unification of the country.

16. The success of the anti-imperialist popular front depends in many ways on the strengthening of the positions of the CCP in the Guomindang territories in China. Here the party faces the task of preserving and nourishing its cadres, of strengthening its ties with and influence among the masses, of struggling for the political legalization of the party, of rebuilding and strengthening party organizations in the major centers of the country. The tremendous upsurge of the anti-imperialist struggle in the country and the creation of a series of anti-imperialist organizations are extending the legal possibilities, which the CCP can and must utilize in its work. It is necessary to ensure that except for a small number of Communists working in the clandestine party apparatus, all other organizations (trade unions, youth, etc.) in which there are Communists be legalized or, at least, semi-legalized. Practical experience has demonstrated that there is no need for any illegal organizations besides the party (leftist trade unions, Komsomol, MOPR, etc.). All these organizations must be rebuilt so as to become mass and, if possible, legal or semi-legal organizations. The Chinese comrades must carefully study and employ any possibility for legal work. A united popular anti-imperialist front, besides [its] other [advantages], must

serve as a powerful shield for the Communist Party and significantly increase the scope of its legal activities.

17. It is necessary to systematically expose the attempts by the enemy to depict the Communist Party as a group of conspirators. It is essential to seize every chance to demonstrate that Communists are the most committed patriots and the most progressive fighters for the national and social liberation of the masses. The recent articles in defense of Chinese Communists published in the Chinese press by such prominent figures as Zhang Ta-ion [Taofen?], Zhang Naiqi, Chen Minshu, and others facilitate the struggle of the Communist Party for legalization.

The party must support and broaden in every way possible the movement in defense of Communists that has begun among the bourgeois intelligentsia and a number of political figures. In particular, it is necessary to prepare and conduct a broad mass campaign in connection with the 15th anniversary of the CCP (July 1936). By that date, it is necessary to publish a series of essays on the party history, biographies of fallen heroes and of the most prominent leaders of the party, etc.

Utilizing the humanitarian spirit of the Chinese people, it is important to conduct mass campaigns through the lawyers' union, the journalists' union, charitable organizations, etc., for better treatment of political prisoners, against torture, executions, and incarceration without trial, for the free choice of defense lawyers, and for public court sessions.

18. The party must step up the struggle for <u>trade union unity</u> more actively than heretofore. The recent merger of the seven sailors' unions demonstrates that there are favorable conditions for this. The party must aim at uniting the proletariat in all kinds of mass organizations that correspond to the traditions and the level of consciousness of the working masses, as well as to the legal conditions: from the most primitive to legal trade unions (including those under the Guomindang label) that will protect the vital interests of the working class. It is essential to use the anti-Japanese upsurge to unleash a struggle in the Japanese enterprises. However, strikes should not be the only resort; other methods of struggle must also be used, according to the conditions, moods, and traditions of the workers—petitions, sabotage, etc.

19. The party must effectuate a radical turn in [its] work among the <u>intelligentsia</u>, students, and other sectors of the urban petty bourgeoisie. By using and inciting their patriotic sentiments against imperialist aggression and the national traitors, the party must strengthen the united front in the student movement and broaden the anti-Japanese agitation of the student unions among the broadest sectors of the Chinese population. Under the slogans of the struggle to save the motherland, for elementary democratic rights, for freedom of thought, speech, press, assembly, unions, etc., against police interference with the work of schools, press, etc., the party must aim at unifying all the cultural organizations into a powerful association for the salvation of the

motherland. The petty-bourgeois and bourgeois intelligentsia can and must be involved in the universal front of the anti-imperialist struggle.

20. The Communist Party must struggle to organize and head the spontaneously growing peasant movement. The party must make sure that the rice revolts, the hunger walks, the partisan actions become part of the struggle of all people against the Japanese imperialists and their Chinese servitors. Under the slogans of the struggle against excessive taxes, against requisitions, high rents, usury, for aid to the starving, for the repair and regulation of the irrigation system, etc., the party must spread its influence over the millions of Chinese peasants. Through their tedious and tenacious work in all the mass legal organizations that unite the peasants—cooperatives, old-type organizations, self-defense units, etc.—the Chinese Communists must involve the peasant masses in the armed struggle to protect their motherland.

21. At the Seventh [Comintern] Congress, C. Dimitrov expressed a special concern about preserving the party cadres, putting great responsibility for this on the party leadership. In China, this concern is not yet sufficiently visible. Failures frequently result from the impermissible situation in which comrades conduct work under illegal conditions in the same place for a number of years. It is essential to move and shift party cadres regularly, sending workers who are already known to the police and who are in danger to the "rear" in a timely fashion. On the other hand, the party uses up significant forces organizing different demonstrations for dates known to the police (the Paris Commune Day, the First of May, an antiwar day, the November anniversary, the Canton Commune, etc.). By demanding that all party members participate in these demonstrations, as well as the open participation of the leading cadres in the strike actions, the party carelessly exposes its cadres, thus depriving itself of the chance to increase its forces.

22. The CCP must improve the party educational work among its members. It is important to popularize the heroic behavior of fallen comrades and the examples of Bolshevik behavior in prison and during their trials of such comrades as Dimitrov, Ichikawa, Fang Zhimin, and others. At the same time, it is necessary to systematically expose national traitors and foster in each party member disgust toward the wicked behavior of provocateurs and renegades.

While refraining from campaigns of mass recruitment to the party, it is necessary to overcome a sectarian attitude toward accepting new members into the party. While protecting its ranks from penetration by alien elements, the CCP must also open wide its doors to those workers and intellectuals who are eager to struggle within the party for the national and social liberation of the Chinese people.

The Communist Party of China, struggling on the two fronts in theory and in practice, must raise its fighting capacity, its ideological and organizational solidity. Mistakes of a leftist character [and] sectarianism are the major obstacles to an anti-imperialist popular front and to the work of the party among the masses. At the same time, the CCP must prevent and overcome the rightist opportunistic vacillations and wavering in its ranks, the danger of which is undoubtedly increasing with the new tactical orientation of the party.

The current situation in China presents the CCP with extremely difficult and extremely responsible tasks. We have no doubt that the Communist Party of China, which has passed through a tough and heroic school of the revolutionary struggle, will be up to these historically important tasks. We are convinced that all party members will rally closely around its tested Central Committee and, under its leadership, do everything in their power to create a popular anti-imperialist front, and will thereby score new victories.

[Early July 1936]

In October 1934, when the Chinese Communists embarked on what became the Long March—the year-long relocation of their forces from their southern strongholds in Jiangxi and Fujian to new headquarters centered in Yan'an, in the north—direct radio contact between the Comintern and the CCP was disrupted.

In this message Dimitrov informs Stalin that radio communication with the Chinese comrades has been reestablished, though for technical reasons there are gaps and unintelligible passages in the messages received from Yan'an. He transmits to Stalin the most important messages that have been received from the CCP in the preceding month. Among other things, the Chinese are requesting Comintern assistance of money, arms, planes, and ammunition. Another message, dated 30 June 1936, assures the Comintern that the CCP is complying with its united-front directives by orienting the fight "against Japan and Chiang Kai-shek"—a complete misreading of the united-front strategy, which was to ally with anyone and everyone, including the Nationalists, against Japan.

Dimitrov lists three broad questions posed by the Chinese messages and solicits Stalin's guidance in resolving them: what the military and political orientation of the CCP should be, how much and what kind of material assistance should Moscow give to the Chinese Red Army, and how to resolve internal disagreements within the CCP.

Document 17

Dimitrov to Stalin, no date (early July 1936), with enclosures. Letter: RTsKhIDNI, f. 495, op. 74, d. 249, ll. 8–17; enclosures (omitted here): f. 514, op. 1, d. 860, ll. 1–11, and d. 862, ll. 2–4. Original in Russian. Typewritten.

No. 1390

Top secret

To Com. Stalin.

The radio communications between the Comintern and the CC CCP, which were interrupted when the bulk of the Chinese Red Army forces left Jiangxi and Fujian in October 1934, have been reestablished over the Comintern radio transmitters.

As a result of a test (a series of check telegrams), stable radio communication with the CC CCP may be considered to have been firmly established.

We are including the following major telegrams from the CC CCP that we have received in the last month.

"TO WANG MING—Telegram No. 1. First of all, we are reporting to you about the <u>situation in the Northwest</u> and about our plans.

"1) The CC and the major forces of the Red Army arrived in Shaanxi Province in the winter of last year, and defeated the offensive of <u>Zhang Xueliang and Chiang Kai-shek</u>, which gave our party an opportunity to establish a base for the revolutionary headquarters in the Northwest.

"2) <u>This February</u> the main forces of the Red Army, under the banner of the <u>Chinese People's Red Army and anti-Japanese vanguard</u> crossed the [Yellow] river into <u>Shanxi Province, and were very successful</u> [there]. Politically, this served as a boost to the resistance to Japan and to the salvation of the mother-land for the whole country. Militarily, it was a heavy blow to General <u>Yan Xi-shan</u>, and the Red Army itself grew in numbers. Since Chiang Kai-shek had sent ten divisions to assist <u>Yan Xishan</u> and had created a menace (a military fortress), the main forces retreated across the river to the west.

"3) At this time, the main forces of the Red Army are going <u>to create a base in the northern part of Gansu Province</u>, in the eastern part of <u>Ningxia and in the northwestern part of Shaanxi</u> Province; they have already had initial successes.

"4) In the soviet <u>part of Shaanxi and Gansu</u>, there is a Red Army composed of the <u>three segments</u> of the Red Army: a) the Red Army of the <u>Central Soviet region</u>; b) the Red Army which had <u>left the soviet regions—the provinces of Hubei, Henan, and Anhui</u>, and c) the <u>Shanxi-Gansu Red</u> Army. It totals 25 thousand people. A significant territory of this soviet region is to the north of the Great Wall of China, to the east at the Yellow River, in the south close to the Wei River, to the west near the Ta River, and comprises the following districts: Yan Chuan, An Sai, Huai Pang, Tin . . . ***Nin [Xian]?***, Tiao Liang, Huan Xian, where the towns are under our control. The landscape there is hilly, unproductive, and not densely populated. In this region live approximately . . .500,000 people. The mood of the masses is combative. Besides that, a new sov[iet] region is being created in the northern part of Gansu, the western part of Ningxia, and in the three bians (i.e., districts Jing Bian, Ang Bian, and Ding Bian in the northwestern part of Shaanxi—[note by Wang Ming]).

"5) The 4th Red Army under the leadership of Com. Zhang Guotao, due to militarization in the Red Army system and opportunist mistakes in policy and military strategy, rejected the political and organizational leadership of the CC of our party in the second half of last year and pursued its own plans to penetrate Sichuan Province (the region of the Han [Fanzhen] national minorities), and created a second CC of our party. However, this January, Zhang Guotao started to change his position, agreed to accept our orientation in favor of creating a united front against Japan and Chiang Kai-shek, and announced the liquidation of the second CC created by him. This May, as a result of a bad harvest in this region, it[2] could not hold on here any longer and significantly decreased [in numbers]. Moreover, Com. Zhu De pushed it to seek to create a government of national defense in northwestern China. Now they are ready to go north. Provided that they meet no other obstacles, they will be able, in the course of two months, to reach the southern part of Gansu Province. However, organizationally, comrade Zhang Guotao does not yet recognize the CC of our party, and calls himself the Northwestern Bureau of the CC, and he refers to our CC as the Northern Bureau of the CC. Thereby he places himself parallel to the CC of the party. At this time, we are trying, in all possible ways, to achieve an agreement with him on the basis of a policy of principle in order to unite into a single whole and carry through the creation of the government of national defense in the northwest, and to move the Chinese revolution up to a higher stage. The 4th Red Army, which used to have more than 40 thousand soldiers, is now probably composed of approximately 20 thousand people.

"6) The 2nd Red Army under the command of Cc. Ren Bishi, He Long, Xiao Ke, and others has followed the correct line. Last December, it left Hunan Province, and by now has reached the upper Ding Xia River and joined with the 4th Red Army. In two months, the 2nd Red Army managed to reach the southern part of Gansu Province; it consists of about 20 thousand people. Politically, [the 2nd Red Army] is stronger than the 4th Red Army.

"7) At present, the enemy's armies in the Northwest are as follows: the Guomindang army of Chiang Kai-shek, 73 regiments; the Zhang Xueliang [army], 65 regiments; the Yan Xishan [army] 69 regiments; and the Yan Hucheng [army], 21 regiments; [the army of] the three Ma generals in Ningxia, 21 regiments; [the army] of the 2 Ma generals in Quinghai Province, about 15 regiments; the Shaanxi [army] (local), 10 regiments; and the Gansu [army] (local), about 12 regiments. 286 regiments altogether. The supreme command in the

---

2. Probably refers to the Communist Party—Trans.

Document 17 *continued*

campaign against the Red Army in the <u>Northwest belongs to Chiang Kai-shek.</u> The immediate commander of the military forces in the Northeast is the deputy commander, Zhang Xueliang. Commissars in the fight against the rebellion are Yan Xishan in Taiyuan, General Yang Hucheng in Xian, General Zhu Shaoliang in Lanzhou. The governors are: Shao Lijing in Shaanxi Province, and General Zhu Shaoliang in Gansu Province.

"8) <u>Last December, in all of these units we initiated the united-front movement for the struggle against Japan for the salvation of China. The greatest success was achieved in the Northeastern Army; Yang Hucheng</u> is in second place. In other units no significant success [has been achieved] as yet. After establishing a united front from above in the Northeastern Army, we [have] very much <u>. . .Our plenipotentiary comrade has conducted several</u> negotiations <u>with Zhang Xueliang</u>. At this time, the question of sending (?) <u>money to Zhang Xueliang</u> is being approved. Political, military, economic, and diplomatic preparations are under way (?) in order to achieve, as soon as possible, the goal of creating the northwestern government of national defense. At this time, taking into consideration that the movement is growing in Guangdong and Guangxi, that there is turmoil involving Sun Yongqin in northern China and Liu Xiang in Sichuan Province, etc., it is essential to accelerate the [growth of the] movement in northwest China. <u>Although the Northeastern Army still has many political and organizational weaknesses, our allied army, which counts more than 80 thousand people, becomes more and more conscious with every passing day, and there is in it a growing mood to struggle against Japan and Chiang Kai-shek and for an alliance with the USSR and the Communist Party</u>. Besides the relatively good workers among the low and the middle rank [soldiers], the most promising are <u>Yang Xiufeng</u> in Shaanxi Province and <u>Deng Baoshan</u> in Gansu Province (?). We have already started negotiations, it has been declared . . . The five <u>Ma generals</u> also maintain contact with us, however, . . . there is still no . . . result.

"After the <u>Red Army and the Northeastern Red Army enter</u> into action, these two most <u>important factors in Northwestern China will play a decisive role in the whole Northwest, and a solid foundation will be created for [the formation of] the northwestern government of national defense.</u>

"10) <u>We are asking for Comintern directives regarding this question</u>. We think that at this time the most difficult issues for us are <u>financial and economic</u>.

"The monthly payroll to the soldiers of the <u>Northeastern Army</u>, which amounts to <u>2,000,000 dollars, completely depends on receipts from Nanjing</u>, and would completely cease <u>if the army moved. Difficulties are rather serious</u>. Shaanxi Province is self-supplied. The **supplies** for the <u>Yang Hucheng army</u>, which has more than <u>30 thousand people</u>, are already insufficient. In Gansu Province there is a <u>population of 6 million, and the tax revenues are also insufficient</u> to supply the <u>200 thousand–strong Red Army and the Northeastern Army</u>. After their merger into the united anti-Japanese army, <u>70–80 thousand</u>

Document 17 *continued*

Red Army soldiers have to be paid the same salary as the [soldiers of the] North-eastern Army, otherwise Red Army growth is in doubt.

"We are asking you to inquire in the Comintern whether it is possible to give us monthly aid in the amount of 3 mil[lion] dollars, and also to begin collecting donations from Chinese émigrés abroad and among the workers of the world. We count on it very much.[3]

"In addition to the financial question, there is a very important military question. We hope to get planes, heavy artillery, shells, infantry rifles, anti-aircraft machine guns, pontoons, . . . etc. Please inquire whether the political situation makes it possible to give assistance, and to what extent. We are waiting for your answer.

"Regarding the action in northwestern China to support the (movement ?) in Guangdong, Guangxi, and northern China, the decisions taken about the time of the action . . . of the army. We assume that the general attack will take place within 2 months . . . units on the principle of approaching the USSR and liquidation of the Chiang Kai-shek forces in northwestern China.

"In general, the 1st Red Army . . . in Northern Gansu, the 2nd and the 4th Armies in the south of Gansu, units of the northeastern armies will occupy Lanzhou and will liquidate Zhu Shaoliang, as well as control the road from Lanzhou to Hami. Due to the obstacles that the Yellow River presents before it freezes, the Red Army has no means to . . . it.

"The seat of the national defense government of northwestern China is Lanzhou. Zhang [Xueliang] was elected chairman of the government and the commander of the anti-Japanese army. We have nominated . . . deputy.

"11) At this time, many of the Politburo members have assembled: Cc. Luo Pu, Zhou Enlai, Bo Gu, Mao Zedong, Deng Fa, Lin Yuying, Kai Feng, Chzi Iui[?], and De Tsui [Peng Dehuai?] (the last three [names] are distorted). The secretaries are the following 4 comrades: Luo Fu, Zhou Enlai, Bo Gu, and Mao Zedong. Next month, we will send Com. Bo Gu to the Beijing-Tiianjing region as a representative of the North. Early this month we sent C. Deng Fa to the Soviet Union. On the 12th [of this month], he was already in Lanzhou. In early July, he will possibly be in the Xinjiang town of Hami. Please make sure that connection is established with him. Currently, there is a lot of work. We hope that you will send us more Chinese comrades. C. Lin Yuying, sent by you in early November, has arrived. Cc. Yang Hunyi and Luo Ying have also arrived. Seven people with a radio arrived in a region bordering on the soviet zone, [but] the Mingtuang soldiers killed 6 of them. The survivor and his radio are in the town of Anbiancheng being held by the Mingtuangs. We received the resolution of the Seventh [Comintern] Congress in March, Wang Ming's speech in May. We will inform you about the rest. From the CC CCP Secretariat, 26/6/ North[ern] Shaanxi, town of Wayaobu."

---

3. The handwritten reference in the margin is illegible—Trans.

Document 17 *continued*

<u>Telegram of 30/6/36 to WANG</u> MING.

"The <u>February</u> political resolution of the <u>CC CCP</u> is written in the spirit of the decisions of the Seventh Comintern Congress. [We] started firmly implementing the Comintern <u>line of the broad united front of struggle against Japan and Chiang Kai-shek</u>. Subsequent numerous meetings of the Politburo have made political decisions on the basis of changes in the real situation and, as a result, have not only consolidated our own forces but also secured ardent support and sympathy of <u>students, intelligentsia, workers, peasants, and all those unwilling to become colonial slaves</u>, as well as the support and sympathy of all armed anti-Japanese forces."

See report by <u>Zhang Wentian and Mao Zedong</u>.

The aforementioned telegrams prompt <u>3 major questions on which</u> we need to consult [you] and receive your directives:

1) <u>Regarding the political and military plan of the CCP and the Red Army in the Northwest and, in connection to this, about the general political orientation of the CCP in the question of creating an anti-Japanese united popular front</u>.

2) <u>Regarding material assistance to the Chinese Red Army</u>, and

3) <u>Regarding differences between the majority of the members of the Secretariat of the CC CCP and its member C. Zhang Guotao</u>.

(DIMITROV).

Sent 2 copies

S E

ATTACHMENT: 1. Circular telegram from the central government of the Chinese Soviet People's Republic on the convocation of the all-China congress concerning the struggle against Japan and the salvation of the motherland.

2. Declaration of the Northern Bureau of the Central Committee of the Communist Party of China about the struggle against Japan and the salvation of the country.

The first enclosure was a circular telegram sent by the "Central government of the Chinese Soviet People's Republic," calling for an all-China congress concerning the struggle against Japan; the document was published in *Jiuguoshibao* in Paris on 20 July 1936. The second was a declaration by the so-called Northern Bureau of the Central Committee of the CCP.

27 July 1936

On 23 July 1936 the ECCI Secretariat discussed and adopted the directives to the CCP printed below, in the presence of four representatives from the CCP (including Wang Ming). Indicating his awareness of the document's importance, Dimitrov sought to secure Stalin's approval. In essence, the Comintern takes issue with several of the CCP's basic policy positions, above all, its tendency to see Chiang Kai-shek and the Guomindang as no better than (and perhaps linked to) the Japanese invaders. The ECCI outlines the terms on which the CCP must offer to negotiate with the GMD. Above all, Moscow directs the Chinese comrades to stop fighting the Nationalists, concentrating instead on the anti-Japanese offensive and mobilizing support for this task.

Stalin writes on the left-hand margin of Dimitrov's handwritten note, "For. I. St." (that is, he votes in favor of the directives). The document did not arrive back at the ECCI until 13 August, and a notation by Dimitrov indicates that it was transmitted on 15 August—presumably, it was encrypted and radioed to the CCP.[4]

Document 18

Dimitrov to Stalin, 27 July 1936, with enclosure. Letter: RTsKhIDNI, f. 495, op. 73, d. 48, l. 54; enclosure: f. 495, op. 73, d. 275. Original in Russian. The letter is handwritten, the enclosure typewritten.

Dear Com. Stalin,

We consider it necessary <u>urgently</u> to send our Chinese comrades (after the latest conversation with you) the enclosed explanation and advice regarding the united anti-Japanese national front.[5]

Due to the particular importance of this document, I would not want to send it <u>before I get your possible comments.</u>

4. Both Dimitrov's statement to the ECCI Secretariat and the message to the CCP Central Committee appear also in the documentary collection of the Academy of Sciences' Far Eastern Institute: M. L. Titarenko, ed., *Kommunisticheskii Internatsional i kitaiskaya revolyutsiya* (Moscow: Nauka, 1986), pp. 263–269. See also f. 495, op. 74, d. 294, ll. 50 and 51, and TsPA (Sofia), f. 146, op. 2, a.e. 3.

5. In the margin, handwritten by Stalin:
For. I. St.

Document 18 *continued*

I beg you to give [us] your directives.
With fraternal greetings

                   G. Dimitrov

27. VII. 1936[6]

MK/2

Top secret.

TO THE SECRETARIAT OF THE CC CCP[7]

Having read your decision of 25 December 1935 and your information sent by telegraph, we approve in general your plans for creating a united anti-Japanese national front. However, we think that the leadership of the party and the Red Army has to have a clear understanding of the essence and character of the united anti-Japanese national front, since making a mistake on this question would have fatal consequences for the toilers of China.

1. Creating a united anti-Japanese national front does not imply weakening the soviets, subsuming the Red Army into a broad anti-Japanese army, and [immersing] the Communist Party in some broad political league of China.

Politically, the united anti-Japanese national front must represent an agreement among the CCP, Guomindang, and other organizations on a common anti-Japanese platform, while each retains its complete political and organizational independence. Militarily, the anti-Japanese front must show an agreement between the Red Army and other armed forces about the organization of a united anti-Japanese army, while each of these forces retains its independence, is responsible for its sector of the front, but is subordinated to the central command in fulfillment of a common military plan. The government of national defense must be representative of all the parties and organizations that participate in the united anti-Japanese national front.

We especially emphasize that the correct line for creating a united anti-Japanese national front presumes a further strengthening of the party and the Red Army. Therefore, we are worried by your decision to admit to the party anyone who wants to join, regardless of social origin, and by the fact that the party is not afraid of certain careerists infiltrating its ranks, as well as by your intention to admit even Zhang Xueliang to the party. Today more than ever, it is necessary to safeguard the purity of the ranks and the monolithic integrity of the party. While you are systematically conducting recruitment into the party, and especially strengthening it in Guomindang territory, it is important to avoid mass admissions and admit only the best, tested people from among the workers, peasants, and students.

6. In the margin, Dimitrov wrote:
Received on 13/8/36.

7. In the margin, the secretary scribbled:
1 excess copy destroyed by us on 7 Jan[uary] 1937.
< . . .> Valter.

Document 18 *continued*

We would also consider it a mistake to admit to the Red Army, without distinction, students and **former** officers of other armies, since this might undermine its concord and unity.

We agree with you that, in the interests of creating a united anti-Japanese national front, the party must introduce substantial correctives into its previous economic policy: to discontinue unnecessary confiscations—in particular, to discontinue confiscations of the land of small property owners which they rent out, as well as the land of soldiers and officers who actively participate in the struggle against the Japanese occupiers—and to permit free trade.

At the same time, we consider it improper to allow the representatives of the propertied classes to participate in the political administration of the soviet regions, since they can undermine the administrative apparatus from within.

2. The current domestic and external situation in China challenges the party with the immediate and most important task of uniting all the anti-Japanese forces to protect the territorial integrity of China and to protect the Chinese people from complete colonial enslavement.

In this connection, it is expedient for the Communist Party of China to declare that it supports a united all-China democratic republic, the convocation of an all-China parliament on the basis of the universal suffrage, and the creation of an all-China government of national defense, which, under present conditions, would be the best means to unite all the democratic forces of the Chinese people in defense of their motherland from the Japanese occupiers.

The Communist Party of China may also declare that, given the creation of an all-China democratic republic, the soviet regions will be included in an all-China democratic republic, will participate in an all-China parliament, and will implement in their territories the democratic regime instituted for all of China.

3. We think that it is incorrect to place Chiang Kai-shek in the same category as the Japanese occupiers. This conception is politically mistaken since the major enemy of the Chinese people is Japanese imperialism, and every resource must be dedicated to fight it. Besides, it is impossible to conduct a successful struggle simultaneously against the Japanese occupiers and Chiang Kai-shek. It is also wrong to consider the entire Guomindang and all of the Chiang Kai-shek army as allies of Japan. A serious armed resistance to Japan also requires participation of the Chiang Kai-shek army, or of its majority.

For all these reasons it is essential to work for the cessation of hostilities between the Red Army and the Chiang Kai-shek army, and for an agreement with [Chiang's army] to struggle jointly against the Japanese occupiers. This is essential despite the fact that Chiang Kai-shek and the Guomindang are still afraid to conclude an anti-Japanese agreement with anybody.

For this purpose, we deem it necessary that the Communist Party of China and the leadership of the Red Army immediately extend an official offer to the Guomindang and Chiang Kai-shek to enter into negotiations to cease hostilities and sign a concrete agreement about the common struggle against the Japanese occupiers. The Communist Party and the Red Army command must immediately express their readiness to send a delegation for these negotiations or to receive a delegation of the Guomindang and Chiang Kai-shek in the soviet regions.

Our demands, to be discussed during these negotiations, must be roughly the following:

1) Ending the civil war and uniting the armed forces of the Chinese people in a genuine struggle against the Japanese occupiers.

2) Creating a unified command and working out a common military plan against Japan, while preserving the complete political and organizational independence of the Red Army, which would be responsible for a particular sector of the front in the struggle against Japan.

3) Securing an appropriate territorial base for the Red Army, along with the necessary arms and supplies.

4) Freeing the imprisoned Communists and the cessation of the persecution of Communists in the Guomindang regions.

If, despite proposals for negotiations and despite all attempts to achieve an agreement with Chiang Kai-shek, he continues hostilities against the Red Army, the army must conduct the struggle against the Chiang Kai-shek units as a necessary defense, while continuing the campaign and concrete measures aimed at achieving an agreement with the Guomindang and its army and at creating the united anti-Japanese national front.

Your declaration calling for support of the actions of the southwestern army group against Chiang Kai-shek seems incorrect to us. Politically, it would have been better to condemn any further stirring up of internal strife, which has been provoked by the Japanese imperialists, and to concentrate the main fire against them.

4. We also recommend that you alter your slogan of the "immediate declaration of war against Japan." Your slogan must reflect the aggressive character of the war waged by Japanese imperialism, and the defensive character of the struggle of the Chinese people. Therefore, it is better to adopt the slogan, "Japanese occupiers out of China," a slogan of the defense of territorial integrity, national independence, and freedom of the Chinese people.

5. It is important to maintain contact with Zhang Xueliang, using it to perform our work in the army of Zhang Xueliang, to strengthen our positions in all of his units, to broadly disseminate among the soldiers and the officer corps the ideas of a united anti-Japanese national front. However, Zhang Xueliang must not be viewed as a reliable ally. Especially after the defeat of the Southwest, new vacillations from Zhang Xueliang are possible, and even his direct betrayal of us.

We are waiting for your delegate to discuss in detail the whole range of questions raised by us and to receive an exhaustive response to them.

The ECCI Secretariat

G. Dim

9 January 1938

On 12 December 1936, on a visit to Xi'an, Generalissimo Chiang Kai-shek was arrested by rival warlords led by the "young marshal," Zhang Xueliang (Chang Hsüeh-liang). Moscow, Dimitrov included, promptly suspected that the Chinese Communists were part of the plot: the CCP had repeatedly made overtures to the young marshal, and although Moscow had warned it that he was an unreliable ally, the Communists had worked with him to the exclusion of the Guomindang. On 14 December, Dimitrov noted in a letter to Stalin that "it was hard to imagine that Zhang Xueliang would have undertaken his adventurist action without coordination with them [the Communists] or even without their participation."[8]

Dimitrov was right, although he may have exaggerated the CCP's role. Soon Moscow heard directly from the Chinese. The Chinese Communists—still a weak and marginal presence—had found extremely tempting the occasion to rid themselves of their most prominent and perhaps most menacing Chinese enemy.

8. RTsKhIDNI, f. 495, op. 74, d. 294, l. 6; enclosure in d. 292, ll. 19–28. The Xi'an incident, one of the most dramatic episodes in contemporary Chinese history, has been the subject of numerous and somewhat contradictory accounts. For analyses that provide both detail and context but antedate the recent revelations of the documentary sources, see Lyman Van Slyke, *Enemies and Friends* (Stanford: Stanford University Press, 1964), chap. 4, and Wu Tien-wei, *The Sian Incident* (Ann Arbor: Michigan Papers in Chinese Studies, 1976). Otto Braun, a strongly anti-Maoist Comintern representative in China (who was cut off from the ECCI at this time), asserts that there was a formal agreement between the CCP leadership and the young marshal. Though suspect in other regards, his account generally corresponds to other sources (Otto Braun, *A Comintern Agent in China, 1932–1939* [Stanford: Stanford University Press, 1982], pp. 182–190). For the orthodox (anti-Maoist) Soviet version, see K. V. Kukushkin, "Komintern i yedinyi natsional'nyi antiyaponskii front v Kitae," in *Komintern i vostok* (Moscow: Glav.red. vostochnoi lit., 1969). For another Soviet version, see S. L. Tikhvinskii, *Put' Kitaya k ob"edineniyu i nezavisimosti* (Moscow: Vostochnaya literatura, 1996), pp. 290–301. The most recent scholarly controversies are well presented in Michael M. Sheng and John W. Garver, "New Light on the Second United Front: An Exchange," *China Quarterly*, vol. 129, March 1992, pp. 149–183, and the sources cited therein. Insofar as the documents offered here help shed new light on the question—essentially, the scope and nature of the disagreements between Stalin and Mao Zedong—they seem to give more support to Garver's position. See also his *Chinese-Soviet Relations, 1937–1945* (New York: Oxford University Press, 1988), and "The Soviet Union and the Xian Incident," *Australian Journal of Chinese Affairs*, July 1991, pp. 145–175. For an insightful discussion, see Jonathan Haslam, *The Soviet Union and the Threat from the East, 1933–41* (London: Macmillan, 1992), chap. 3.

Chiang's liquidation could have seriously weakened the Nationalist government and triggered a crisis in the Nationalist Army as well.

But Moscow saw the crisis in a vastly different light. The united-front policy adopted at the Seventh World Congress demanded that the Communists work with their domestic adversaries and rivals against the "enemy number one"—in this case, the Japanese. The ECCI had already informed the Chinese comrades that the united front was above all to include the Nationalists. Moreover, the Soviet Union was in the process of establishing and improving relations with the Chinese Nationalist government in Nanjing (Nanking), for a variety of geopolitical and diplomatic reasons. The aggressive actions of the Chinese Communists were the last thing the Soviet leadership wanted.

On 16 December, Stalin received Dimitrov in the Kremlin, in the presence of several other Soviet leaders (Molotov, Kaganovich, Voroshilov, and Ordzhonikidze). At the meeting, the leaders approved the following telegram, which the ECCI Secretariat sent to the CCP Central Committee:

> In response to your telegrams, we recommend that you take the following positions:
>
> 1. Whatever his intentions, the move by Zhang Xueliang can objectively badly hurt the concentration of the forces of the Chinese people into a single anti-imperialist front and can stimulate Japanese aggression against China.
>
> 2. Inasmuch as these moves [the Xi'an incident] have taken place and one must deal with realities, the Communist Party of China takes a decisive stand in favor of a peaceful resolution of the conflict on the basis of
>
> (a) the reorganization of the government by including in it several representatives of the anti-Japanese movement, advocates of the integrity and independence of China;
>
> (b) assurance of the democratic rights of the Chinese people;
>
> (c) the cessation of the policy of destroying the Red Army and the establishment of cooperation with it in the struggle against Japanese aggression;
>
> (d) the establishment of cooperation with those governments which support [soputstvuyut] the liberation of the Chinese people from the advance of Japanese imperialism.

To this negotiated text, Dimitrov had added, "Finally, we advise you not to put forward the slogan of alliance with the USSR," and sent it off over his own signature.[9]

The Comintern "advice" to the Chinese comrades was unmistakably that they should release Chiang—something they found very hard to accept. It is worth citing Edgar Snow's notes on the subject: "It now seems probable that the Communists had encouraged Chang Hsüeh-liang to detain the Generalissimo. . . . *Pravda's* shattering denunciation of Chang as a traitor and Japanese agent enormously weakened the Chinese Communists in their relations with him and threw them into confusion."[10] One witness asserts that Mao, at a meeting on 13 December, declared, "Since April 12, 1927, Chiang has owed us a blood debt as high as a mountain. Now it is time to liquidate the blood debt. Chiang must be brought to Pao-an for a public trial."[11]

Snow quotes an eyewitness: "Mao Tse-tung flew into a rage when the order came from Moscow to release Chiang. Mao swore and stamped his feet. Until then they had planned to give Chiang a public trial." "We didn't sleep for a week, trying to decide," Zhou Enlai ostensibly told Wang. "It was the most difficult decision of our whole lives."[12]

Finally the Chinese Communists' sense of discipline prevailed against their better judgment, and they did what Moscow had told them to do. Although the Soviet leadership may have underestimated the Chinese comrades' pain at this action, no doubt the Xi'an incident left a strong memory in the minds of Chinese leaders, beginning with Mao and Zhou Enlai.

Dimitrov continued to pressure the CCP leadership from afar. On 16 January 1937 he sent Stalin the draft of a telegram to the Chi-

9. Published in Titarenko, *Kommunisticheskii Internatsional*, p. 270. According to Sheng, the Chinese have published five ECCI telegrams to the CCP over the Xi'an incident.

10. Edgar Snow, mimeographed version of *Random Notes on China (1936–1945)* (Cambridge: Harvard University Press, 1957), pp. 1–3.

11. Wu, *Sian Incident*, p. 101.

12. Snow, mimeographed version of *Random Notes on China*, pp. 1–3. Snow's interpretation is challenged by other China specialists. The *Pravda* condemnation of the incident (in a front-page editorial, "Sobytiya v Kitae") appeared on 14 December 1936 and a similar treatment in *Izvestiia* on 15 December—curiously, ahead of the decision by Stalin and the Comintern transmitted to the CCP.

nese stressing the need for joint action with the Guomindang. At a meeting with Stalin on 19 January the text of two directives was agreed upon. The first chastised the CCP for striving to split the GMD instead of working with it: the main task of the Chinese Communists was supposed to be bringing about an end to the civil war and supporting all measures of the central government to defend China's integrity and independence. The second urged the Communists to reorganize the local government in their areas from a "soviet" system to a national-revolutionary system on a democratic basis, renouncing land confiscation from the large landholders in the interests of national unity and the creation of an "all-Chinese democratic republic."[13]

In essence the Chinese accepted Moscow's terms.

For the Soviets, this policy was vindicated when in July 1937 Japanese forces began a full-scale invasion of China, soon capturing Beijing and Shanxi Province, and a few months later advancing to Shanghai and Nanjing. In return for the Communist role in creating a national anti-Japanese front, the GMD now recognized the "border area" held by the Communists, and the Red Army was renamed the 8th National-Revolutionary Army.

On 11 November, Stalin received Dimitrov and several CCP representatives (including Wang Ming, Kang Shen, and Wang Jiaxiang, who worked in the Comintern under the pseudonym of Kommunar). Now that the struggle with the Japanese appeared to have begun in earnest, Stalin was prepared to pledge help with weapons and equipment. Wang Ming soon returned to China, and on 4 January 1938 Dimitrov reported to Stalin that the CCP Central Committee had unanimously accepted the ECCI directives. During the following days the Chinese consulted Moscow about the advisability of participating in various government bodies and requested material and monetary support from the Kremlin.[14]

---

13. Titarenko, *Kommunisticheskii Internatsional,* pp. 271–272.

14. In a related matter, the Kremlin needed to decide the fate of the so-called Western Army—the remnants of the Red Army that were cut off in October 1936 and decimated in March 1937. As the army moved westward into Xinjiang, its leaders requested asylum in the Soviet Union. On 13 April, Dimitrov forwarded the request to Stalin and the CPSU Politburo (RTsKhIDNI, f. 495, op. 74, d. 294, l. 19). A fraction of this group made it to Urumqi by 8 May. On 17 June, Dimitrov sent Stalin another request from the surviving 393 men who had made their way into Xinjiang,

Document 19

Dimitrov to Stalin, 9 January 1938. RTsKhIDNI, f. 495, op. 74, d. 294, l. 49. Original in Russian. Typewritten, with handwritten note by Dimitrov.

Ev "2" 9. 1

Copy.

To Comrade Stalin.

We have received, from the Secretariat of the CC CCP, the following telegram:

"1. At this time, the Guomindang has not received any requests from the Communists to participate in the government.

"The Guomindang has expressed a desire to ask the Communists to send their people to the political department of the military committee, [to] the mass movement, and to the trade unions but has not proposed any concrete measures in this regard.

"2. The State Defense Council (Guo Fang and Weiyuanhui), which includes representatives of all parties and groups, expresses—in time of war and in narrow forms—public opinion.

"Please give us a prompt answer on whether we can participate in this body in case we are invited."

Regarding participation in the government, we have **previously** instructed the CC to refrain from such participation. As to participation in the State Defense Council, we tend to believe that it is possible to participate.

We are asking you to give your opinion and directive in regard to this question.

p. p. With fraternal greeting

(Dimitrov)

9 January 1938

No. 145/ld.

Informed via C. Poskr[ebyshev] that it is sanctioned to participate in the State Defense Council. 10. 1. 38. GD

---

urging that they be admitted to the Soviet Union; Dimitrov proposed that they be temporarily housed in a camp in the Crimea, and that 100–150 of them be admitted to "our Chinese school." But on the same day Molotov turned him down, writing on Dimitrov's request, "Better to instruct them in Xinjiang. We might provide partial help with instructors and support, but partial help should also come from Duban Shen" (RTsKhIDNI, f. 495, op. 74, d. 294., l. 20). "Duban Shen" refers to Sheng Shicai, the Soviet-supported ruler of Xinjiang. There is no evidence that Dimitrov raised any objections to the refusal. On Xinjiang, see Garver, *Chinese-Soviet Relations,* chap. 6, and Allen Whiting and Sheng Shih-tsai, *Pawn or Pivot?* (East Lansing: Michigan State University Press, 1958).

29 January 1940

On 17 and 19 January 1940 the Presidium of the ECCI discussed a report given by Zhou Enlai, a prominent member of the CCP Politburo. Dimitrov forwards a summary of the talk and discussion to Stalin and asks for instructions for the Chinese comrades on dealing with the Nationalists (rather paradoxically anticipating not only the possible "capitulation" of the Chiang Kai-shek government to the Japanese but also an onslaught by the Nationalist armed forces to overwhelm the Yan'an area and the 8th Army).

Document 20 also included an excerpt (here omitted) of the declaration of the Communist members of the National-Political Council, an advisory body to the Chinese government established in July 1938. An earlier version of Zhou's report, a lecture in Russian delivered on 29 December 1939, was amplified by him into a 132-page document.[15]

Document 20

Dimitrov to Stalin, 29 January 1940, with enclosure. RTsKhIDNI, f. 495, op. 74, d. 317, ll. 10–36. Original in Russian. Typewritten.

TO COMRADE STALIN.

Dear Comrade Stalin!

The Presidium of the Executive Committee of the Comintern has recently heard at its closed session a report by C. ZHOU ENLAI, a member of the Political Bureau of the Chinese Communist Party, who has arrived from China.

The main points of his report are reproduced in a very condensed form in the enclosed material. A congress of the Communist Party will take place in China in the very near future.

In view of the situation in China and the exceptionally difficult conditions of the struggle of the Communist Party, the CC of the Chinese Communist Party needs advice on two major issues:

1) What the line of the Communist Party should be and how it should try to prevent the capitulation of the ruling circles in China to the Japanese imperialists.

---

15. The declaration was published in *Xinhua ribao*, 9 September 1939; Zhou's 132-page document is in RTsKhIDNI, f. 495, op. 18, d. 1309.

2) What the line of the Communist Party should be and what measures it should take to further the struggle under the present circumstances, in particular, considering the policy pursued by the leading circles of the Guomindang of persecuting the Communist Party and liquidating the special region and the 8th Army.

These questions are currently being discussed by the commission created by the ECCI Presidium, together with representatives of the Communist Party of China.

We beg you to give your advice and directives.

Attached are the materials about the position of the Communist Party and the measures it plans to take.

With fraternal greetings

(G. DIMITROV)[16]

29. 1. 1940.

Enclosure: 1) Summary of the report by Zhou Enlai.

2) Abstract of the declaration by the Communist Party representatives in the National Political Council.

The main points of the report by Com. Zhou Enlai amount to the following:

Evaluation of the military situation.

At present, the war has entered its 2nd stage, which is characterized by the fact that both the army of the Japanese occupiers and the Chinese army are stable. The Japanese army can no longer conduct a major offensive, but the Chinese army has not yet met all the necessary conditions to initiate a strategic offensive.

During the 1st year of the war, the Japanese occupiers advanced 1,800 km; during the 2nd year, 310 km; and during the last half a year, approximately 200 km. Lately, the Japanese occupiers have been concentrating their major efforts on liquidating the partisan movement, exploiting the resources of the occupied regions, and cultivating them. In the past year, 85 percent of the armed forces, i.e., about 28–29 divisions, have been used to liquidate the partisans and for defense.

In order to evaluate the military situation, it is important to take into consideration the situation in Japan. As of 1937, Japan can provide 5 million, 332 thousand men for the army. During the war in China, the Japanese troops have lost 520 thousand killed and heavily injured (316 thousand of the heavily injured and sick have been evacuated home). According to military experts, in Japan half the draftable men have been drafted. In addition to the existing 13 divisions that have not been employed in the war, Japan can muster 17 more fighting divisions from its reserve units.

16. In the margin, handwritten by the secretary:
Sent on 31.1.40 in package no. 21. < ...>

Document 20 *continued*

During the war, the military spending of Japan has reached 16 billion yen. The major source of the military budget is loans and taxes. Because Japan receives the bulk of the military matériel and strategic raw materials from abroad, and has to pay for them with gold, the gold reserves of Japan are now almost exhausted. It is believed that by 1939, 505 million yen's worth of gold was left in Japan, and 200 million yen's worth of gold must have been panned out. In 1939 Japan's payments for deliveries [from abroad] had to exceed 500 million yen, which is leading to a complete exhaustion of its gold reserves.

The war against China affects the morale of the Japanese people and the army. The lengthy war and tremendous losses have led to a sharp deterioration of the morale in the army. The antiwar sentiment, a desire to end the war and go home, is more and more common among the soldiers.

Whereas previously Japanese soldiers did not as a rule surrender but preferred to die in battle, the instances of surrender have become more frequent lately.

The Japanese army has occupied a large portion of Chinese territory and now is trying hard to assimilate it. However, in this respect, the Japanese have to overcome enormous difficulties. It is important to note that the rulers of Japan did not expect such a development in the war, and it is clear that the plan of a "lightning war" and the "lightning defeat" of China has failed.

Taking into account the results to date of two and a half years of war, the Japanese occupiers are pursuing a new policy at this stage of the aggression. They are striving to put an end to the war. Perceiving that it is impossible to enthrall China by military force only, and fearing that a prolonged war might lead to complications in Japan itself, the Japanese imperialists are undertaking a series of maneuvers. First of all, pursuing a policy of "subjugating China by the Chinese themselves," they are attempting to lure China into capitulating. They are trying to attract traitorous elements from among the bureaucracy, bourgeoisie, and landowners, and to make them their foremen. That is why they are placing so much hope on Wang Jingwei.

Accordingly, they have modified their policy in the occupied regions. If during the first stage the Japanese occupiers used to rob, murder, and ravage the population, which provoked the hatred of the Chinese people, during the past year they have been pursuing a policy of "pacifying" the occupied regions using demagogic methods, throwing some crumbs to the population, stirring up the struggle between landowners and peasants, attempting to discredit the partisan movement, and bribing gentry and other elements everywhere in order to create puppet authorities.

The Japanese imperialists are trying to provoke dissension among the peoples of China by juxtaposing the Chinese and the Mongols, Buddhists and Muslims, etc. They are employing Trotskyists and other traitors to conduct subversive and espionage activities. The Japanese occupiers are making a special effort to incite dissension between the Guomindang and the Chinese Communist Party, provoking conflicts between them. The Japanese conduct a provocative policy in regard to the Soviet Union intimidating [the people] with the prospect of socialism in China, threatening the isolation of China from the major capitalist powers of the world—the USA, England, and France.

In the occupied regions, the Japanese are trying to revitalize the economy. First of all, they are trying to start up enterprises producing iron, steel, coal, and cotton in order to increase supply to Japan. To develop the occupied regions, the Japanese drew up a special plan for 1938 to 1941.

The Japanese imperialists are endeavoring a large penetration of Japanese goods in the internal markets of China, and in this regard have achieved considerable success in the central, northern, and southern parts of China.

The Japanese are striving to undermine the Chinese currency. For this purpose, they have issued a large number of banknotes, which are circulating, under pressure from the Japanese, in the occupied regions.

In order to develop the occupied regions of China, the Japanese are working on rebuilding and expanding the transportation network: they are repairing and building paved and dirt roads and, in some places, are building railroad lines.

The Japanese pursue a policy of resettling Japanese [immigrants] in the regions of China occupied by the Japanese, and sometimes they are trying to convert their military units into militarized settlers in the occupied regions.

The Japanese are striving to isolate China from the outer world and, in particular, are trying to cut transportation links in the Southwest, between Yunnan and Indochina and Burma.

Thus, the plan of the Japanese imperialists is <u>to subjugate China using Chinese human and material resources.</u>

Lately, the Japanese have been actively striving to isolate China in the international arena.

Taking into consideration, first, these maneuvers of the Japanese imperialists and their persistent attempts to generate discord among the Chinese people and to select their servitors from among the traitors, and, second, the existence of vacillating and clearly capitulationist elements in the ranks of the Guomindang, it must be pointed out <u>that capitulation is the main danger at the present moment. The policy of splitting the unity of the Chinese people and of undermining the united front between the Guomindang and the Communist Party, on which the Japanese are concentrating their subversive activities, is particularly dangerous.</u>

Nevertheless, one must realize that if all these measures by the Japanese imperialists prove unsuccessful, they will try to assemble [their] armed forces into a single striking force and deliver a new blow to China.

<u>What is the situation of the Chinese side?</u> The Japanese have occupied, entirely or in part, 15 provinces of China with more than 900 towns; they occupy most of the industrial and administrative centers. The Japanese have captured

the major seaports of China and its railroad lines, as well as a significant number of the coal, iron, and copper mines. In the course of the war, China has lost more than one million soldiers killed and wounded.

Nevertheless, in the past two and a half years, China has had a number of successes. The Chinese nation has launched a war for liberation that is unparalleled in its history. The government has united all the forces of the nation for this war. The Chinese army is fighting against the external enemy under unified leadership. All the anti-Japanese parties, starting with the Communist Party of China and the Guomindang and including different anti-Japanese groups as well as all classes and social strata of China, are cooperating in this struggle.

Thanks to its tactics, China managed to preserve the bulk of its armed forces and a number of provinces, which form a base for launching a protracted, extended war.

In the occupied regions, a broad partisan movement is developing; this pins down significant forces of the enemy, delivers heavy blows to it, and hinders the "development" of the occupied territories.

Thanks to the united front, the fighting spirit of the entire Chinese people has been mobilized against the Japanese occupants. Lately, the successes of the Chinese army have been affecting the ratio of losses. If at the beginning of the war the ratio of Chinese losses to Japanese was 3:1, today it is 2:1.

The 16 provinces of China where mobilization can be carried out have a population of some 277 million, of whom only 2 percent have been drafted, who can still provide significant reinforcements to the Chinese army.

Since the crucial part of Chinese industry was captured by the enemy or destroyed, and only a small part was evacuated to the rear, Chinese industry finds itself in very difficult conditions. Military supplies, except for a few local stocks, are coming from abroad.

Regarding the position of different classes in China and their attitude toward the war against Japan, it is necessary to say the following. The Chinese proletariat has suffered the greatest losses during the war. The majority of the workers were evacuated from the occupied regions along with the Chinese troops. Some of them joined the army, some left for the countryside, a small portion are employed in enterprises controlled by the Chinese government, but the majority are unemployed. As a result, some of these workers had to return to the occupied zones; however, the Japanese occupiers hire primarily impoverished peasants coming to the cities.

The Chinese peasantry, which comprises the majority of the population, is in a state of permanent warfare. The peasants form the bulk of the army [and] the major part of the partisan units. They are being mobilized for war-related tasks (digging, carrying heavy loads, building fortifications).

It is worth mentioning that the atrocities of the Japanese occupiers have provoked tremendous dissatisfaction among the broad masses of peasantry, and now the national spirit of the Chinese peasants has been forged as never before.

The petty bourgeoisie plays a rather important role in the anti-Japanese struggle and supports it.

Among the bourgeois-landowner class, a certain split is taking place: some are already wavering in their resistance to the Japanese and are striving to come to terms with them. No doubt such attitudes will become stronger in the course of war. The officer corps, regardless of class origin, has demonstrated determination, courage, and selflessness in the anti-Japanese war. Throughout the war, there have been almost no cases of desertion at the front.

The anti-Japanese national united front and cooperation between the Communist Party and the Guomindang

The foundation of the anti-Japanese struggle and the guarantee of its success is the united anti-Japanese front, which has been in place for three years. The united front in China has no officially proclaimed common program, platform, or any other official manifestation. Indeed, all classes in China participate in the anti-Japanese front. The working-peasant masses have contributed the most to it, but the bourgeois-landowning class still remains in power. Local governments are already united under the leadership of the central government, although in a number of cases they still retain a certain independence.

The political foundation of the national front comprises the three people's principles of Sun Yat-sen. However, these three principles are interpreted differently by the representatives of the Communist Party and of the Guomindang. The parties that form the united front have armies of their own. The Guomindang, the Communist Party, and some local authorities each have armies. In the course of the past three years, the anti-Japanese national front underwent and is still undergoing significant changes. The policy of the Communist Party in the united national front is based on the following principles:

1. Everything is subordinate to the interests of the anti-Japanese war. The anti-Japanese war is above all else.

2. The three people's principles are the political basis of the united front.

3. Cooperation between the Communist Party and the Guomindang is the organizational basis of the united front.

4. The progress of the Guomindang and the strengthening and growth of the Communist Party and the army are the guarantee of the united front.

5. The central task of the united front is the steadfast continuation of the protracted war, the struggle against capitulation and schism.

6. Principles of democratization must be implemented and a democratic republic must be built in China on the basis of the united front.

During these three years, the Communist Party has been conducting its policy based on these principles: it has struggled against traitors and national deserters, criticized vacillators and hidden capitulators, and instructed its organizations not to expand their influence within friendly parties and friendly armies (Guomindang), to support progressive elements in these organizations, and to attack the hard-liners.

The Communist Party of China has been struggling in the National-Political Council and other organizations, in its press, and in its everyday activities for the democratization of the regime and for the betterment of the lot of the masses. It has been organizing the worker-peasant masses to conduct the war, and has mounted a broad propaganda campaign.

The Communist Party has defended its ideology and maintained the struggle against the hard-line elements in the Guomindang. In case of military attacks, it followed its policy on the basis of the principle proclaimed by Com. Mao Zedong: "If they do not trouble us, we will not trouble them. However, if they trouble us, we will surely trouble them."

The Communist Party pushes the Guomindang to pursue progressive policy. The Communist Party supports the progressive elements within the Guomindang and its leaders who firmly champion the anti-Japanese struggle and turns them against the backward, regressive tendencies in the Guomindang.

Whenever the Guomindang took an erroneous position, the Communist Party criticized it, demanding that [the GMD] recognize these mistakes.

Regarding Chiang Kai-shek and the Guomindang government, the Communist Party pursued the following policy:

1. Support of the Chiang Kai-shek leadership in the anti-Japanese war;

2. Recognizing the key position of the Guomindang in leading the organs of power and the army throughout the country;

3. Recognizing the programs of the anti-Japanese war and of state-building as the basic political line of all government measures.

The Communist Party has always tried to influence Chiang Kai-shek to conduct a policy of tenacious resistance to Japan. Cases where Chiang Kai-shek made unfounded charges against the Communist Party were not infrequent. In such cases, the Communist Party clarified its position, cited relevant facts, and worked to refute those charges.

Participating in the work of the National-Political Council, Communists submitted various proposals. The National-Political Council represents the ruling elements. The Communist Party uses the National-Political Council as a rostrum for agitation and propaganda and tries to make it play the role of a national bloc. The opinion of the Communist Party representatives in the National-Political Council always attracts public attention. Nevertheless, it is rather difficult to promote serious measures via the National-Political Council, since a significant role is played by the financial compradors[17] of Anglo-

17. This refers to the commercial bourgeoisie who, in Marxist theory, are a reactionary force in colonial nations, as opposed to the "national bourgeoisie."—Trans.

American orientation, who are occupying key positions in the central government and exert influence upon Chiang Kai-shek.

Despite repeated discussions, the question about the forms of cooperation between the Communist Party and the Guomindang has not yet been resolved. The line of Chiang Kai-shek amounts to absorbing the Communist Party. Chiang Kai-shek repeatedly offered to merge the Communist Party and the Guomindang, explaining that this does not mean liquidation of the Communist Party—the Guomindang could even join the Comintern. Obviously, the Communist Party did not go for this. Then Chiang Kai-shek introduced a theory of "remaking the Communist Party," which in fact means its liquidation. At one point, Chiang Kai-shek was offering to divide the authority and development of the organizations of the Communist Party and the Guomindang by region; however, later he stopped talking about this.

The Guomindang definitely does not want to recognize the legal existence of the Communist Party and does not consider the Communist Party equal to itself. Therefore, the Guomindang representatives reject any organizational cooperation with the Communist Party and the formation of the united national bloc. Even in northern China, where the Communist Party is a formidable force and where local organizations of the Guomindang have created united committees or councils along with the Communist Party, the CEC [Central Executive Committee] of the Guomindang does not permit it.

In practice, the Guomindang conducts a line aiming at the liquidation and eradication of the Communist Party.

Recently, there have been many cases where, following the orders of Guomindang generals and officials, Communists and soldiers of the 8th Army were killed and even buried alive. Armed clashes have occurred between individual units of Guomindang troops and the 8th Army. After the Communist Party protested to Chiang Kai-shek, he would order the military clashes stopped, and the conflicts would cease for a while. If the command of the Guomindang is not improved, the danger of military clashes will persist.

The border region.

The border region of Shaanxi-Gansu-Ningxia covers the territory of approximately 18 districts. The population of this region numbers 586 thousand. Besides agricultural products, the region produces a little oil, coal, iron, and, relatively speaking, a lot of salt. Most of the land in the border region is divided among the peasants.

In the border region universal suffrage has been introduced, on the basis of which a political council has been elected and a government of the border region has been formed. The composition of the political council is as follows: workers, 15 percent; peasants, 30 percent; soldiers, 5 percent; intelligentsia, 38 percent; merchants, 4 percent; and others, 8 percent.

15 percent of the entire population is bearing arms. For the past several years, agricultural and industrial output have grown. The workers' wages, compared

to the prerevolutionary period, have risen 15–30 percent, taxes have decreased, and a public education network has been developing, although in this regard there has been insignificant success.

The major shortcoming in the border region remains the insufficient implementation of democratism under the new conditions. This can be explained by the fact that until recently there has been a strong tradition in which the Communist Party administered this region exclusively.

The border region has not been formally recognized by the central government and the Guomindang. At one point, Chiang Kai-shek issued an order to the executive chamber to publish provisions about the border region; however, since the ruling circles of the Guomindang and the representatives of the northwestern provinces of China were against it, the order was not carried out. Therefore, the border region remains recognized and not recognized at the same time. The hard-line elements in the Guomindang are conducting a campaign against the border region. They have surrounded it with commissioners and guard detachments, who incite tensions that sometimes lead to military raids against the troops of the border region.

In the opinion of the Communist Party, the border region is needed as a base for the 8th Army, as the bulwark for the activities of the party, and as a model for establishing a democratic regime for all of China.

The 8th and the 4th Armies.

The 8th Army is active in the provinces of Hebei and Shanxi and in parts of Shandong, North Henan, Suiyuan, and Qahar. In most cases, units of the 8th Army have been occupying regions that were not penetrated by the units of the Guomindang army.

Chiang Kai-shek thinks that the 8th Army should not act on its own but must obey his orders. Therefore, he has not yet recognized activities of the 8th Army in Shandong Prov[ince] and in the regions to the south of this province. However, when the units of the 8th Army gain a victory, he praises and encourages them, and orders his units to establish contact [with them.] Chiang Kai-shek permitted the 8th Army to create three armies and promised to increase its supply. At the same time, he insisted on limiting the area of operation and growth of the 8th Army. The resources and armaments that Chiang Kai-shek provides to sustain the units of the 8th Army are quite insignificant (since the [beginning of] war, only 120 light machine guns have been received). The Communist Party urges that the supplies and weapons of the 8th Army be improved. The Guomindang sent several staff officers to the 8th Army who do not play any important role and are engaged, for the most part, in informing Chiang Kai-shek about the situation in the army.

The 8th Army has about 240 thousand soldiers, plus 21 thousand men in the border region.

The 4th Army differs from the 8th Army both in its activities and numbers. It counts about 30 thousand soldiers. It operates to the rear of the enemy, for the most part near Nanjing and along the Nanjing-Shanghai railroad. The 4th Army strictly follows Guomindang directives and conducts mass work with the population in the spirit of these directives and of the corresponding orders of the provincial governments. It accomplishes operational tasks according to the directives of the Guomindang army headquarters and operates in the regions designated by these headquarters. Therefore, Chiang Kai-shek and the Guomindang leadership have no reason to interfere with the activities of the 4th Army, although he tries from time to time.

Although the 4th Army is not large, it has strong leadership, its cadres have lived through a long period of partisan struggle and been well forged, and, therefore, as a whole it is a tightly knit military unit.

During the 2 years of their struggle against the Japanese occupiers, the 8th and the 4th Armies have been engaged in many battles and have captured a lot of military supplies. The 8th Army has conducted 2,689 large and small battles, captured 385 soldiers of the Japanese army and 9,615 soldiers of the puppet government army. [It has] captured 20 thousand rifles, 384 light and 78 heavy machine guns, 24 mountain cannons, and 3 airplanes. In the course of the battles, the 8th Army lost about 30 thousand killed and wounded, and the enemy 70 thousand.

The 4th Army has conducted 344 battles, captured 826 soldiers and 1,747 rifles and 54 machine guns. It lost about a thousand killed and wounded, and the enemy about three thousand.

A number of partisan bands and popular armed self-defense groups are growing up around the 8th and the 4th Armies. In northern China, in the zone of the 8th Army's activities, there are about 300 thousand people, and in the zone of activities of the 4th Army about four to five thousand partisans.

Both in the 8th and the 4th Army the military-political cadres are the strongest cadres of the Communist Party. 30 percent of the personnel of these armies are party members. Currently, there are 90 thousand Communists in the 8th Army, and about 10 thousand in the 4th Army.

Basing itself on the units of the 8th and 4th Armies, the Communist Party is launching the partisan movement in the enemy's rear. The military-political staff of these armies conducts all the political work in the zones of partisan activities and creates organs of local administration in the regions liberated from the Japanese occupiers.

Pursuing a policy of maximum growth in partisan warfare, the Communist Party has broken the territories occupied by the enemy into 20-plus partisan regions. Of those, in the Shanxi-Hebei-Qahar, Shanxi-Hebei-Henan, Hebei-Shandong-Henan, eastern Shandong, and southern Shandong regions, [and in] the region of the southern Yangtse River [and] Eastern Anhui, strong bases have been created that have become the bulwark of the partisan movement.

Moreover, the party conducts work in the big cities occupied by the enemy. In this regard, particularly notable success has been achieved in Shanghai.

Document 20 *continued*

The work of the Communist Party.

Compared to the prewar period, the number of party members has increased sevenfold. As of June–July 1939, the number of party members was 498 thousand; in northwestern China, 233 thousand; in the Guomindang regions, 108 thousand; in the zones of activities of the 8th and 4th Armies, 100 thousand; in the border region and in the regions under direct control of the CC, 56 thousand.

The majority of party members are peasants. The number of workers among the party members does not exceed 10 percent. The Communist Party has about 30 thousand party cells. It must be noted that the political [consciousness] of some party members is rather low, and the party educational work is still very weak.

Lately, the Communist Party has been paying close attention to the question of educating [its] cadres. At this time, under the direct guidance of the CC, the Marxist-Leninist Academy, the party school of the Central Committee of the Communist Party, there are courses of instruction at the Administration of Affairs Department and 4 party schools in the border region. In addition, there is an anti-Japanese Academy, the North-Shaanxi College, the workers' school, the Lu Xun Academy of Arts, classes for young people, a women's university. Outside the border region, there are [other] local schools or classes.

The Communist Party conducts its work according to the situation, which varies in different regions of China. For example, in the border region, legal forms of work are being used; in the 8th and 4th Armies, semilegal forms of work, in the zones of partisan activities, legal is combined with illegal [work], since it is important to consider the possibility of occupation of the partisan territory by the enemy and of the Chinese troops being on the move. In the regions under Guomindang control, for the most part illegal forms [of work] are used. In the regions occupied by the Japanese, the work is strictly underground.

In March–April 1940 a party congress is to take place. All the preparatory work for it has been done. The Communist Party is awaiting the return of its representative from Moscow.

---

23 February 1940

Zhou Enlai lingered in Moscow, hoping to consult with Stalin and receive assurances of more tangible help from the Soviets. On 19 February 1940 Dimitrov again wrote Stalin, forwarding the ECCI Presidium's draft resolution on China and the draft outlining the line the CCP Central Committee ought to take in anticipation of the impending party congress in China.[18]

On 25 February, Stalin told Dimitrov by telephone that he could not meet with him and the Chinese and that he had been unable to read the materials sent him because he was too busy. One may surmise that he was preoccupied, among other things, with the crisis in the Winter War with Finland. As for what advice to give the Chinese, Stalin added over the phone, "Decide by yourselves."[19]

Meanwhile, on 23 February, Dimitrov had sent Stalin another document concerning the financial needs of the Chinese party and its army, with the recommendation that the Soviet Union provide $350,000 in 1940. In their telephone conversation on 25 February, Stalin told Dimitrov that the CCP would receive $300,000.

Document 21

Dimitrov to Stalin, 23 February 1940, with enclosure. Letter: RTsKhIDNI, f. 495, op. 74, d. 317, l. 52; enclosure: ll. 53–55. Original in Russian. Typewritten, with handwritten annotations by Dimitrov.

To Comrade STALIN.

Dear Comrade Stalin,

The CC of the CP of China charged C. Zhou Enlai with presenting a budget of party and military expenditures to us, explaining the extremely difficult financial situation in the party, and requesting financial support.

It is clear from this budget (see enclosure) that the monthly deficit of the party is, for party spending, 58,280 U.S. dollars, and for the military, 300,000 U.S. dollars.

We, of course, have explained to C. Zhou Enlai that the party must mobilize all existing resources in the country to cover these enormous deficits and that he should not count on outside help.

However, considering the situation of the party and the urgent necessity of supporting the party press and propaganda and the existing network of party schools for educating party and military cadres, we would consider it appropriate to provide assistance to the Chinese Communist Party for these pur-

18. RTsKhIDNI, f. 495, op. 74, d. 317, ll. 38–51. The final version of the Comintern documents, signed on 2 March 1940, contains some changes from the draft sent to Stalin. See RTsKhIDNI, f. 495, op. 2, d. 275, ll. 2–14.

19. TsPA (Sofia), f. 146, op. 2, a.e. 6.

Document 21 *continued*

poses in the amount of 350,000 U.S. dollars in 1940.

We are asking, if you find it possible in the current situation, to give a directive to the appropriate organs to offer financial help to the Communist Party of China in this or some other amount.

With fraternal greetings

(G. Dimitrov)

23 February 1940.
Sent on <. . . >40
Outgoing No.<. . .>/39
<. . .>

BUDGET OF THE PARTY AND MILITARY EXPENDITURES OF THE CP OF CHINA

I. BUDGET OF PARTY EXPENDITURES.

The total of monthly expenditure amounts to <u>707,960 Chinese</u> dollars = <u>101,137 American dollars</u>.

Of which

1) Publishing expenses	<u>190,000 Chin. dol.</u>
a) "Xinhua Ribao" *(Chongqing)*[?]	60,000
b) Northern edition of "Xinhua Ribao" *(Shaanxi)*	25,000
c) "Xin Sijun Hua bao" *(Yanan)*	15,000
d) "Kang Di bao," a newspaper of the border region Shanxi-Hebei-Qahar	10,000
e) Subsidy to five daily newspapers <. . .>	20,000
f) Publishing of magazines <. . .>	10,000
g) Subsidy for book publishing and literature[20]	40,000
2) Expenses for cadre training	<u>218,060 Chin. dol.</u>
a) For schools, under direct supervision of the CC CCP of China <. . .>	146,760 " " " "
(Currently, all schools have a total of <u>9,784 students,</u> 15 dol. each)	
b) For local party scools	71,300 " " " "
(Currently, the schools under the auspices of the Bureau of the CC have a total of <u>1,080</u> st[udents]; schools under the auspices of the provincial committees have <u>3,810</u> st[udents])	
3) Expenditures of the CC (including special expenses)	<u>60,000 Chin. dol.</u>
4) Expenditures of the provincial and regional committees	<u>189,900 Chin. dol.</u>
a) For district committees	84,700 " " " "

20. Handwritten note in the margin:
<u>3 publishing houses:</u> *Chungun, Yan'an — <. . .> — Lenin, Stalin, Marx, Engels.*

(There are 1,210 district committees in the
country; 70 Chin. dol. each)
b) For special and regional committees   27,000   " "   " "
(There are 180 special and regional committees
in the country, 150 Chin. dol. each)
c) For provincial and territorial committees   36,000   " "   " "
(There are 36 provincial and territorial committees
in the country; 1,000 Chin. dol. each)
d) For communications and transfer of workers   18,000   " "   " "
(500 Chin. dol. to each provincial committee)
e) For agitation and propaganda of the district
committees   24,000   " "   " "
(20 Chin. dol. to each district committee)
5) Spending on communications between the CC and
local [committees]   50,000   " "   " "

The monthly income of the party is   300,000 Chin. dol.
(Collections in the partisan regions
and party membership dues.)
Each month, the deficit is 407,960 Chin. dol. = 58,280 American dollars.
(Annually—696,000)

II. BUDGET OF MILITARY EXPENDITURES
Each month, the total expenditures amount to 4,200,000 Chin. dol.
= 600,000 American dollars.

The 8th Army has	261,246 soldiers
The new 4th Army has	30,448 " "
The military school has	10,000 students
The military staff in Yan'an has	1,500 people

Total   303,195   " "
Each [of them costs] on average 13 Chin. dol. 85 cents a month (including
food, clothing, money for ammunition, repairs of military equipment,
medical expenses, transportation, miscellaneous purchases, forage, office
equipment, pocket money).
We receive from the Chinese National government 770,000 Chin. dol.
every month.
This includes: a) For the 8th Army 650,000 Chin. dol.
b) For the 4th Army 120,000   " "   " "
The monthly income of the army is 1,330,000 Chin. dol. (we receive this
income, for the most part, from local government organs under the control
of our party in the partisan zones of Northern China).
The deficit amounts to 2,100,000 Chin. dol. = 300,000 American dollars

each month.

1) From the government	*770,000 Chin. dol.*
2) Army collections	*1,330,000* " " "
	2,100,000 " " "

General spending: *Deficit:*
4,200,000 Chin. dol.   *2,100,000 Chin. dol.*
<. . .>
Annual[?] deficit
3,600,000 Amer. Dol.

The minimum necessary for the party
up to 35,000 Am. dol. <. . .>
420,000 dol. per year
For the army: 250,000 dol.
3,000,000 dol. per year

---

23 November 1940

In the summer of 1940 Zhou Enlai had transmitted a surprisingly positive report on the Nationalists' attitude toward the Soviet Union and the Chinese Communists. In essence, he argued that there was no longer any prospect of Chiang Kai-shek's capitulating to the Japanese, but there was a need for military support—particularly airplanes—for the Nationalist armed forces from the Soviet Union. In the general context of international relations, Zhou Enlai suggested, Chiang Kai-shek needed to improve relations with Moscow, and he now realized that this meant that he had to stabilize his relations with the Yan'an regime. The Guomindang leadership, though split on the issue, was reportedly considering sending T. V. Soong to Moscow for negotiations and was exploring the possibility of asking the CCP—and Zhou Enlai personally—to join him and others in this task. Zhou urgently desired Stalin's opinion about whether he should get himself involved in this effort.[21]

21. CCP Central Committee to Dimitrov, 3 August 1940; Dimitrov to Stalin (with identical notes to Molotov and Zhdanov), 4 August 1940, in RTsKhIDNI, f. 495, op. 74, d. 317, l. 66; enclosure in f. 495, op. 184, vkhod. 1940, d. 13, ll. 101–98.

No reply to this inquiry has been located.

By late 1940 the tone of CCP communications to the Comintern had changed considerably. Mao Zedong sent Moscow a coded message that he expected the Nationalists to attack the Communist forces and was therefore considering a preemptive counteroffensive. Dimitrov instructed the Comintern staff to prepare a reply warning the Chinese comrades against starting a fight with the Guomindang forces, in effect breaking the united front.

Mao's message to Moscow was dated 7 November and was received on 12 November; it was distributed to Stalin, Molotov, and Timoshenko; Dimitrov also showed it to Gottwald and "Ercoli." The ECCI reply to Mao was approved by Dimitrov, "Ercoli," Manuilsky, and Gottwald on 23 November, and the final text was signed by Dimitrov on the 25 November.[22]

Document 22

Dimitrov to Stalin, 23 November 1940, with enclosures. Letter: RTsKhIDNI, f. 495, op. 74, d. 317, ll. 68–70; enclosures: f. 495, op. 74, vkhod. 1940, d. 13, ll. 176–174. Original (decoded from Chinese) in Russian. Typewritten.

Dear Comrade Stalin,
We forwarded to you a telegram from C. Mao Zedong in which he informed us that Chiang Kai-shek had demanded that the units of the 4th and 8th Armies

22. In a message to Mao Zedong on 27 November, Dimitrov had written, "If you could secure the whole road between your territory and the Mongolian People's Republic, it would be possible to send you a significant quantity of arms by that road. This question needs to be examined urgently and seriously. Inform us of your considerations and concrete proposals" (RTsKhIDNI, f. 495, op. 184, iskh. 1940, d.2, l. 91). On 18 December, Mao replied, outlining three possibilities: periodic cavalry detachments to protect incoming shipments from Mongolia; an extension of the area controlled by the Communist partisans; and an effort to bribe and win over a general who had control of the area (ibid., op. 184, vkhod. 1940, d. 13, ll. 361–359). On 29 December, Dimitrov (after consultation with Stalin) told Mao: "The variants proposed by you are being studied. This will require some time. It is essential for you to keep this whole issue in strict secrecy" (ibid., op. 74, d. 317, l. 74 [Dimitrov to Stalin]; f. 495, op. 184, iskh. 1940, d. 2, l. 113 [Dimitrov to Mao]). Timoshenko's involvement (he had been sent a copy of Mao's 7 November request) suggests that the Soviet military might have been interested in the Mongolian variant, but Dimitrov may have gone too far in suggesting the possibility to Mao in the first place. There is no evidence that it was ever discussed again.

leave central China and Shandong Province in the north within a month, and that furthermore, if this demand was not fulfilled, Chiang Kai-shek would undertake a punitive expedition against them; and 200 thousand central government troops had been assembled for that purpose.

Based on his belief that Chiang Kai-shek had already decided to capitulate to the Japanese and was therefore preparing to smash and liquidate the people's armies, C. Mao Zedong informed us that the Chinese comrades were planning to undertake a "preventive counteroffensive in order to defeat the punitive troops and Chiang Kai-shek's fortified zones." However, since doing so could lead to a final split with Chiang Kai-shek, C. Mao Zedong asked for our opinion before the Chinese comrades made a final decision on this question.

Immediately after receiving this telegram, we told Com. Mao Zedong that their plan caused us great doubts, and we asked if he could delay making a decision on this question until we had thoroughly studied it.

After reviewing the materials and discussing the problem, we are thinking of sending the following reply to C. Mao Zedong:

"The current situation in China seems to us very ambiguous and unclear. In any case, one cannot conclude, as you do, that Chiang Kai-shek has firmly decided to capitulate to the Japanese. On the contrary, there are indications that despite his usual vacillations, he has not yet dared to take this course. The mood of the masses in favor of continued resistance and the existence of a rather strong army under the leadership of the Communist Party, which is determined to continue the anti-Japanese war, obviously restrain Chiang Kai-shek. Moreover, the Americans and the British, to whom Chiang Kai-shek listens, are eager, after the signing of the tripartite pact,[23] for Chinese resistance to continue and grow in order to prevent Japan from seriously stepping up military activity in areas other than China. And they have influence on Chiang Kai-shek in this sense. The friendly position of the Soviet Union likewise cannot be unimportant to Chiang Kai-shek. Under these conditions, it will be clear to every Chinese patriot that it is precisely now that the national-liberation struggle against the Japanese occupiers has the best prospect, despite domestic problems. Chiang Kai-shek cannot go against this, since he does not want to commit political suicide as leader of the Chinese people, which he considers himself to be.

"Therefore, it seems to us that for the time being, you ought to follow a policy [that allows you] to gain time, to maneuver, and to bargain with Chiang Kai-shek in every possible way over the evacuation of your troops from central China and from Shandong Province. It is important to gain as much time as possible. It is essential that you do not initiate military action against the expeditionary forces and do not give Chiang Kai-shek an opportunity to portray

23. A treaty signed by Germany, Italy, and Japan on 27 September 1940.

you to the Chinese people as the violators of the unity of the anti-Japanese struggle, and to use your actions to justify his attempts to sign a compromise peace with the Japanese.

"However, if Chiang Kai-shek nonetheless attacks the people's armies, you must strike with all your might at the attacking forces. In this case, the responsibility for the split and the internecine warfare will fall entirely on Chiang Kai-shek, and your armies will get immeasurably stronger support from the masses than if you decided to engage the central government troops now, as a preemptive measure against a possible attack."

We ask your advice and directives on this question. Please reply as soon as possible since Mao Zedong's inquiry was sent from Yan'an on 7 November 1940, and we are afraid that our Chinese comrades, being in a very difficult position, may undertake some action without thorough reflection.

With fraternal greetings,

(G. Dimitrov)

23 November 1940

Copy No. **2**
TOP SECRET.[24]

To Cc. DIMITROV and MANUILSKY.[25]

Preparing for capitulation, CHIANG KAI-SHEK has lately been inspiring a broad anti-Communist campaign to clear the way to direct capitulation to Japan. The propaganda about China's alleged adherence to the Anglo-American bloc is merely a smokescreen to camouflage capitulation. However, CHIANG KAI-SHEK still takes into account the position of the Soviet Union and fears protests by the Chinese people. After Com. STALIN's telegram to CHIANG KAI-SHEK arrived, there were signs that the Guomindang was relenting toward the Soviet Union. If the Soviet Union can further increase its pressure on CHIANG KAI-SHEK and we, on our part, increase our activity, it may be possible to delay his capitulation and the broad anti-Communist military expedition; and if it is possible to delay them for two to three more months, our situation will very much improve. Currently, CHIANG KAI-SHEK is trying to push us out of central China and SHANDONG Province (where we have 300 thousand people, including 200 thousand troops and 70–80 thousand activists of different kinds) and make us retreat into northern China. We cannot accept these demands of CHIANG KAI-SHEK, since the Japanese are relentlessly organizing punitive expeditions in northern China: our bases are

24. In the margin, handwritten:
Sent from China 7.XI.40. Rec[eived] 12.[XI.40]
25. In the margin, handwritten by Dimitrov:
Send to Cc. Manuilsky, Ercoli, Gottwald. 14.11.40.
Also signed: *Gottwald, 15.XI.40. Ercoli 19.XI.40.*

diminishing and shrinking daily. There are serious problems with food and supplies, and we already have 500 thousand people in northern China, including 300 thousand troops and various kinds of activists, and their lives and struggle are extremely difficult.

CHIANG KAI-SHEK's plan is to drive our forces to northern China, i.e., to the valley of the old tributary of the Yellow River. Our forces are being surrounded by fortified zones (the construction of these zones is already going at a fast pace) in order to expose us to Japanese fire and to CHIANG KAI-SHEK and so liquidate us.

CHIANG KAI-SHEK demands that we evacuate our troops from central China and SHANDONG Province to the provinces of HEBEI, QAHAR, and SHANXI in one month. If this demand is not met on time, he will start a war against us. The military units of TANG ENBO or PIN XIANG, totaling about 200 thousand people, have already started moving toward the eastern and northeastern regions of ANHUI. The anti-Communist war may break out at any moment.

At this time, we are stepping up the struggle throughout the country against capitulation to Japan and against the splitting of the united anti-Japanese national front. On the one hand, we will soften our stance toward CHIANG KAI-SHEK and agree to evacuate part of our 4th Army, which is located in the southern valley of the Yangtse River and in its northern valley in order to delay CHIANG KAI-SHEK's attack against us. However, there is no way that we can agree to his demand that all our units leave central China and move to the three provinces of northern China, since we cannot put ourselves in a situation where we will be surrounded by a new wall of China, where we will have both CHIANG KAI-SHEK and the Japanese confronting us, where we will be eliminated by them and thus give CHIANG KAI-SHEK an opportunity to quietly capitulate to the Japanese. If we take a conciliatory position, before CHIANG KAI-SHEK attacks us, we will begin a counteroffensive for defensive purposes, in order to smash his troops and fortified zones. In this case, our military plan will be to leave the bulk of our forces (about 350 thousand soldiers) to struggle against the Japanese in different anti-Japanese bases, assemble some of our auxiliary and shock troops (about 150 thousand soldiers) to deliver a blow at the rear of the enemy's expeditionary force, i.e., in Henan, Gansu, and other provinces, in order to completely smash CHIANG KAI-SHEK's expedition and turn the political situation around (this is possible).

If a combined offensive of CHIANG KAI-SHEK and the Japanese [takes place], and if we do not undertake the aforementioned military action, it will be impossible to forestall their attack and deter it, and as a result, our situation will be very precarious. However, there is also a danger that if we do proceed with this useful (for us) undertaking, CHIANG KAI-SHEK will make sure to accuse us, in order to deceive the people, of disrupting the anti-Japanese struggle. This may result in a final split between us and CHIANG KAI-SHEK. Therefore, politically it [the attack] is not advantageous to us, even though the mere fact of our troops moving into the rear of the expeditionary force does not imply any desire on our part to break with CHIANG KAI-SHEK.

Although at this time our slogans will be: "To ask CHIANG KAI-SHEK to remove and punish HE YING QIN; withdrawal of the anti-Communist expeditionary forces; ending the capitulation campaign; implementing the three principles of SUN YATSEN; reforming the government organs; freedom [to hold] popular anti-Japanese demonstrations; freedom for the anti-Japanese political prisoners; convocation of the national council, etc."—which will find a positive response with the majority of the people—CHIANG KAI-SHEK may break with us permanently. Therefore, although we are now ready to undertake the necessary military measures, we have not yet made a final decision. The plan of CHIANG KAI-SHEK is very dangerous and harmful for us. If we fail to resolve this question correctly, it could cause countless disasters in the future. Consequently, we now need to seriously approach this problem, for which purpose I am informing you about it and asking that you give directives as soon as possible.

MAO ZEDONG

7/XI/40

No. 1240/138

Copies sent to: Cc. Dimitrov, Stalin, Molotov, Timoshenko

Outgoing No. 940

16/XI/40

To Mao Zedong

Due to the exceptional complexity of the problem, we will be able to give you an answer only after studying a number of important points. You should prepare, but we ask you to wait for the final decision.

No. 12   **Dimitrov.**

15.11.40. G. D.

Copy No. 2

TOP SECRET.

Incoming 1273/144

To C. DIMITROV

A SECRET DIRECTIVE OF THE CC CCP DISTRIBUTED ON 7 NOVEMBER 1940[26]

1. Japan is most actively wooing China into capitulation. The German ambassador Trautmann sent a telegram in which he seeks to persuade the Chi-

---

26. Handwritten in the margin:
Show to Cc. Manuilsky, Ercoli, Gottwald. 23.11.40. G. D. Ercoli 29.11.40. Gottwald. D. Man[uilsky]

nese ruling circles to agree to peace. Plotters from among the pro-Japanese elements and instigators of civil war exert pressure on the ruling circles, incite civil war, and seek capitulation. The goal of Japan and the pro-Japanese elements is to divide China, to make the Guomindang and the Communist Party fight each other, so that they can seize China without any difficulties. The current crisis is very serious. In order to overcome this critical situation, our entire party must mobilize to struggle against the capitulation and schism.

2. [It is essential] to immediately mobilize all the party and non-party activists so that they can explain, directly and indirectly, by word of mouth and in writing, with all possible means, persistently and honestly to the ruling circles, to the Guomindang, to the army, and to the different parties and groups that the campaign against the CCP will result in destruction of the country and of the Guomindang itself. Capitulation will result in a divided China, disorder in the anti-Japanese army, loss of authority, and ruin for the leaders of the anti-Japanese struggle. It is important to mention that all this is a scheme by Japan and the plotters among the pro-Japanese elements and the instigators of the civil war. Under no circumstances should we fall into this trap. Turning bayonets against our allies will only provoke hatred within our ranks and make our enemies happy. From the very beginning, our Communist Party has been supporting CHIANG KAI-SHEK, the Guomindang, fraternal armies, and all the leaders of the anti-Japanese parties and groups. But it resolutely demands and insists on unifying China and on the tenacious continuation of the war of liberation; it demands that there be no capitulation, no disunity, no instigation of civil war. On this basis, we have been implementing in practice all the declarations and promises outlined in the manifesto of the CC of our party of 7 July of this year, and the united-front measures we have been undertaking all this time. We wish to continue on this road along with the Guomindang and the different parties, groups, strata, and armies. Our party, the 8th and the 4th Armies, as well as the entire people of the country, will not for a moment tolerate the pro-Japanese elements and instigators of civil war. We are urging all the parties, all groups, all the circles and armies to pay serious attention to the 200 thousand–strong Guomindang armies advancing against the 4th and the 8th Armies. In Henan Province the danger of civil war is imminent. We must demand, all together, that the government cease these military actions and prevent a civil war.

3. In their work of agitation and propaganda, party and non-party activists must watch their behavior. Do not curse CHIANG KAI-SHEK, do not curse the Guomindang, the Guomindang armies, different local military Whampoa groups, or the youth organizations of the three people's principles. It is also inappropriate to curse England and America and the pro-Anglo-American elements. This is not key to today's struggle. We must concentrate on consistently exposing the plotters among the pro-Japanese elements and the instigators of civil war. It is essential to stress Japan's plan to woo China into

capitulation, to make more visible the slogan of struggle against capitulation, against civil war, to pay [more] attention to the rear and to the external enemy. Chinese must not fight Chinese. [It is necessary] to launch the slogan "The entire people and the entire country must unite to prevent civil war." Expel the pro-Japanese elements. We must ardently and actively utilize all opportunities to propagandize and explain this danger everywhere. Thus we will show ourselves honest friends of the unification of the entire people to defend their nation. The central task of our party at this crucial moment must be the struggle against capitulation and civil war. The main thrust of our struggle, which in the past used to be focused on the hard-liners, must now be aimed against the pro-Japanese elements and the instigators of civil war.

Once the pro-Japanese elements and the instigators of civil war are defeated, it will be much harder for the hard-liners to go for capitulation.

4. It is important to determine precisely who is a plotter among the pro-Japanese elements and the instigators of civil war. According to the specific information from the provinces, their leaders on the national level are a group of pro-Japanese elements under the leadership of HE YING QIN. This group, connected to Japan and WANG JINGWEI by QIN, surrounds CHIANG KAI-SHEK and urges him to issue an order to start a punitive expedition against the CCP. The goal of this group, following directives from Japan, is to instigate a civil war and thus to make it easier for the Japanese army to end the war in China and [instead] fight England and America. China would have to capitulate as a result of the civil war. However, for this to happen all of China would have to capitulate, and CHIANG KAI-SHEK would have to be involved in the civil war. Thus, the pro-Japanese elements, who started by supporting CHIANG KAI-SHEK's anti-Communist policy, are encouraging him in every possible way to struggle against the CCP. They think that as soon as the anti-Communist war is started, CHIANG KAI-SHEK will be trapped and there will be no way out for him, and then capitulation will come and they will ask Japan to get rid of CHIANG KAI-SHEK, and HE YING QIN will become a Chinese PÉTAIN. This is what HE YING QIN has in mind. From this perspective a great danger can be foreseen that CHIANG KAI-SHEK and his supporters may be lulled by the pro-Japanese elements and fall into a trap. They will start with the anti-Communist struggle and end with capitulation to Japan. This is the greatest danger that CHIANG KAI-SHEK can present. We must be extremely vigilant and avoid the smallest blunder that could destroy us. However, while CHIANG KAI-SHEK is still at the crossroads of the three international fronts and the three tendencies in the Chinese government (capitulation, joining the Anglo-American bloc, or continuation of the liberation struggle), while he has not yet decided to become a PÉTAIN, we must take measures to prevent his attack on us, in order to win time to continue the anti-Japanese struggle for at least a while longer. Today, the greatest danger comes from the pro-Japanese elements with HE YING QIN at the head and

with the instigators of civil war. Our party must expose, by word of mouth, the great plot of HE YING QIN and others to all the parties, groups, circles, and armies. Explain, in all possible ways, the criminal activities of HE YING QIN and others so that everybody knows [about them] and expresses hatred toward him. Nevertheless, it is necessary to avoid mentioning HE YING QIN's name in the official [party] press.

5. It is essential now to step up the united-front work. It is important to establish, concretely and at every opportune moment, contact with every possible concrete object. It is necessary to explore ways to pursue this goal against capitulation, against civil war. [It is important] not to make excessive demands. We must realize that even small, individual oral agreements will be useful for us. It is essential daily, hourly to check on and expose the shortcomings in our work. It is essential to carefully study the situation and condition of all the strata, all the parties, groups, armies, organizations, and leaders, [so that we can] skillfully detect contradictions among them and find ways to establish contact with them.

6. It is necessary, according to the directives of the CC, to conceal entirely the [party] leadership. All our organizations in the Guomindang region must be ready to go underground for a long time. [All our organizations] must be prepared to counter the double attack of the pro-Japanese elements and of Japan.

7. It is necessary to explain to all the party and non-party activists and anti-Japanese figures that we all have to conduct a decisive struggle while there is still time and while there is still a possibility of preventing capitulation and civil war.

If we, our army, and the people of the nation contribute more today to the work against capitulation and civil war, tomorrow we will achieve a bigger victory. In essence, the policy and the work of our party will determine what the outcome of the current situation will be.

8. No matter how the current situation develops, the final victory will belong to China and the Chinese people. Our party deploys a 500 thousand–strong armed force and 600 thousand party members. The Chinese people have great sympathy for our party; there are many intermediate elements who may join us or else become enemies or neutrals. We enjoy the sympathy and support of the great forces in the USSR. The world revolution is maturing. There is an unprecedented aggravation of contradictions among the imperialists, severe difficulties in the enemy camp, serious contradictions between the pro-Japanese elements and the hard-liners, between the hard-liners and intermediary elements, as well as contradictions within each of these groups. All this leads us to assert with confidence that the final victory undoubtedly belongs to China and the Chinese people. No matter how difficult the situation is, the Communist Party has strong faith in victory. Only a solidly united party and a revolutionary people, self-reliantly conducting a persistent struggle, will

emerge victorious. This confidence can be created and strengthened in our party and among the people of the country. The inevitable pessimistic moods in the ranks of our party must be resolutely overcome.

CC CCP

Copies sent to:
C. Dimitrov
C. Stalin
C. Molotov
C. Zhdanov
C. Timoshenko
<. . .>

---

6 February 1941

The leaders of the Chinese Communists, and Mao Zedong in particular, continued to insist that a break with Chiang Kai-shek was inevitable, while Dimitrov repeatedly warned against hasty action and civil war. In January 1941 the Communist-commanded 4th Army was decimated by superior Nationalist forces, and Mao painted a gloomy scenario of the prospects.[27] Dimitrov, who had been forwarding the messages from Yan'an to Stalin and other Soviet leaders, here informs Stalin about a message sent the previous day from the Comintern to Mao taking direct issue with his policy.

27. By contrast with his sharply critical view of Mao's analysis and policy preferences, Dimitrov had a positive opinion of the analysis provided to the Comintern by Lin Biao (Lin Piao), commander of the 115th Division of the 8th Army, who was in Moscow at the time. Lin Biao's sober analysis foresaw no inevitable rift between the GMD and the CCP and no inevitable civil war (Lin Biao to Dimitrov, received 6 February 1941, distributed to Stalin and others, 7 February; RTsKhIDNI, f. 495, op. 74, d. 97, ll. 76–77; enclosure, d. 322, ll. 8–25). For a message sent to Mao on 4 January 1941, see Titarenko, *Kommunisticheskii Internatsional,* p. 291.

Document 23

Dimitrov to Stalin, 6 February 1941, with enclosures. Letter: RTsKhIDNI, f. 495, op. 74, d. 317, l. 75; enclosures: f. 495, op. 184, vkhod. 1941, d. 4, ll. 9–8, 31–30. Original in Russian. Typewritten.

TO COMRADE STALIN

Dear Comrade Stalin,

Regarding the recent telegrams from C. Mao Zedong from which it is evident that the Chinese comrades consider a break with Chiang Kai-shek inevitable and are thoughtlessly pursuing this rift themselves, we have decided, even before the whole question about relations between the Communist Party and the Guomindang is clarified, to draw C. Mao Zedong's attention to his incorrect position on the question of a rift [by sending] the following telegram:

"We believe that breaking with Chiang Kai-shek is not inevitable. You should not strive for the rift. On the contrary, the Communist Party, basing itself on the masses, which support the united anti-Japanese front, should do everything in its power to avoid the rift and the onset of civil war. We ask to analyze the present situation you soberly and thoroughly, to reconsider your present position, and to inform us about your considerations and suggestions."

I urge you, Com. Stalin, to receive me in order to give me your directives regarding any further urgent advice to give to the CC of the Chinese Communist Party.

With fraternal greetings,

(G. DIMITROV)

6 February 1941

Sent on 6/II/41

Package No. 27

Stern.

INCOMING TELEGRAM

After the creation of the bloc comprising Germany, Italy, and Japan, the struggle between Japan and America has intensified. England, America, and the USSR provided assistance to China. Chiang Kai-shek has dared to wage a more open struggle against the CCP and now has sunk into lawlessness—[has come] "to the extreme."

Secretariat of the CC of the CCP

Made *6* copies and sent to:

1. *Addressee*
2. *C. Stalin*
3. *C. Molotov*
4. *C. Zhdanov*
5. *C. Timoshenko*
6. *C. Beria.*

Document 23 *continued*

Copy No. *2*
TOP SECRET
To Com. DIMITROV[28]

Since Chiang Kai-shek published his counterrevolutionary decree of 17 January, all the circles have been expressing their dissatisfaction with CHIANG KAI-SHEK. Intermediate elements believe that from now on the internal unity will be undermined. Some individuals in the Guomindang are also dissatisfied with CHIANG KAI-SHEK. The masses sympathize with us. Anglo-American diplomatic personnel and journalists are, for the most part, afraid of a civil war in China and are displeased by CHIANG KAI-SHEK's measures. The Japanese and WANG JINGWEI are rejoicing. For the past few days, a number of reports unfavorable to CHIANG KAI-SHEK have been published, which forced him to make an announcement on 27 January in which he justified his counterrevolutionary behavior, stressing that this incident was a local rather than an all-China military question, [that it was] not a political [question], [it was] an internal question which should not affect foreign relations.

CHIANG KAI-SHEK is already preparing the extermination of all progressive, anti-Japanese forces on a national scale. Representatives of the 8th Army are in danger.

Taking into consideration that there will be a transitional period between this incident and the final rift, we are using this time to thoroughly prepare [ourselves] in order to capitalize on the rift. At the same time, we are delaying, in all ways possible, the final rift. Nevertheless, the rift is inevitable. After the final split, CHIANG KAI-SHEK will certainly capitulate to Japan. Then we will undoubtedly find ourselves in a difficult situation, under dual attack from Japan and CHIANG KAI-SHEK (in central China, we are already under dual attack). If then you are not able to help us openly, we will have tremendous difficulties.

At this point, we are politically exposing, in all ways possible, CHIANG KAI-SHEK's plotting, [we are] mobilizing the masses to struggle against his policy of splitting and preparing for capitulation. Militarily, we are waging defensive battles so that the masses can see the actual disposition, can see who is to blame for the impending civil war, and at the same time looking forward to changes in the international arena. As to the diplomatic relations between England and America and Chongqing, we will also use them.

MAO ZEDONG

No. 159/10
1/11/41 [*sic*]

28. In the margin, handwritten:
Show to Cc. Manuilsky, Ercoli, Gottwald, as well as Cc. Li Ting and Ziuzin. 4.1.41.
G. D. Ercoli. Manuilsky, Gottwald, 4.2.41.

Document 23 *continued*

Copies sent to:
Addressee
C. Stalin
C. Molotov
C. Zhdanov
C. Voroshilov
C. Timoshenko
C. Beria

---

13 February 1941

In his reply to Dimitrov's telegram, Mao retreats somewhat from his previous position, professing to agree with the ECCI argument, but then spells out his own, more complex position. Dimitrov promptly distributed Mao's message to Stalin and other Soviet and Comintern leaders, asking the CC to reconsider its current position and then present its proposals to the ECCI.

Document 24

Mao Zedong to Dimitrov, forwarded to Stalin and others, 13 February 1941. RTsKhIDNI, f. 495, op. 184, vkhod. 1941, d. 4, ll. 38–35. Original (decoded from Chinese) in Russian. Typewritten, with handwritten comments by Dimitrov.

Copy No. **2**
Top Secret.
To Com. DIMITROV[29]
Your telegram has been received. Our decision conforms to your directives. However, achieving unity depends on altering our position in view of the pressure CHIANG KAI-SHEK is putting on us. The more determined we become,

29. In the margin, handwritten by Dimitrov:
1) Show to Cc. Manuilsky, Ercoli, Gottwald, Li Ting (via Ziuzin), and Sukhanov.
13.2.41. G. D.
2) Send to Cc. Stalin, Molotov, Zhdanov, Voroshilov, Timoshenko, Beria. 13.2.41.
G. D.
Signatures in the margin: *Ercoli. Gottwald. Manuilsky. Ziuzin.*

ТОВ. ДИМИТРОВУ.

38

Ваша телеграмма .... получена. Принятое наше решение соответствует Вашим указаниям, с которыми не имеет расхождения. Способы достижения единства заключаются в необходимости изменения нашей позиции в отношении оказываемого на нас давления со стороны ЧАН КАЙ ШИ. Чем мы становимся решительней, тем будет больше возможности уступок со стороны ЧАН КАЙ ШИ, чем больше ему уступать, тем больше и сильнее он будет наступать и тогда раскол будет неизбежным.

ЧАН КАЙ ШИ способен преследовать слабых и уступчивых и бояться сильных и решительных. Чем тверже проводить политику в отношении его, тем мягче и уступчивее он становится и наоборот. Поэтому мы намерены проводить твердую политику в отношении ЧАН КАЙ ШИ, иначе можем проиграть.

Ведь с прошлого года во время подъема антикоммунистической волны мы заняли позицию решительного контр-наступления, показав, что мы боимся раскола и повседневно отвечаем контрударами, не делая ни шагу в сторону уступок. В результате мы завоевали поворот обстановки в лучшую сторону за период с апреля по сентябрь месяц. В октябре-декабре прошлого года, когда вторично начался подъем антикоммунистической волны, мы заняли умеренную позицию для урегулирования положения, опубликовав телеграмму от 9-го ноября, показывающую наше умеренное отношение и решив эвакуировать свои войска из южной части Аньхуей. Но ЧАН КАЙ ШИ усмотрев в этом нашу боязнь раскола стал усиленно наступать на нас, в результате 13 января сего года им было уничтожено десятитысячное войско 4-й армии, вернувшейся из южного Аньхуей. Им опубликован контрреволюционный приказ от 17-го января.

С 18 января мы заняли новую позицию. Предпринимаем решительное контр-наступление, показывая, что мы не боимся раскола. В политическом отношении мы предъявили 18 условий, нами самими был назначен начальствующий состав 4-й армии, поднято общественное мнение во

DOCUMENT 24. First page of Russian decoded translation of Mao Zedong to Dimitrov, 13 February 1941

the more likely it is that CHIANG KAI-SHEK will make concessions. The more we give in, the more and more strongly he will advance, and then the rift will be inevitable.

CHIANG KAI-SHEK is capable of hunting the weak and soft, but he is afraid of the strong and resolute. The harder the policy toward him, the softer and more tractable he becomes, and vice versa. Therefore, we intend to conduct an uncompromising policy toward CHIANG KAI-SHEK, or else we may lose.

Starting within the past year, during the anti-Communist upsurge, we have taken a position of decisive counteroffensive and have demonstrated that we are not afraid of a rift and respond with daily counterblows without making any concessions. As a result, we changed the situation in our favor between April and September. In the period from October to December last year, when there was another anti-Communist upsurge, we took a moderate position to balance the situation, publishing our telegram of 9 November, which demonstrated our moderate attitude, and evacuating our troops from the southern part of Anhui. Nevertheless, CHIANG KAI-SHEK interpreted this as our fear of a rift and launched strong attacks against us. As a result, on 13 January, he destroyed a 10 thousand–strong force of the 4th Army that had returned from southern Anhui. On 17 January, he published his counterrevolutionary decree.

Since 18 January we have assumed a new position. We are making a decisive counterattack to demonstrate that we are not afraid of a rift. Politically, we stated 12 conditions, we independently named the commanders of the 4th Army, and we have stirred up public opinion throughout the country to the point that the Anglo-American diplomats reproached CHIANG KAI-SHEK. We have recalled several representatives of the 8th Army, refused to negotiate on issues we did not want to negotiate, and [prepared to launch] a broad offensive against the leader of the pro-Japanese elements, HE YING QIN. Militarily, we are preparing forces under the slogan of struggle against civil war. If they attack us, we will beat them. As a result, CHIANG KAI-SHEK has taken a position which demonstrates the possibility of concessions on his part and asked ZHOU ENLAI to find ways to straighten things out. On 1 February, CHIANG KAI-SHEK sent YE JIANYING by plane to Yan'an to convey CHIANG KAI-SHEK's opinion regarding straightening out the issues. His demands: to create a single corps out of the 4th Army and subordinate it to the leadership of the 8th Army, but [also] move it from central China to the north. However, these conditions are not yet acceptable to us.

We believe that the rift between the Guomindang and the CCP is inevitable in the future, but not now. If we continue with our soft attitude toward CHIANG KAI-SHEK, he will undoubtedly continue [his] advance, and if we are defeated in the military sense, there will be danger of a rift. However, if we win, he will realize the difficulties of attacking us. This is a general rule that has been tested more than once and has always proven accurate.

At this time, it is essential to continue the measures we have adopted, exploiting contradictions between Japan and CHIANG KAI-SHEK, his destruction of part of the 4th Army on 13 January, and his "mistaken" order on 17 January about the "betrayal" of the 4th Army. [It is necessary] to continue to inflict political counterblows, stressing the struggle against the pro-Japanese elements represented by HE YING QIN, firmly insisting on our twelve conditions, expanding our propaganda, and under no circumstances making any concessions. At the same time, [it is important] to keep open the option of reaching an agreement with him.

At this time, the population is upset, the intermediary elements sympathize with us, the Anglo-Americans also reproach him. Never before have we had such a mass of people on our side. CHIANG KAI-SHEK has already found himself in isolation. Two to three months from now, when we create better conditions [for ourselves], it will be possible to close this issue.

Militarily, it is necessary to continue the defensive policy. If they attack us, we will certainly beat them, resolutely destroy [them], but we will not attack [first].

Contradictions between Japan and CHIANG KAI-SHEK remain the fundamental contradictions. On this ground, there is a new proposal concerning cooperation between the Guomindang and the CCP. Lately, the Japanese have been launching an offensive in Henan Province, so CHIANG KAI-SHEK has transferred some 200 thousand troops from the anti-Communist front to the anti-Japanese front. He is eager to settle the issue by sending YE JIANYING to Yan'an. At this time, a massive offensive by the anti-Communist army against us is already impossible. Nevertheless, our military preparedness must not weaken. The better we are prepared, the more CHIANG KAI-SHEK will be afraid of a rift.

The current moment offers us the best opportunity to gain the upper hand, and we must not lose it. At the same time, we have to be rather careful in applying our new tactics, considering the existing possibilities.

Here are the twelve conditions that we set for CHIANG KAI-SHEK: 1) At once to stop provoking a civil war; 2) to revoke the reactionary order of 17 January and declare that the person who issued it was completely mistaken; 3) to punish the inspirers of the south Anhui events, KUO CHUN TUNG and SHANG KUAN YUNSIANG; 4) to liberate YE CHING and reinstate him as the army commander; 5) to return all the people and arms that were captured from the south Anhui group of the 4th Army; 6) to provide support to the families of all the killed and injured officers and soldiers of the south Anhui group of the 4th Army; 7) to withdraw the anti-Communist troops from the fronts of central China; 8) to eliminate the siege line in the Northwest; 9) to free all political prisoners, patriots of the motherland; 10) to abolish the one-party dictatorship and institute a democratic regime; 11) to implement the three people's principles of Sun Yatsen; 12) to arrest the leaders of the pro-Japanese

Document 24 *continued*

groups and put them on trial.

   13/II/41

          MAO ZEDONG *13.2.41*

No. 186/14

Copies sent to:

C. Dimitrov

C. Stalin

C. Molotov

C. Zhdanov

C. Voroshilov

C. Timoshenko

C. Beria.

Comment [by Dimitrov]

This telegram is a reply to C. Dimitrov's telegram, in which he informed C. Mao Zedong that the ECCI did not consider the rift with Chiang Kai-shek inevitable and suggested that the CC of the Chinese Communist Party not strive for a rift but, on the contrary, relying on the masses which support the united anti-Japanese front, do everything possible to avoid the rift and the internecine war. Com. Dimitrov asked the CC to reconsider its current position and to present its considerations and proposals to the ECCI.

18 July 1941

When the Germans attacked the Soviet Union, the ECCI sent out an appeal to the Communist parties of the world to rally to the Soviet Union. On 9 July, Dimitrov sent the CCP Central Committee a general ECCI directive; Document 25 is the Chinese reply. A handwritten note by Dimitrov on the document indicates that Molotov expressed agreement with the CCP's line on 20 July (evidently by telephone) but instructed Dimitrov to make no promises, for the time being, regarding military equipment.

Document 25

Dimitrov to Stalin and Molotov, 18 July 1941, with enclosures. RTsKhIDNI, f. 495, op. 74, d. 317, ll. 80–81. Original in Russian. Typewritten, with a handwritten note by Dimitrov.

<u>Top secret</u>
<u>Confidential</u>
No. 128
TO COMRADE STALIN[30]
TO COMRADE MOLOTOV
Dear Comrade Stalin,
Dear Comrade Molotov,

In response to the directive sent out to the Communist parties about providing all possible support to the Red Army by [conducting] military operations in their respective countries, the CC of the Communist Party of China informs us of the following:

"When the Soviet-German war broke out, we immediately intensified our monitoring of the movements of the Japanese forces and are preparing to destroy transportation lines in northern China to paralyze the enemy. In the current situation, we will with all means provide resolute support to the Red Army in its struggle. Nevertheless, because the enemy has been holding northern China for four years and has built strong fortifications in the big cities, on the railways, in the mines, etc., and because the enemy is better armed and equipped than we—our human and material resources [are diminishing], regions of operation [are getting smaller], ammunition is running out—and the situation is becoming more difficult by the day, if Japan attacks the Soviet Union, our abilities in terms of coordinating military operations will not be great. If, however, we act despite all the sacrifices we will incur, there is a possibility that we will be defeated and will not be able to long defend our partisan bases in the enemy's rear. Such an action will not be good for either side. Therefore, we decided to fortify the partisan bases in the enemy's rear, to wage broad partisan warfare, as well as a protracted struggle against the Japanese invaders, to gain time.

"However, if we receive support in the form of ammunition, machine guns, artillery, and explosives, the effectiveness of our actions will be much greater. Ammunition for rifles will be the most precious help to us, since we have only twenty rounds per rifle [left]. The number of [our] machine guns is insignificant, and the number of cannons is even less. There is no place for us to get the explosives (glycerin) from.

"Is our decision correct? Please give us your directive. We also ask you to convey our opinion to the State Defense Council of the USSR."

30. In the margin, handwritten by Dimitrov:
<u>*Molotov's reply:*</u> *"[We] agree with the line of the comrade from the CC CP of China. Regarding ammunition, do not make any promises yet." G. D. 20.7.41.*

Document 25 *continued*

We are asking for your directive regarding the answer to give to the Chinese comrades, in particular, whether they can count on a certain amount of ammunition to step up broader operations against a possible attack by Japan against the USSR.

With fraternal greetings,

(G. DIMITROV)

18 July   ***Sent to the addressees indicated. <. . .>***

16 July   611

10   16–18

19

To C. DIMITROV[31]

On 23 June we received your directive of the 22nd. On the same day, we discussed the issues and made a decision, which you were informed of.

We received your directive to the Communist parties to create a national united front on 12 July, and discussed it on 13 [July]. We decided to take measures to improve relations between the CCP and the Guomindang, to improve [our] work abroad, to improve intelligence monitoring of the activities of the Japanese army and prepare for the destruction of the transportation network, and to improve the [political] education of the cadres from Manchuria, as well as to introduce a new school discipline—classes of the Russian language.

CC CCP

No. *2*

TOP SECRET.

To Com. DIMITROV[32]

When the Soviet-German war broke out, we immediately intensified our monitoring of the movements of the Japanese forces and are preparing to destroy transportation lines in northern China to paralyze the enemy. In the current situation, we will with all means provide resolute support to the Red Army in its struggle. Nevertheless, because the enemy has been holding northern China for four years and has built strong fortifications in the big cities, on the railways, in the mines, etc., and because the enemy is better armed and equipped than we—our human and material resources [are diminishing], regions of operation [are getting smaller], ammunition is running out—and the situation is becoming more difficult by the day, if Japan attacks the Soviet Union, our abilities in terms of coordinating military operations will not be great. If, however, we act despite all the sacrifices we will incur, there is a pos-

---

31. In the margin, handwritten by Dimitrov:
Send to Cc. Stalin, Molotov, Beria, Malenkov. 19.7.41. G. D.

32. In the margin, handwritten by Dimitrov:
Show to Cc. Manuilsky, Ercoli, Sukharev. 18.7.41. G. D.

sibility that we will be defeated and will not be able to long defend our partisan bases in the enemy's rear. Such an action will not be good for either side. Therefore, we decided to fortify the partisan bases in the enemy's rear, to wage a broad partisan warfare, as well as a protracted struggle against the Japanese invaders, to gain time.

However, if we receive support in the form of ammunition, machine guns, artillery, and explosives, the effectiveness of our actions will be much greater. Ammunition for rifles will be the most precious help to us, since we have only twenty rounds per rifle [left]. The number of [our] machine guns is insignificant, and the number of cannons is even less. There is no place for us to get the explosives (glycerin) from.

Is our decision correct? Please give us your directive. We also ask you to convey our opinion to the State Defense Council of the USSR.[33]

CC CCP

18 July 1941
No. 603/13–25
C. Dimitrov will convey [this letter]
to Cc. Manuilsky and Ercoli. <. . .> [34]
19.7.41 <. . .>[35]

To Com. DIMITROV[36]

1. The CC of the CCP fully agrees with the measures outlined in your telegram of 22 June and will resolutely implement them.

2. The CC of the CCP has already issued the enclosed directive of 23 June "About the Struggle Against the Aggression of Fascist Germany Against the Soviet Union."

The directive read: 1) On 22 June, the German fascist rulers began a massive invasion of the Soviet Union. This perfidious crime, the aggressive attack, is aimed not only against the Socialist state, but also against the freedom and independence of all peoples. The sacred war of the Soviet Union against the aggression of fascist Germany is not only to defend the USSR but also to protect all the people who conduct a struggle against the fascist oppressors. 2) Today's international task is to mobilize the people of the entire world to organize the international united front of struggle against fascism, to struggle against in-

---

33. In the margin, handwritten by Dimitrov:
Send to Cc. Stalin, <u>Molotov,</u> Malenkov, Beria. 18.7.41. G. D.
34. Signature unclear.
35. Signature unclear
36. In the margin, handwritten by Dimitrov:
Send to Cc. Stalin, Molotov, Zhdanov, Voroshilov, Timoshenko, Beria. <. . .> 41. G. D.

ternational fascism in defense of the Soviet Union, in defense of China, in defense of the freedom and independence of all people. At this stage, everything must be concentrated on the struggle against the fascist enthrallment and not on the socialist revolution. 3) The tasks of our party are: 1. To resolutely insist on the continuation of the anti-Japanese national united front. To resolutely insist on cooperation with the Guomindang to drive the fascist Japanese imperialists from Chinese soil. 2. To conduct a resolute struggle against any anti-Soviet, anti-Communist activities on behalf of the reactionary elements from among the large bourgeoisie. 3. In foreign policy, to contact all the public figures in England and America who are struggling against the German-Italo-Japanese fascist enthrallers to struggle against the common enemy.

CC CCP

Dimitrov continued to pressure the Chinese Communists to do all they could to avoid a split with Nationalist China. On 20 July he inquired about press reports that fighting had resumed.[37] On 25 July, Mao replied with a message, which Dimitrov distributed to Stalin (and also to Molotov, Malenkov, Beria, Zhukov, Shcherbakov, and Lozovsky), that ignored Dimitrov's question. Mao wrote:

> For the past several months we have avoided friction with the Guomindang in every possible way. In this period the outbreak of conflicts between our army and the army of the central government declined to a minimum. . . . But since the outbreak of war between the USSR and Germany, the pro-Japanese and pro-German elements, the special service organs of the Guomindang and its party organizations are hoping

37. In another minor conflict, Dimitrov received word, evidently from Soviet military intelligence, of unpleasantness between Soviet Major-General Kalganov and the Chinese leadership in Yan'an. Dimitrov thereupon asked Mao about relations with Soviet comrades assigned to Yan'an. On 15 September 1941 Mao sent a message, which Dimitrov sent on to Stalin, Molotov, Golikov, and Panfilov (deleting the name of the Soviet officer but failing to cross out a Chinese reference to "Kar."), which said: "We understand the great importance of the work being done here by the Soviet comrades. We have helped them in every possible way and will continue to do so. They are working very hard, but their work suffers from great shortcomings. Comrade Kar. is a devoted comrade but his work methods are unsuitable; moreover, he does not wish to take account of our opinion. Our representative will give you a report on the details of this matter on arrival [at the ECCI]" (Mao to Dimitrov, 16 September 1941, and Dimitrov to Stalin and others, September 1941; RTsKhIDNI, f. 495, op. 184, vkhod. 1941, d. 3, l. 78).

for a German victory and the defeat of the USSR; they also wish for Japan to fight against the USSR. Beginning on 19 July, when the German troops advanced to Smolensk, there suddenly began an anti-Communist howl.

Charging that the Nationalists had fabricated "conflictual affairs," Mao reported that according to Zhou Enlai this had been the work of Zhang Qun, the ostensible head of the pro-Japanese elements, "with Chiang Kai-shek's tacit consent." This tactic had been opposed by the pro-Anglo-American members of the Guomindang, like Guo Taiqi and Wang Shijie. "We are taking advantage of these contradictions," Mao reported, "between the pro-Anglo-American and the pro-German-Japanese elements to attract [the former] . . . and paralyze [the latter]."[38]

13 December 1941

After the Japanese attack on Pearl Harbor and Hong Kong, China formally declared war on Japan. On 10 December, Mao Zedong sent Dimitrov the two messages below, which Dimitrov (from the Comintern's wartime headquarters in Ufa) had forwarded to Stalin and Molotov in Moscow.

Document 26

Dimitrov to Stalin and Molotov, 13 December 1941. RTsKhIDNI, f. 495, op. 74, d. 317, ll. 85–86. Original in Russian. Typewritten.

To Cc. STALIN, MOLOTOV

We have received the enclosed two telegrams from Yan'an from MAO ZEDONG, dated 10 December:

"1. After the Pacific war broke out, we issued a declaration. We took the position of supporting England and America. We gave directives regarding work in the South Seas countries, but probably only in Hong Kong will the work suffer somewhat."

"2. After the war in the Pacific broke out, the following changes have occurred or may occur [soon]:

38. RTsKhIDNI, f. 495, op. 74, vkhod. 1941, d. 4, ll. 241–240.

Document 26 *continued*

"a) The pro-Japanese and pro-Hitler elements will suffer a serious setback.

"b) Chiang Kai-shek's deployment of He Wen Den's division to occupy an important position in the border region will probably be terminated.

"c) The broad and extremely ferocious assault on our army initiated by the Japanese since the beginning of the German-Soviet war in northern and central China (where we have already sustained heavy losses) is getting weaker. We think it will get even weaker in the future.

"d) Relations between the Guomindang and the CCP will improve to some extent. There are already some indications of this.

"e) Ties between the USSR and China will further strengthen."

I would recommend that Mao Zedong contact Chiang Kai-shek directly in order to quickly eliminate existing misunderstandings between the Communist Party and the Guomindang, to strengthen the unity of the Chinese people, to unite its armed forces and to organize a bold offensive against the Japanese armies in China. In doing so, the Communist Party must demonstrate maximum reasonable willingness to reach agreement. I am requesting your directives on this question.

DIMITROV

13 December 1941

To Com. NIKITIN
Please send the enclosed cipher telegram to Cc. STALIN and MOLOTOV in Moscow.

(G. DIMITROV)

13.XII.41.

Throughout the years that followed the dialogue continued—Dimitrov, on behalf of Stalin, admonished the Chinese comrades neither to provoke the Nationalists nor fall for their provocations; the Chinese Communists reported on the nefarious doings of the Guomindang, assuring Moscow of their total devotion, and hinting that sooner or later they would need to fight Chiang Kai-shek.[39]

39. See RTsKhIDNI, f. 495, op. 184, vkhod. 1942, d. 15, l. 146; f. 495, op. 184, iskh. 1942, d. 17, l. 51; op. 184, vkhod. 1943, d. 9, ll. 37–32, 50, 51; op. 74, d. 32, ll. 50–51; also Titarenko, *Kommunisticheskii Internatsional,* pp. 291–296.

Dimitrov speaking for the defense at the Reichstag Fire trial in Leipzig,
10 December 1933

Top Soviet and Comintern officials, Moscow, 1934: The original photo-graph (at top), located in Dimitrov's files, shows ten persons: (from left to right) Wilhelm Knorin, Vyacheslav Molotov, Valerian Kuibyshev, Grigory (Sergo) Ordzhonikidze, Blagoi Popov, Vasil Tanev, Georgi Dimitrov, Dmitry Manuilsky, Joseph Stalin, and Kliment Voroshilov.

The cropped version (at right; from Elena Savova, ed., *Georgi Dimitrov* [Sofia: Bulg. Akad. na Naukite, 1952]), repeatedly published in the Soviet Union and Bulgaria in later years, deletes the six on the left, presumably because Ordzhonikidze committed sui-cide when faced with arrest, and Knorin, a high Comintern official, was purged in 1937.

Comintern leaders, Moscow, 1935: The original photograph (at top) shows: (front row, left to right) Mikhail Moskvin (Trilisser), Georgi Dimitrov, Palmiro Togliatti, Wilhelm Florin, and Wang Ming; (standing, left to right) André Marty, Otto Kuusinen, Klement Gottwald, Wilhelm Pieck, and Dmitry Manuilsky. This picture was also edited (at bottom; from Louka Zoulamski and Georgi Stoichev, *You, I, and Dimitrov* [Sofia: Sofia Press, 1968]) to omit the two figures on the left: after Moskvin became an "unperson" his name and likeness were cropped.

Stalin and Dimitrov at the May Day parade, Moscow, 1936

Dimitrov in conversation with Spanish Communists, notably Dolores Ibárruri (La Pasionaria) and José Diaz, Moscow, 1939

Dimitrov (right) and Marshal Tito, 15 April 1945

Georgi Dimitrov

CHAPTER FIVE

Strange Interlude

THE NAZI-SOVIET NONAGGRESSION PACT, signed in Moscow on 23 August 1939, was a bombshell for Communists and non-Communists alike. Even though its full scope—to say nothing of the secret protocol that accompanied it—was not yet apparent, it marked the end of the protracted period in which Hitler's Germany, and fascism more broadly, had been identified by Moscow, and therefore Communists everywhere, as the main enemy. For years both Soviet diplomacy and the Comintern had striven to mobilize all forces into broad alliances, fronts, and coalitions, using all their available ideological, organizational, and psychological resources.[1] Now all this had to come to a halt—indeed, needed to be reversed.

The reaction among Communists, especially in the West, was inevitably disorientation and confusion. Should they continue

1. On the eve of the conclusion of the Nazi-Soviet Pact, the ECCI Secretariat clearly did not fully understand the reorientation the agreement signaled. Though assailing the "bourgeois and social-democratic media," the Secretariat also called for stepping up the struggle against "German fascism" and foresaw that the pact might prompt Britain and France to conclude a similar agreement with the Soviet Union (protocol, in RTsKhIDNI, f. 495, op. 18, d. 1291, ll. 141–143, cited in Mikhail M. Narinsky and N. S. Lebedeva, eds., *Komintern i vtoraya mirovaya voina* [Moscow: Pamyatniki istoricheskoi mysli, 1994]; hereafter cited as *KI*), vol. 1, pp. 69–71.

their antifascist campaigns? Should they support the defense efforts and military build-ups in their own countries—say, in Britain and France—that they had backed since 1935? Would they justify and endorse the Soviet diplomatic coup?

In the end, although many party members demurred and defected, all the parties placed loyalty to the International—that is, to the Soviet Union—above patriotic duty to their national states: for many this required some heavy breathing and rhetorical acrobatics. Indeed, Dimitrov himself seemed initially to be trying to uphold the antifascist line even while rallying in support of Moscow's policy. There is no indication that Dimitrov had had any clue of the coming shift in Soviet orientation.

27 August 1939

On 27 August 1939 Dimitrov sent Stalin, Molotov, and Zhdanov information about the positions taken by various Western Communist parties with regard to the Nazi-Soviet Pact (focusing rather selectively on the positive responses of these parties).[2] On the same date, Dimitrov and Manuilsky asked for Stalin's guidance: although they were being persecuted at home, the French and British Communist parties were continuing to oppose Nazi Germany's aggressive policies. Was this the right line to take? There was evidently no reply to this letter.[3]

---

2. RTsKhIDNI, f. 495, op. 73, d. 67, ll. 44–59. The secret protocol attached to the Nazi-Soviet Pact delineated the respective spheres of influence in eastern Europe of the Germans and the Soviets: these included the partition of Poland, and the assignment of Soviet "interest" in Bessarabia, the Baltic States, and Finland (a revision at the end of September ceded Lithuania to the Soviet sphere in return for a larger area under German control in Poland).

3. See, for this as well as subsequent developments discussed in this chapter, Fridrikh I. Firsov, "Arkhivy Kominterna i vneshnyaya politika SSSR v 1939–1941 gg.," *Novaya i noveishaya istoriya,* 1992, no. 6; and the excellent introduction to *KI.*

Document 27

Dimitrov and Manuilsky to Stalin, 27 August 1939. RTsKhIDNI, f. 495, op. 74, d. 517, ll. 41–42. Original in Russian. Typewritten.

TO COMRADE STALIN

Dear Comrade Stalin,

We request your advice regarding the following question.

Communist parties of the capitalist countries, the French and the English Communist parties in particular, have taken the correct position on the Soviet-German nonaggression pact, which foils the plans of the anti-USSR warmongers. The Communist parties have reacted appropriately to the rabid anti-Soviet campaign in the bourgeois and social-democratic press. It is important to note that the French bourgeoisie started an offensive against the Communist Party by shutting down "L'Humanité" and "Ce Soir" and all the local Communist press, as well as by prohibiting meetings of the Communist Party. The French bourgeoisie wants to outlaw the Communist Party, to isolate it and rouse the entire country against it. It is obvious that despite the persecution, the Communist Party will continue to defend, with all means possible, the Soviet-German pact as an act of peace, an act that corresponds to the interests of the international working class and the French people. However, in the complex current situation, a question arises about the position of the Communist Party on the measures taken by the Daladier government in the cause of the so-called national defense of the country. We think that the Communist Party must maintain its position of resistance to the aggression of fascist Germany. It must support the measures aimed at strengthening the defensive capacity of France but, at the same time, condition its support of those measures by demanding that the party be allowed to express its views openly and to promote its activities. Simultaneously, the party must indicate that the current government of Daladier-Bonnet does not enjoy the confidence of the people and does not provide guarantees of either a sound policy that matches the interests of the French people or the proper defense of the country.

We request your advice on whether such a position is correct.

With fraternal greetings,

(G. Dimitrov)
(D. Manuilsky)

27 August 1939.

26 September 1939

On 1 September 1939, the day German troops invaded Poland on a broad front, starting World War II, the ECCI Secretariat in Moscow heard Dimitrov and others discuss the position of several Communist parties abroad. The meeting resolved to approve the general Comintern position regarding the Soviet-German pact but also to inform the French party that it was "incorrect to declare its unconditional support of the Daladier-Bonnet government." Instead, the party should argue that the French government, by its "betrayal" of Czechoslovakia and Spain and the September 1938 Munich agreement, which surrendered the Sudetenland to Germany and excluded the Soviet Union from the settlement of central and eastern European problems, and by its torpedoing of the collective security policy, had strengthened Germany; following the lead of British warmongers, it had rebuffed the Soviet Union and brought France to the brink of war. Such a government did not deserve the confidence of the people.[4]

On 5 September, Dimitrov brought Andrei Zhdanov up to date on the Secretariat's ongoing work on a set of theses regarding the war and the tasks of Communist parties; he volunteered that the Secretariat was encountering "exceptional difficulties" in arriving at a proper formulation and would like instructions from Stalin himself. Accordingly, on 7 September, Stalin received Dimitrov, in the presence of Molotov and Zhdanov and, according to Dimitrov's notes, made several revealing comments. The war, he said, was being waged by two groups of capitalist countries (poor and rich, as judged in terms of colonies, raw materials, and the like) for the repartition of the world and global dominance. As for the Soviet Union's position, "we have no objection to their having a good fight, weakening each other. It wouldn't be bad if by the hands of Germany the position of the richest capitalist countries (especially England) were shattered. Without himself understanding it or wishing it, Hitler upsets, undermines the capitalist system." The Soviet calculation was: "We can maneuver, nudging one side against the other so that they come to big-

---

4. See RTsKhIDNI, f. 495, op. 18, d. 1292, ll. 8–9; also in *KI*, pp. 85–86. For the cable to France's Thorez with this message, see f. 495, op. 184, iskh. 1939, d. 16, l. 123.

ger blows. To some degree the nonaggression pact helps Germany. The next step is to nudge the other side forward."

The Communist parties, Stalin went on, must take a decisive stand "against their own governments, against the war." Clearly, there was no fundamental difference between the democratic and fascist regimes. Before the war, the juxtaposition of democratic regimes and fascism was justified, but "during the war between imperialist powers this is already incorrect. The division of capitalist states into fascist and democratic ones has lost its previous meaning." Thus the Comintern's advocacy of an antifascist popular front should be cast aside. Instead of directing its arrows against fascism as the primary source of aggression, henceforth the Comintern's efforts must be aimed against imperialism in general, including that of the Western democracies.[5]

The next day a directive prepared by Dimitrov on the basis of Stalin's remarks was sent out to all Communist parties on behalf of the ECCI Presidium. (The rush to get the word out was so great that the ECCI Secretariat got around to the formality of approving the text only a day later.) In terms reminiscent of Lenin's reaction to the outbreak of World War I in 1914, the document described the war as imperialist and unjust. "The international proletariat can under no circumstances defend fascist Poland, which refused the assistance of the Soviet Union and which oppresses other nationalities" (this was presumably a reference to Ukrainians and Belorussians in prewar Poland). The tactics of the Communist parties at this stage of the war, the Comintern instructed, were to oppose the war, expose its imperialist character, vote against war credits (when Communist deputies were present), and inform the masses that the war would bring them only suffering and destruction. Once again the Communist parties were to wage an offensive against the "traitorous policy of the social democrats."[6]

Especially in western Europe and North America, the Communist parties had some difficulty accepting and absorbing this sharp

5. TsPA (Sofia), f. 146, op. 2, a.e. 5; also cited in F. I. Firsov, "Komintern: Opyt, traditsii, uroki," in *Komintern . . . materialy nauchnoi konferentsii* (Moscow, 1989), pp. 21–22; also in Anatoli Latyshev, "Dva predatel'stva," *Rossiya*, 22–28 June 1991.

6. RTsKhIDNI, f. 495, op. 18, d. 1292, ll. 47–48; also cited in "Komintern i sovetsko-germanskii dogovor o nenapadenii," in *Izvestiia TsK KPSS*, 1989, no. 12, p. 207.

turn in their general strategic orientation. The challenge was further aggravated by the entry of Soviet troops into eastern Poland on 17 September, who occupied (and later annexed) the territory according to the secret protocol between Berlin and Moscow. To some extent coming up with a coherent and acceptable argument was also a problem in the drafting of the Comintern's theses. The archives contain several variants of the same draft with comments and changes introduced by Dmitry Manuilsky and probably Otto Kusinen, and others at the ECCI Secretariat, like Wilhelm Florin and Wilhelm Pieck (the Germans advocated an immediate peace since the Polish state no longer existed, and the Franco-British goal of overthrowing Hitler had "an imperialist character").[7] On 26 September 1939 the following text was sent to Stalin, Molotov, and Zhdanov for review and approval.

For reasons that remain unclear, the theses were never approved. It may well be that at this moment of great fluidity, the Kremlin decided that any theses of this sort risked being an embarrassment. In all likelihood the theses were also considered too explicit about Germany's intentions.

Document 28

Dimitrov to Stalin, 26 September 1939, with enclosed draft theses of the ECCI. Letter: RTsKhIDNI, f. 495, op. 73, d. 67, l. 73; enclosure: f. 495, op. 18, d. 1302a, ll. 1–18. Original in Russian. Typewritten.

DEAR COMRADE STALIN!
We are sending you the draft theses of the Executive Committee of the Comintern regarding the war.
We request your directives.
With Com[munist] greetings
                              (G. Dimitrov)
26.9.39.
Sent on 26/IX/39
in package No. 198
Stern.

7. RTsKhIDNI, f. 495, op. 18, d. 1302a, ll. 133–134.

<u>Draft</u>

THE WAR AND THE TASKS OF COMMUNISTS
(Theses of the Executive Committee of the Comintern)

Twenty-one years after the end of the first imperialist world war, which raged for four years and cost mankind 10 million killed and over 20 million wounded and maimed, the ruling classes and the governments of the large capitalist countries have again plunged the peoples into bloody carnage. Long before this war Communists had been tirelessly warning the masses that the bourgeoisie was preparing this heinous crime and called on them to struggle against the impending war. Nevertheless, the dark forces of imperialism once again succeeded in imposing their will on the peoples and in dragging them into war for alien interests. The working class, disorganized by the treacherous policy of social democracy, was unable to prevent the war. Now the international proletariat must solve its main tasks in this situation, when the European war has already broken out.

1. The current war is an unjust, imperialist war. The bourgeoisie of all the capitalist countries and the ruling classes of the warring states bear primary responsibility for it. Lenin taught [us] to determine the character of war by resolving "what its class content is, which class wages the war, which policy is being carried out in the form of war" (<u>Collected Works</u> [Russian ed.], vol. 24, p. 284). The character of war is determined not by who first started the hostilities but by why is it being waged, in the interests of which classes it is being waged, which classes dominate and hold power in each of the warring states. In both warring camps of the current war the dominant and leading force, i.e., the force which determines the goals of the war, is the reactionary bourgeoisie, while the working class and the masses have been made into cannon fodder and must shed their blood to support the interests of their own exploiters and oppressors. This is not a war between fascism and democracy, but a <u>war for world domination</u>, a war between the exploiters for further enslavement of the working class and toilers of the metropolis and the colonies. It is an antipopular, reactionary war for all the imperialist countries at war.

2. The current European war is a direct continuation of the struggle for domination between the two groups of imperialist states, the rich states and the inferior states, although not all the states that side with these groups have as yet directly entered the war.

The three richest bourgeois countries—England, France, and the USA—control immense territories, have subdued more than half of humanity, dominate the major world routes and commodity markets, have concentrated in their hands the major sources of raw materials, tremendous economic and financial resources, a lion's share of the world's gold reserves; they keep the majority of the capitalist countries in economic financial dependence. They have amassed these reserves through wars, by pillaging other peoples, and by exploiting the workers in their [own] countries. Over a period of decades, the bourgeoisie of these countries has set up a strong apparatus for enslaving the masses. By camouflaging the exploitation of the subdued countries and peoples with the forms of so-called bourgeois democracy, it is all the easier for [this bourgeoisie] to defraud the masses and keep them in subjection. [The bourgeoisie] uses the excess profits pumped out of the colonies to fatten the "labor aristocracy," to bribe and corrupt it, to maintain, through the power of its state apparatus, its influence in the workers' movement, and thus to weaken the working class. The ruling classes of these states have built their power on the bones of Indians, Chinese, Negroes, Malays, Arabs, and [American] Indians. These states are the backbone of the entire capitalist system.

In the other camp are three other large capitalist states: Germany, Japan, and Italy, which were the latecomers in colonial expansion, and which did not get their share of colonies and sources of raw materials in the war of 1914–18; [these are] countries without oil, iron, coal, and rubber, without nonferrous metals and cotton, countries that are hungry for commodity markets, areas of influence, and territories that are already occupied by the rich imperialist states. These countries, exhausted by the feverish arms race, but having managed to build a stronger military machine than that in the rich countries, are striving to redistribute sources of raw materials, food, gold reserves, to redistribute the human resources of the colonies.

The struggle between these two groups of countries for a new repartition of the world aggravates and sharpens the crisis of the entire capitalist system.

3. English and French imperialists are waging the war not only to preserve [what they have] stolen but also for a chance to conquer and steal further. They are struggling for a worse Versailles [Treaty], for making Germany into a vassal state serving their imperialist goals.

English and French imperialists lie when they claim that they are waging the war against fascism. Their entire policy has been aimed at strengthening fascism, while they planned to use Germany in the war against the USSR. With their loans, they have been salvaging the most reactionary governments of Europe from bankruptcy and have supported reaction on all the continents of the globe. The regime of colonial domination established by them (India, Morocco, Indochina) is no less reactionary that the regime in the fascist states.

The English bourgeoisie lies about struggling to establish a stable peace among nations. For centuries, the English bourgeoisie has been setting peoples against one another, has been constantly creating coalitions of some states against others, provoking bloody wars between them in order to weaken them and thus make it easier to rule the world.

It is a lie that England wanted to establish a united front of peace with the USSR. The English bourgeoisie did everything in its power to provoke a war by others against the USSR.

It is a lie that the English bourgeoisie is waging a war for the independence of Poland. The entire history of English imperialism is a violation of the independence of countries, rights, and the freedom of peoples.

The statement by the French imperialists that they are waging the war in fulfillment of their obligations to Poland is just as shameless a lie as well. On dozens of occasions, the French bourgeoisie violated those obligations when they contradicted its imperialist interests. It turned its mutual assistance treaty with Czechoslovakia into a piece of paper. In Munich, it grossly violated its obligations to the USSR and thus derailed the Franco-Soviet pact. The French bourgeoisie is not fighting for a legitimate [cause] and for justice but for a new injustice and lawlessness toward the defeated. Not by right but by the law of force did it suppress the national liberation struggle of the Druzes in 1925, of the Moroccans in 1926, and occupy the Ruhr region in 1923. Not by right but by the law of the jungle did the Versailles masters divide peoples by artificially creating vassal states in order to create a counterrevolutionary encirclement of the Soviet state. The ruling classes of England and France, as well as of the other warring capitalist countries, are not fighting for the freedom of peoples but for their enthrallment, not for lasting peace but for continued imperialist robbery.

4. The collapse of the reactionary Polish state, which exposed its internal rottenness, its military impotence, its complete political incapacity, is a historic retribution for the entire counterrevolutionary domestic and foreign policy which the Polish landowners and capitalists have been waging since the creation of the state. Poland was not a national but a multinational state. It was not 1848 Poland which struggled for its national independence against Russian tsarism, it was a prison of peoples which took the place of tsarism in oppressing Ukrainians, Belorussians, Jews, Lithuanians, and other nationalities. Seeking further expansion, the Polish bourgeoisie was ripping apart Lithuania and participating in the partition of its ally, Czechoslovakia. The Polish bourgeoisie has also paved the way for the destruction of its state by perpetually serving alien interests of foreign capitalists, by always claiming to be the outpost of world reaction against the Soviet state, by politically discrediting itself in the eyes of the toiling masses of the world by its counterrevolutionary war against the USSR. By its entire reactionary foreign and domestic policy, it has generated hatred of itself among the masses, who refuse to defend such a state.

The Polish people and the international proletariat are not interested in reestablishing the old multinational bourgeois-landowner Polish state, which was brought to collapse by the corruption and treachery of its ruling classes. The Polish people will be able to secure its future not by oppressing other peoples but through a common struggle with the workers of other countries for liberation from capitalist slavery.

5. Under the pretext of struggling against the Versailles [Treaty], for the "unification of all Germans," for "Lebensraum," the German imperialists strive to conquer more countries and enslave more peoples. They seek to establish their hegemony in Europe, to divide the colonial possessions of England, to under-

mine the power of the rich leading imperialist states. The German bourgeoisie wages a war to establish its own domination over the capitalist world.

Playing the role of broker between the warring countries, Italy is still waiting to see who gains the upper hand militarily. Being afraid of the excessive empowerment of Germany, Italian imperialists do not mind selling their neutrality to England and France in return for influence in the Balkans, the Mediterranean, and further colonial expansion in Africa.

In the Far East, the Japanese imperialists, with their [adherence to the] bankrupt anti-Comintern pact, defeated on the Mongolian-Manchurian border, are getting more and more entangled and entrapped in China. Having lost a chance to crush the resistance of the Chinese people on their own, they are seeking agreement with England in order to jointly partition China. At the same time, reactionary elements of the Chinese bourgeoisie weaken the national anti-imperialist front by their persecutions of Communists and thus facilitate the aggressive plans of Japanese and English imperialism.

6. The "peaceful" posture of the so-called neutral states and in particular the leading capitalist power, the USA, is hypocritical through and through. The American bourgeoisie did not lift a finger when Japan attacked China. Throughout the entire Japan-China war it has been and remains the major military supplier of Japan. Under the banner of "neutrality" American imperialists are fanning the flames of war in the Far East in order to weaken both Japan and China, so as to establish themselves afterward in China, relying on [America's] financial power. Along with England, they are trying to push the Japanese military clique into war with the USSR, hoping in this manner to resolve to its advantage the imperialist rivalry with Japan over domination in the Pacific. The American bourgeoisie is using its "neutrality" in the European war to profiteer, weaken Europe by the war, remove its competitors from the world markets, and establish its domination over seas and oceans.

Equally, the policy of "neutrality" of other noncombatant capitalist countries serves, directly or indirectly, the cause of stirring up the war. The bourgeoisie [of these countries] is eager to trade and profit. Therefore, [each nation's bourgeoisie] is for peace for its own country but for war between other countries. The bourgeoisie of these countries is either trying to get the best deal for trading its neutrality as a commodity or is waiting for the outcome of the war so as to seize on the defeated one and snatch [that bourgeoisie's] piece of booty.

7. Imperialist countries have been fomenting the war for a long time, each in its own way. The Versailles bosses have been preparing for years under the Pharisaic mask of securing a "lasting peace." They have been preparing by their collusions, blocs, conferences on the "pacification" of Europe; they have been preparing by their predatory Versailles [Treaty], by the Washington [conference] imperialist collusion,[8] by the fettering Dawes Plan, by the perfidious

---

8. A reference to the Washington naval disarmament conference of 1922.

Locarno agreement, and by the anti-Soviet pan-European plans. The bourgeoisie has been fomenting the current carnage by counterrevolutionary wars against the Soviet state and, after the failure of these wars, by machinations to create anti-Soviet coalitions. It fomented [the war] by numerous provocations against the USSR (assassination of diplomatic representatives, raids on trade missions, the breaking of diplomatic relations, organization of sabotage by foreign intelligence services, conflicts on the border, etc.). It fomented [the war] by systematically declining proposals of the USSR aimed at removing the most dangerous focuses of war. It fomented [the war] by disrupting collective security and by making a laughingstock of the League of Nations, its own creation.

The ruling circles of Japan, Italy, and Germany, backed by the bourgeoisie of England and France, have been fomenting a European war by new colonial seizures (Manchuria, Abyssinia), by military intervention in China, by the annexation of Austria, by the strangling of revolutionary Spain, by the partition of Czechoslovakia. The bourgeoisie has been fomenting this war directly by the <u>Munich pact</u>, which opened the gates to the military flooding of Europe.

<u>The bourgeoisie started this war because it is hopelessly tangled in its own contradictions, because it cannot survive without imperialist war.</u>

8. For twenty years the Soviet Union has been tirelessly struggling to preserve peace. If in the course of these twenty years the people have not been dragged into a new world massacre, it is because of the Soviet Union. The USSR has demonstrated great patience and tenacity in the face of never-ending anti-Soviet provocation; it did not let the warmongers drag it into the war. Continuously exposing to the masses the villainous schemes of the imperialists, it disrupted their machinations and frustrated their military plans by its peaceful policy. It suggested universal disarmament to all the capitalist countries, but the imperialists, primarily England and France, rejected this proposal. It offered a project of partial disarmament, but the imperialist powers hastened to arm themselves [instead]. At the most dangerous moments of impending war, the USSR repeatedly suggested that international conferences be convened to [agree on] common action to preserve peace. Still, the bourgeois governments persisted in their insane policy of isolating the USSR. Finally, when the cause of peace was hanging on a thread, the Soviet Union made one last attempt to prevent the war by entering into negotiations with England and France. However, the English and French bourgeoisie, by consciously delaying negotiations, sought to disrupt them and tried to use them to achieve agreement with Germany at the expense of the USSR, to draw Germany into war with the USSR, and to camouflage the preparation of this anti-Soviet war from the masses. Having satisfied itself that England and France do not defend the cause of peace, but rather seek a worse variant of the Munich plot against the USSR, the Soviet Union signed a nonaggression treaty with Germany and thus disrupted the insidious plans of the instigators of an anti-Soviet war.

Document 28 *continued*

With this step, [the USSR] protected its people from the European imperialist clash. However, the position of the USSR differs fundamentally from the "neutrality" of bourgeois states. The Soviet Union is a socialist country that follows its own path and pursues its particular goals—goals which serve the toiling humanity. Imbued with concern for the happiness of its people, the USSR values every drop of blood of its sons and daughters. It determines its foreign policy in the interests of socialism, which coincide with the interests of the working class and toilers of all countries. In peace and in war, the USSR defends the cause of socialism by ways and means corresponding to the international situation. With its action to help the workers of Western Ukraine and Western Belorussia, the Soviet Union has accomplished its liberating mission: it has snatched 11 million people from capitalist hell, joined them with the great cause of socialism, assured their free national and cultural development, protected them, with all its state power, from foreign intervention and enslavement.

9. Communists have always struggled to preserve peace, but they have never been pacifists. According to the teachings of Lenin and Stalin, they struggled and continue to struggle against unjust, imperialist wars; they supported and continue to support just wars of liberation (revolutionary Spain, China, Abyssinia). The Communists were opposed to the Munich deal because they wanted to fight for a <u>just cause</u>. The masses too wanted to struggle for this cause. They demanded the creation of true popular-front governments, for they strove to repel the forces of internal and external reaction. The masses demanded a united front with the USSR as a guarantee against their struggle being used by reactionary forces for imperialist goals. Nevertheless, the reactionary [forces] in each country, supported by social democracy, did everything to disrupt the liberation struggle of the peoples: destroyed revolutionary Spain, finished off Czechoslovakia, prevented the organization of a popular front in the largest capitalist countries, disrupted a united front of the peoples of these countries with the USSR, and drew them into the war for an <u>unjust</u> cause alien to them. Today, when the criminal war is raging, the gang of the Munich social-democratic capitulators who organized the collapse of the struggle of the Spanish people demands that the masses shed their blood to restore the bankrupt reactionary regime of the Polish landowners and capitalists.

The Communists struggle against the current imperialist war because it is directed against the liberation aspirations of the peoples, because the working class cannot trust any bourgeois government: it trusts only the Soviet Union, which has brought liberation to the workers of Western Ukraine and Western Belorussia, the only country that has protected and will protect a just cause. The working class has nothing to fight for in this war. To protect the freedom of all peoples, the vital interests of its own people, means to wholeheartedly struggle against the war. <u>The struggle against the imperialist war is a vital, just cause of the proletariat of the entire world.</u>

10. The European war has drastically changed the international situation. It exacerbates to the extreme all the contradictions of the capitalist system, the contradictions among the imperialist countries, [between] dominant and oppressed nations, the metropolis and the colonies, labor and capital, the exploited and their exploiters. The war opens a period of the most sharp and profound crisis of capitalism, a period of its great agony.

Contrary to the capitalist world, which is weakened by the war it has unleashed, the great socialist state, in staying out of the imperialist clash and pursuing its independent foreign policy, increases its specific weight in the international arena as a major power that embodies the age-old aspirations of the toiling masses of the world. Supported by the economic, political, and military might of victorious socialism, the might that makes the bourgeois states come to terms with the country of Soviets, the USSR uses its foreign policy to alter the course of international events for the benefit of the toilers, radically changes the balance of forces in favor of socialism at the expense of capitalism, and thus strengthens the positions of workers and toilers of capitalist countries.

In their futile attempts to resolve their contradictions by means of war and to preserve their domination by escalating political reaction, the ruling classes of the warring countries, through their domestic and foreign policy, erase the difference between the so-called bourgeois-democratic states and the fascist states. All of them are equally engaged in criminal war, all of them are aggressors and defendants in this war, all of them increase the brutal exploitation of the toilers and the terror of the bourgeois dictatorship in the warring countries. Further pursuing the Munich policy of provoking war against the country of Soviets, the bourgeoisie of England and France have now taken a more aggressive stance toward the USSR than the fascist states. The leaders of the Second International who offered their services to Anglo-French imperialism are foully misusing the antifascist attitude of the toilers in capitalist countries for imperialist purposes, supporting with chauvinist propaganda the democratic illusions of the masses, and thus helping the bourgeoisie to lead the people to slaughter.

But the more the imperialist reaction rages in the warring states, the greater the indignation it provokes among the masses. Although still held back by terror of the bourgeois dictatorship, the dissatisfaction of the masses with the war is growing, dissatisfaction that is deeper and maturing faster than in 1914. The longer the war goes on, the more it undermines the faith of the masses in capitalism. The masses realize more and more that this is not their war. They assimilate the universal historical experience of the Russian Bolsheviks' termination of the war. With its socialist victories, with its might and the independence of its policy toward the capitalist countries, the Soviet Union increasingly strengthens [the masses'] confidence in their own forces. Therefore, the liberation of masses from the influence of democratic illusions, the divorce from social democracy, the switch to Communism by the major groups of the working class are inevitable. "The era of the decline of capitalism is also the era of the decline of social democracy in the workers' movement" (Stalin).

Objective and subjective conditions are ripe for the proletariat to achieve its goal of its own liberation, the liberation of all the toilers, and perhaps the conjunction of imperialist, anti-popular wars with popular liberation wars.

11. The new situation created by the war requires a change of tactics by the Communist parties. Before the European war broke out, the tactics of the united workers' and popular fronts had been correct. They are still appropriate for China and may be appropriate for other colonial and dependent countries and peoples struggling against imperialism for their national liberation. These tactics permitted the proletariat and the workers temporarily to delay the advance of capital and reaction (France), to step up the armed struggle against reactionary rebels and interventionists (Spain), and to delay the European war.

Nevertheless, this tactic is no longer applicable; first, because the leaders of social democracy and of the petty-bourgeois "democratic" parties have completely gone over to the side of the bourgeois governments that are waging the imperialist war and that are attempting, by perverting the slogans of the united front, to draw the workers into supporting the imperialist policies of the bourgeoisie in both the warring and the neutral countries. Second, because today's central task for the working class and the toilers is the struggle against capitalism, [which is] the source of wars, [and] against all forms of bourgeois dictatorship. The faster the leaders of the petty-bourgeois parties, including social democracy, are moving into the camp of bourgeois counterrevolution, the stronger the "idea of an assault matures in the masses' consciousness" (Stalin).

The attempts by Communists to organize common action with social democracy were disrupted before the European war started. They were disrupted by the refusal of social democracy to struggle for the basic rights and liberties of workers, for the improvement of their living conditions under capitalism; they were disrupted by Blum's "nonintervention" policy and by support of the Munich deal by French social democracy; they were disrupted by the capitulationist betrayal of Prieto by Caballero; they were disrupted by the systematic rejection of the Comintern's proposals to organize common action against the reaction and war by the Executive Committee of the Second International and, primarily, by the English Labourites; they were disrupted by the participation of social democracy in the preparation and unleashing of the current war; they were disrupted by its policy of inciting the war against the Soviet country, by its present role as vigilante of the Anglo-French bourgeoisie, which has seized the bankrupt banner of the anti-Soviet struggle and the anti-Comintern pact. Communists can have no united front with a party that has created a united front with its national bourgeoisie, including its most chauvinistic, most imperialist, most reactionary elements.

The forging of the militant unity of the proletariat and the realization of the alliance of workers and peasants will not be achieved by agreements with the leaders of social democracy and the petty-bourgeois "democratic" parties but despite them and against them, on the basis of the independent mobilization of the broadest masses by Communists to struggle against reaction and war.

12. At this stage of the war, the tasks of Communists in the capitalist countries are:

a) To oppose the war courageously, as real Bolsheviks should, notwithstanding the terror of the bourgeoisie, through votes in the warring and non-warring countries with Communists in the parliaments, against war appropriations and the bourgeois governments, by patiently explaining the criminal character of the war to the masses of workers, peasants, and soldiers, and by demonstrating to them that the current war, similar to the imperialist war of 1914–18, offers nothing for the toilers except sacrifice and White-guard terror; it will bring them greater exploitation, hunger, and unemployment and will entail new, still bloodier wars if the workers do not finish with capitalism.

b) To launch an attack against provocateurs and warmongers in every country, against the bourgeoisie as the instigator of war, against social democracy as the accessory of the imperialist gangsterism, mercilessly exposing the attempts by the ruling classes of the warring countries to shift the responsibility for the war on each other, their cynical deception of the toilers with the slogans of "antifascist war" and "national unity," by exposing the bourgeoisie of the "neutral" countries as war speculators and marauders capitalizing on the tragedy of other peoples; to step up the struggle against the chauvinism inspired by the imperialist bourgeoisie and its social-democratic servitors.

c) To strengthen, despite the attempts of the class enemy to corrupt the Communist movement, the unity and strength of the Communist ranks, the iron discipline among Communists; to concentrate the fire, within the Communist parties, against right opportunism (sliding down [i.e., descending the slippery slope] to the defense of the bourgeois motherland, "national unity," support of the bourgeois myth of the antifascist character of the war), opportunism nourished by the chauvinist propaganda of the bourgeoisie, the democratic illusions of the masses, and the pseudo-antifascist demagogy of social democracy.

d) To support, nourish, and organize the intangible, but deep, spontaneous dissatisfaction of the masses with the war that ripens under the surface of "national unity"; to mobilize for the struggle against it popular masses who increasingly realize, from their own experience, that the bourgeoisie is using the war as a pretext to eliminate all their rights and gains in order to establish its military dictatorship; and thus to direct the antifascist hatred, accumulated over the course of years, against the growing oppression of the bourgeois dictatorship, against the raging imperialist reaction in all the capitalist countries.

e) To unite, to unify the forces of the proletariat for the struggle against the war, to fortify [the proletariat's] union with the toilers, divorcing and snatch-ing them from the influence of social democracy and other petty-bourgeois parties, not forgetting for a moment that, in time of war and the sharp crisis of capitalism caused by the war, the combative front of all the toilers of the city and countryside—workers, peasants, and soldiers—can be created only on the basis of revolutionary policy, and only by the Communist Party in a re-lentless struggle against all other parties that act as agents of imperialism in the ranks of the working class and [other] toilers.

f) To strengthen, in all possible ways, the bonds of fraternal solidarity of the proletarians of capitalist countries with the victorious Soviet working class, tirelessly explaining to the broad toiling masses the profound internationalist meaning of the wise Stalinist policy of the USSR, a policy that facilitates the struggle of the proletariat and the oppressed of all countries for their libera-tion.

* * *

The Communist International calls on the workers to conduct a selfless struggle against the imperialist war, for the sake of protecting the lives and fu-ture of their people. It calls on all the workers and toilers to rally closer around the great country of socialism and thus to multiply its forces and hasten the triumph of its just cause. The Communist International calls on all Commu-nists and conscious workers to "be faithful to the end to the cause of proletar-ian internationalism, to the cause of the fraternal unity of the proletariat of all countries" (Stalin), to be faithful to the end to the invincible banner of Marx-Engels-Lenin-Stalin, to the banner of the Communist International.

THE PRESIDIUM OF THE EXECUTIVE COMMITTEE
OF THE COMMUNIST INTERNATIONAL

---

17 October 1939

With the theses unapproved and undistributed, Dimitrov felt the need to provide other guidance to the Comintern's sections abroad. He hit on publishing an article with his signature in the monthly *Communist International*. But getting a text approved by all con-cerned (and above all, by Stalin) proved inordinately difficult. On 17 October, Dimitrov sent Stalin (and Zhdanov) a draft, referring to "a certain perplexity concerning the character and causes of the war" among foreign Communists.[9] On 24 October, Zhdanov in-

9. RTsKhIDNI, f. 495, op. 73, d. 67, l. 78.

formed Dimitrov that Stalin had made some changes in the draft. The next day Stalin received Dimitrov and gave him a number of critical comments. Thereupon the article underwent some revision, with the major changes introduced by Otto Kuusinen. On 29 October, Dimitrov sent Stalin the revised text. The article was finally sent to press in early November.

Document 29

Dimitrov to Stalin, 17 October 1939. RTsKhIDNI, f. 495, op. 73, d. 67, l. 83. Original in Russian. Typewritten. The enclosure, not printed here, is in f. 17, op. 121, d. 8, ll. 100–120; the later, revised version is in f. 495, op. 18, d. 1302-a, ll. 135–158. The article was published in *Kommunisticheskii Internatsional* (Russian ed.), 1939, nos. 8–9; in English in *Communist International* (New York), 1939, no. 11, pp. 1100–1110.

Dear Comrade STALIN,

Although the Communist parties have, in the main, rectified their position in regard to the war, there is still some confusion in their ranks regarding the character and causes of the war, as well as regarding the new tasks of the working class and the necessary changes in the tactics of the Communist parties that emerge now.

Considering this, we would deem it necessary to publish the enclosed article in the magazine "Communist International" and in the Communist press abroad.

Since this action acquires great importance under present conditions, I request your advice.

With fraternal greetings,
(G. Dimitrov)

17 October 1939

If anything, Moscow's pro-German orientation became more explicit in the following weeks. In his speech to the Supreme Soviet on 31 October, Molotov contrasted Germany's offer to make peace with the desire of England's and France's ruling circles to continue the war in order to maintain their global dominance. "One may accept or reject the ideology of Hitlerism as well as any other ideological system, that is a matter of political opinion," he explained.

"But an ideology cannot be destroyed by force, it cannot be eliminated by war. It is therefore not only senseless but criminal to wage such a war for the 'destruction of Hitlerism' camouflaged as a fight for 'democracy.'" Stalin's remarks at dinner after the 7 November parade suggested that he was at least considering it possible that Germany would take an anti-capitalist turn.[10]

Throughout the following months the anti-Western orientation of the Comintern was explicit in the directives approved, for example, for the Austrian and Scandinavian Communist parties, or in identifying with the German proletariat against the Western aggressors and "exposing" the "legend of the antifascist character of the war" waged by Britain and France.[11]

This line became particularly pronounced during the so-called Winter War, after the Soviet Union invaded Finland on 30 November and set up a puppet government in Terijoki, headed by Communist Party and Comintern veteran Otto Kuusinen. In the face of stubborn Finnish resistance, Western opinion rallied in support of the Finns: the League of Nations expelled the Soviet Union as an aggressor, and Britain and France considered military action against the Soviet Union. This seemed to give Moscow proof of its contention that the Western powers were planning to convert the anti-German into an anti-Soviet war. On 12 March 1940, Finland and the Soviet Union finally signed a treaty putting an end to their conflict, with modest territorial gains by the Soviet Union but also with the unintended consequence of swinging Finland into the German camp a year later.[12]

---

10. The confusion was particularly apparent in the public statements issued in the name of the German Communist Party. At the end of December 1939 the ECCI Secretariat approved the Political Platform of the KPD, whose main points Dimitrov and Manuilsky then sent Stalin on 7 January 1940. The platform argues, in essence, that Germany's independence was threatened by the Anglo-French imperialists, who were supported by Catholics, social democrats, and some businessmen within Germany; these groups should become the major targets of the KPD (RTsKhIDNI, f. 495, op. 18, d. 1301, l. 106; d. 1302, ll. 27–37; op. 74, d. 155, ll. 1–3. See also KI, pp. 218–222). In May–June 1940, during the crisis in France, the KPD found nothing better to demand than the nationalization of banks and the confiscation of German war profits (RTsKhIDNI, f. 495, op. 10a, d. 31, ll. 22–27; also KI, pp. 347–352).

11. See also KI, pp. 18–21.

12. Moscow began pressuring its neighbor states to conclude treaties of mutual assistance, in line with the free hand it had acquired under the Nazi-Soviet Pact. On

10 June 1940

The Comintern's sharp anti-Western line continued throughout the spring of 1940. Meanwhile the "phony war" between the Western powers and Germany came to an end with the German attacks on Denmark and Norway in April and on Belgium, Luxembourg, and the Netherlands in May, leading to a massive assault on France, whose forces were soon in headlong retreat.

On 10 June, Dimitrov and Manuilsky requested Stalin's advice in view of the complexity of developments abroad. Leading French Communists—Maurice Thorez, André Marty, Arthur Rammette, and Raymond Guyot—had gathered in Moscow (some, like Thorez and Rammette, to escape arrest in France) and there, at the Comintern's headquarters, had drafted a declaration which they now forwarded to Stalin for review and approval. Even as the Germans were approaching Paris and the French government was on the verge of collapse, the thrust of the document was directed against French imperialism and the French bourgeoisie.[13]

---

25 December 1939 Stalin remarked to Dimitrov that "we think that in the mutual assistance pacts (with Estonia, Latvia, Lithuania) we have found the form that will allow us to bring a number of countries into the sphere of influence of the Soviet Union" (TsPA [Sofia], f. 146, op. 2, a.e. 5, cited by Mariia Isusova, "Iz 'Dnevnika' na Georgi Dimitrov ot godishnite na Vtorata svetovna voina," in *Letopisi,* 1992, nos. 7–8, p. 51).

13. On the French Communists in 1939–40, see also A. Rossi (pseud. of Angelo Tasca), *Les Communistes français pendant la drôle de guerre* (Paris: Iles d'Or, 1951), and *Les Cahiers du bolchévisme pendant la campagne 1939–1940* (Paris: Wapler, 1951), which is a facsimile of the illegal PCF journal, with an introductory essay by A. Rossi. An earlier declaration drafted by the French Communists ("We accuse") was approved by the ECCI Secretariat on 23 May and published in the London and New York *Daily Worker* the next day. Its thrust was against the Daladier-Bonnet government; it appealed to the French people to take their fate into their own hands. See also *KI,* pp. 28–38.

Document 30

Dimitrov and Manuilsky to Stalin, 10 June 1940. RTsKhIDNI, f. 495, op. 74, d. 519, ll. 20–30. Original in Russian. Typewritten.

To Comrade STALIN

Dear Comrade Stalin,

The international situation that has become complicated as a result of the escalation of military operations in the West prompts us again to disturb you and to seek your advice.

The question concerns the position of the French Communist Party. Comrades Thorez, Marty, Rammette, and Guyot have prepared a declaration that defines the party's position at the current stage of the war. This declaration is based on the following considerations:

a) The military defeats that France has suffered in the course of one month have once again exposed the bankruptcy of the French bourgeoisie and of all its parties. The working class and the masses of France are facing the problem of how to save themselves from the horrors and disasters into which the bourgeoisie has plunged them.

b) The invasion of France by the German army does not alter the imperialist character of the war for France, since the bourgeoisie still retains power in that country, pursues imperialist goals in this war, and continues to oppress the subjugated colonial peoples.

c) More than a million Communists and sympathizers of the party who are now in the French army are obliged to fight, because Communists, while opposing the imperialist war, have never considered desertion, "sabotage," or boycotting the war a means of struggle against the imperialist war.

d) Given the current balance of class forces in the country, in a situation where a civil war in France would facilitate the task of the invading German army, the French Communist Party does not raise the question of creating a revolutionary government. However, continuing to expose the bankruptcy of the French bourgeoisie and of the leaders of the Socialist Party to the masses, and their responsibility for the disasters that have happened, the Communist Party regards it as its obligation to act and struggle for a number of measures that might alleviate the suffering of the people by shifting the costs of war onto the bourgeoisie, measures that might create more favorable conditions for the French people in their struggle for survival against the internal and external imperialist forces.

With this declaration, the French Communist Party tries to prevent the bourgeoisie from shifting the blame for its pernicious policy onto the Communists, to channel the dissatisfaction and rage of the workers, peasants, and soldiers against the bourgeoisie and its social-democratic agents, to contribute to the unification of the working class and the masses with the Communist Party.

Along with the question of the position of the French Communists is the

Document 30 *continued*

question of the line for German Communists to take in regard to the aggressive policy of the German ruling classes.

The German Communists have issued a document, which was published in the foreign Communist press, in which they expose the imperialist plans of their bourgeoisie and they put forward the slogan of peace without territorial annexations and contributions, without oppression of one people by another, a peace based on the free expression of the will of peoples in determining their fate.

Cc. Pieck and Florin are raising with us the question whether it would be expedient for the German Communist Party to put forward a demand to confiscate war profits and to nationalize banks and large trusts and concerns in order to shift the burden of the war to the propertied classes, to alleviate the lot of the families of mobilized soldiers, and to improve the difficult situation of workers and peasants.

We do not deem the positions of the French and German Communists mistaken. However, the current international situation is so complex, and the moment is so crucial, that every political mistake we make can negatively affect the interests of the USSR.

We ask you, Comrade Stalin, to give us your advice and directive.

With fraternal greetings,
G. DIMITROV
D. MANUILSKY

Moscow, 10 June 1940

Enclosure: Draft declaration of the French Communist Party.[14]

In the days that followed, under pressure from the events in France, the ECCI Secretariat and the French team were busy revising their draft. On 14 June, after consulting with Zhdanov, who had transmitted to them Stalin's comments, Dimitrov sent Stalin a revised text. But the next day the ECCI Secretariat concluded that it was inappropriate to publish the declaration in view of the collapse of the French government.[15]

14. Enclosure omitted here. See *KI*, pp. 359–364.
15. See RTsKhIDNI, f. 495, op. 18, d. 1321, l. 147.

16 June 1940

The collapse of France caused considerable alarm in London and, behind the scenes, in Moscow as well: it left England alone against Germany, and it destroyed the rough balance between the Western democracies and the Nazis that Stalin had assumed would produce a weakening by attrition of both "capitalist" blocs. Hitler was now essentially in control of the continent—except for the Soviet Union. By 15 June the Secretariat of the ECCI had decided that "in view of the rout of the French army and the capitulation of the French government, we consider it inappropriate to publish the declaration adopted by the Com. Party of France." The Secretariat therefore asked its French comrades to revise the declaration in accordance with the new circumstances "on the basis of the exchange of views at the Secretariat."[16] The earlier text had been sent on to the Kremlin, where Zhdanov had authoritatively responded on behalf of the CPSU leadership. The revised text, printed below, evidently met the Kremlin's objections, and it was approved on 19 June.

The principal issue in contention continued to be the attitude toward the Germans and the French war effort. At the outset of the war, the thrust of the PCF's propaganda had been directed against the French government. Now, with France collapsing, Moscow began to signal that it was all right for the French and other European comrades (but not the Soviets) to take an explicit stand against "German imperialism": French patriotism demanded mobilization against the invaders and condemnation of the French government and army command for their ostensible betrayal and incompetence. This set the theme which the PCF was to echo and elaborate in the next year. For Moscow this was an awkward position to espouse at a time when the Soviet government was on seemingly friendly terms with Berlin and was seeking to negotiate new and more far-reaching agreements with the Germans.

16. Ibid.

Document 31

Dimitrov to Stalin, 16 June 1940, with enclosure. Letter: RTsKhIDNI, f. 495, op. 74, d. 518, l. 31; enclosure: f. 495, op. 74, d. 519, ll. 42–50. Original in Russian. Typewritten. The declaration, in the name of the PCF, was published in abbreviated form in the German-language Comintern-sponsored *Die Welt* (Stockholm), no. 27 (28 June 1940), pp. 747–749.

To Comrade Stalin

Dear Comrade Stalin,

After [our] consultation with them, the French comrades revised the draft declaration of the Communist Party of France that had been sent to you, having considered the comments passed on to us by Comrade Zhdanov.

Sending you this revised text of the draft declaration, I request your opinion so that [the declaration] can be sent to be published abroad.

With fraternal greetings,

(G. Dimitrov)

16.6.40.

16.06.40.

Top secret

Translated from French

DECLARATION OF THE FRENCH COMMUNIST PARTY
(Draft)

The French people are living through tragic times. Tremendous disasters, which the Communist Party tried to prevent, have descended upon them. A foreign army has invaded France. The government has surrendered Paris. Having unleashed the war, having brought the people to this catastrophe, having ruined millions of workers and peasants on the battlefields, the French imperialists, behind the backs of the people, are preparing to capitulate in order to preserve their privileges. France faces the danger of disappearing as a nation, as an independent state.

The complete bankruptcy of the French bourgeoisie, of its regime, its corrupt politicians, its talentless generals, is manifest. It is a bankruptcy of the imperialist policy of the French bourgeoisie that nourished the chauvinist propaganda of revenge by the German reaction and facilitated its coming to power.

It is a bankruptcy of Laval, Flandin, Daladier, Bonnet, and Blum, who, contrary to the interests of our people and to the detriment of the cause of peace, have supported in all possible ways the schemes of international reaction. It was the Laval types who signed the Roman agreements that freed Italy's hands to occupy Abyssinia and who prepared the current aggression of Italian fascism against France. It was the Flandin types who strengthened German imperialism by permitting it to remilitarize the left bank of the Rhine. It was the Blum types who, with their criminal policy of "nonintervention," endangered the Pyrenees border and cleared the way for the invaders. It was Daladier and his ministers who handed over to Germany, along with Czechoslovakia, the equipment of its 40 divisions, including 1,600 airplanes and 500 tanks that are now being used to kill French soldiers. It was the protégés of the stock market like Bonnet who systematically sabotaged the Franco-Soviet pact of mutual assistance. All these cads are directly responsible for the imperialist war. They have plunged our people into this criminal massacre.

It is a bankruptcy of radical and socialist politicians, of the reactionary leaders of the General Confederation of Labor who betrayed the workers, who exploded the popular front—which had been an obstacle to starting the imperialist war—who betrayed its program, who unleashed the forces of reaction, and who caused the current war. It is a bankruptcy of the Socialist Party and its miscreant leaders, who are the instigators of the imperialist war, who have done everything to stupefy the workers and to derail their struggle for peace, which accorded with the interests of the people. With their foul slander against the Soviet people, against its socialist regime, against its worker-peasant government, they contributed more than anyone else to the alienation of our country from the Soviet Union, contrary to the feelings of the French people, and to the isolation of France.

Would France be in its present tragic situation if the French government had pursued a loyal and honest policy of friendship toward the great Soviet people, if it had accepted the Soviet proposals for preserving the peace and organizing collective security instead of systematically rejecting them?

This is the bankruptcy of talentless generals with their archaic conceptions of warfare, who ignored the possibilities offered by the advances in modern military technology and the inevitable changes in the conduct of military operations. It is the bankruptcy of the General Staff which, contrary to common sense, had been stubbornly arguing that the current war would be exclusively one of position. With the direct responsibility of Daladier, who was war minister for eight years, the General Staff wasted billions on constructing the Maginot Line, thus dooming France to passive defense. He ignored the importance of the two most important types of weapons of modern war, of the war of maneuver: the tank and the airplane.

The French bourgeoisie and its General Staff had eight months [at their disposal], a sufficient time to catch up and organize a genuine defense of the country. But they could not and did not want to use this time to accelerate the production of tanks and airplanes. They did not even build fortifications or continue the Maginot Line up to Dunkirk, although it was easy to foresee that the German offensive would be directed through the Netherlands and Belgium. During these eight months, the French bourgeoisie did not undertake a single military operation against its adversary. It was too busy organizing a perfidious strike against the Soviet Union, which was not at war with France. For this purpose, it armed and hounded Finnish White-Guardists [at the Soviet Union], it sent an expeditionary corps to Syria in preparation for an attack on Baku and the Soviet Black Sea coast. In the course of these eight months, the imperialist bourgeoisie, considering only its narrow class interests, did not care at all about the defense of France itself, about organizing the defense of the northern approaches to France and to Paris, but only thought about how better to preserve and strengthen its domination over the colonies. In the course of these eight months, the bourgeoisie conducted warfare not against the German armies but against the working class of its own country, by throwing into prisons and concentration camps thousands of vanguard workers, thousands of the best sons of the people, by banishing the most qualified workers from the military plants only because they were Communists or sympathizers of the Communist Party. The bourgeoisie subjected the most staunch and honest defenders of the people to brutal persecution, at the same time promoting the Cagoulards, the agents of German imperialism, to the highest positions in the army and the state apparatus. By pursuing a policy of suppressing and eliminating the most active part of the nation—the Communists—the bourgeoisie undermined the morale of the people and the army, weakened the defense of the country, and doomed it to military defeat. At the time when Germany was systematically and tenaciously preparing its great offensive, Daladier and Blum were busy hunting Communists and secretly getting ready to abandon to the flood and looting by the foreign reaction the proletariat of the North and Paris, the most revolutionary, the most advanced, and the most battle-fit part of the working class of France.

Today, our people are paying for the crimes of their capitalist masters. They are paying for the treason of their bourgeois and "socialist" rulers, are paying today with their suffering and with their blood. Together with them, more than a million Communists and [their] sympathizers are shedding their blood in the army. Today they are feeling the horrors of war on their own backs, together with the rest of the people, since they are part of the people, their bone and flesh.

Today we Communists are saying to the people: the imperialist bourgeoisie has brought our country to the edge of the abyss. We Communists have always been implacable adversaries of imperialist war. We struggled against this war of the French bourgeoisie when the two imperialist predators were struggling to divide the world, when the French bourgeoisie, under the pretext of creating a federated Europe, was planning to dismember Germany, to enslave new peoples, and to establish its domination over Europe. However, today the situation has changed. As a result of the military defeats, these imperialist plans of the French bourgeoisie have collapsed. Today the survival of the French people as an independent nation, the survival of France as an independent state, are at stake. Today German imperialism is implementing its plan of enslaving France. In order to safeguard its privileges, the oligarchy of the two hundred families is ready to capitulate. It is ready to sacrifice the independence and integrity of our country, to sacrifice once again the vital interests of our people. It is ready to ally with the occupier, to hide behind German bayonets from the reckoning that is being prepared by the indignant people.

Communists have always struggled against capitalist exploitation, against the yoke of the national bourgeoisie. They have all the more reason to struggle against the enslavement of our people by a foreign conqueror. Like the entire French people, they do not want to permit [such] double bondage.

That is why today Communists are supporters of a most decisive defense against the foreign invasion and are calling on the army, the workers, the peasants, and the masses to strain every nerve in order to repulse the foreign invasion and secure the independence and integrity of the country.

In the present, exceptionally difficult situation, the Communist Party demands that the following measures be urgently taken:

1. Immediate removal from the government of all pro-capitulationist elements; reorganization of the high command; removal of talentless generals, purging all the capitulationist elements from the army; bold promotion of young officers' cadres who are loyal to the people and have proven courageous and talented commanders.

2. Recruitment of a popular militia; calling up of all those capable of carrying arms, purging of the staffs and offices in the rear of entrenched deserters.

3. Immediate removal of those responsible for the disorganization in supplying the army with military matériel; replacing them with honest and efficient organizers [drawn] from the people, capable of organizing the efficient supply of the front.

4. Reestablishment of workers' delegations in the factories; establishment of workers' control over the production of war matériel; granting factory delegates broad rights in protecting the interests of the workers.

5. Securing the supply of food to the army, as well as to the workers and toilers and especially to the families of draftees.

6. Immediate restitution of democratic and trade union freedoms. Liberation of all arrested and convicted Communists, workers, soldiers, and peasants; immediate release of Communist deputies; resumption of "L'Humanité," the organ of the working class; legalization of the Communist Party; reinstatement to their positions of the Communists elected by the people; termination of tyranny toward the toilers.

7. The arrest, trial, and application of the highest punishment to the traitors of the people (Daladier, Bonnet, Blum, Laval, Flandin, and others), the major culprits of the war, the criminal agents of the "Comité des Forges," the bankers of the City and of the politically bankrupt Chamberlain.

8. The arrest, trial, and application of the highest punishment to the hirelings in the "fifth column," members of parliament and generals who have been exposed as traitors, speculators, marauders, and the war profiteers, the spies and subversives responsible for the sufferings of the French people and for the deaths of hundreds of thousands of its sons.

9. Confiscation of war profits; taxation of large capital; nationalization of banks, insurance companies, mines, railway companies, merchant fleet; na-

tionalization of the trusts of the iron, steel, and chemical industries; nationalization of large mills, sugar trusts, and milk trusts.

10. Requisition of the castles, palaces, mansions, and apartments of the rich for refugees, injured soldiers, and workers without shelter. Cancellation of rents for the toilers throughout the entire war period.

Selflessly protecting the interests of our people, the Communist Party declares that it is ready to cooperate with everyone who will actually struggle for the realization of these measures. In particular, Communists are voicing a fraternal call to the socialist workers, to all the members of the General Confederation of Labor, to all the toilers who are members of the Radical Party, to unite in a common front of struggle.

What the people are imperatively demanding of the government in this difficult situation is, first of all, the implementation of these measures.

Declining any responsibility for the domestic and foreign policy of the bourgeoisie, decisively condemning this criminal policy, exposing it before the masses, the Communist Party declares that it is ready to support the government in implementing these measures, that it is ready to support it as long as it mobilizes all the means and all the forces in the country and honestly organizes the defense of the people and France against the invasion.

The Communist Party of France has always courageously struggled for the cause of peace. Its deputies were imprisoned for suggesting that peace negotiations be opened, at the time when the conditions were favorable, when the Soviet Union was doing everything in its power to prevent the spread of the fire of war across Europe and to France in the first place. Today more than ever, our party continues to struggle for a just and lasting peace based on preserving the integrity and independence of France and securing the independence of the colonies. However, the Communist Party calls on the masses to struggle against a capitulationist peace, against the secret plans of the French reaction, which is preparing the enslavement of the French people by foreigners. The Communist Party calls on the soldiers, workers, and peasants to prevent this new crime.

---

3 August 1940

On 3 August, Dimitrov forwarded a report by Jacques Duclos on developments in France to Stalin. The message, reflecting some of the confusion in the PCF leadership—as paraphrased by Dimitrov—referred to their efforts earlier that summer to conduct negotiations with the German occupation forces and to secure permission to publish the Communist Party's newspaper *L'Humanité* in occupied France. Duclos' letter arrived on 11 July. On 17 July the ECCI Secretariat endorsed the PCF line, but three days later it sharply rebuked the French comrades for negotiating with the Germans and threatened to exclude anyone dealing with the Germans from the party.

Document 32

Dimitrov to Stalin, 3 August 1940, with enclosure. Letter: RTsKhIDNI, f. 495, op. 74, d. 519, ll. 51–58; enclosure: f. 495, op. 74, d. 519, ll. 58a–58g. Original (partly translated from French) in Russian. Typewritten. The original of Duclos' letter is in f. 495, op. 10a, d. 92, ll. 39–45. See *KI*, pp. 394–396, 401–411, for further documentation.

We are sending this text!
TO COMRADE STALIN
Dear Comrade Stalin,
On <. . .> July, the ECCI Secretariat received a report from Paris by C. DUCLOS dated 6 July with very detailed information about the state of affairs in France, the mood of the population, and the work of the Communist Party, its political line, and its tactical concepts. The essence of this report is as follows:

In Paris and other cities occupied by the Germans the overwhelming majority of enterprises have stopped working. Unemployment has reached a terrible level. There is an acute shortage of food. There are long queues near stores and shops. In the occupied zones, the Germans have issued special banknotes and introduced a forced exchange rate of twenty francs to the mark; they are using these marks to buy up everything, literally robbing France. The attitude of the population toward the German occupiers is very hostile. No less hostile is the attitude toward the French bourgeoisie, whom the people rightfully consider the culprit in their misfortune. One can generally hear people talking in queues, in the streets, in the metro:

"They have betrayed us. The rich, who escaped in their cars, betrayed us, the government of national treason betrayed us, corrupt politicians and talentless generals betrayed us."

This is being discussed openly and everywhere not only by the workers but by petty shopkeepers, who only yesterday were frantic jingoists. The prestige of the Soviet Union has grown enormously. Everywhere one can hear people say: "Only the USSR can save us." Along with that, the authority of the Communist Party has been growing notably, the only one among the French political parties that has not been compromised. The masses are saying:

"The Communists were right."

Not a single voice is raised to oppose this statement in public gathering places. Housewives are particularly active in expressing their dissatisfaction, since they are feeling the pressure of poverty and the impending hunger more than anyone else.

Document 32 *continued*

From the first days of the German invasion, the Communist Party resumed publication of "L'Humanité" on a hectograph. French comrades assert that never before during the war has "L'Humanité" enjoyed such a success as it does now. The ordinary newspaper sellers in the streets and in the metro stations are selling it almost openly. The crowd pounces on each seller, literally snatching each issue of the newspaper from their hands. Passersby stop to read "L'Humanité" right on the street. The French police are passive and observe these scenes without intervening.

Duclos reports further that the Germans are trying to maintain outward correctness and have instructed their soldiers to "establish contact with the population." The Parisian workers are taking advantage of this and conduct group or individual conversations with German soldiers, as much as they can, about the goals of the war, about the USSR, about socialism.

The line of the leadership of the French Communist Party, as it is summarized in the report by Duclos and in "L'Humanité" is as follows:

The Communist Party, while avoiding a challenging tone toward the German occupiers, is conducting extensive work to expose the government of Pétain, Laval, and other perpetrators of the military disaster for France, and thus aims over their heads at the German patrons of Pétain-Laval.

The party demands that all those who struggled against the imperialist war be freed from prison, that all the perpetrators of war, all those who oppressed, imprisoned, and killed Communists, the true protectors of the interests of the French people, be put on trial. The party demands that the municipal councilors whose mandate was revoked by the Daladier government only because they were members of the Communist Party be reinstated.

The party demands that trade union freedoms be reestablished, that the elected workers' delegates in the enterprises be reestablished, that the democratic rights and freedoms of the people be reestablished.

The party demands that [the government] open the enterprises, pay unemployment benefits, and create a "national solidarity" fund to provide help to war victims and refugees.

The party demands the confiscation of war profits and merciless taxation of large capital, the nationalization without indemnity of banks, mines, railways, electric power stations, and other large enterprises.

The party demands that [the government] protect small and medium peasants and transfer without compensation the lands belonging to bankers and landowners to agricultural workers and small peasants.

In foreign policy, the party pledges to support colonial peoples in their struggle for liberation.

The party demands further that [the government]:

First, scrupulously "observe the armistice and take decisive measures against any action aimed at once again involving the French people in war."

Second, "sign a pact of friendship with the USSR, a pact that would supplement the German-Soviet pact and that would become an important factor in the cause of European pacification."

Here we must point out that the wording of these two last points about "European pacification" and the "armistice," along with the campaign that "L'Humanité" initiated against General de Gaulle, caused us doubts, which we expressed in our telegram to the French Communist Party, discussed below.

In his report, Duclos further noted that the party has initiated the creation of legal and semilegal coordinating centers to organize the masses under the guise of various committees of mutual assistance (food supplies, providing help to the families of soldiers and refugees), that the party leadership is taking measures to reinvigorate the work of the trade unions, to establish contact with the party organizations in the zone not occupied by German troops, to locate all the party cadres available in France and to use and distribute them as needed in the new situation. Duclos informed us that the party leadership took steps to secure legal publication of "L'Humanité," but the German authorities not only rejected the petition, they even kept the comrades who had been sent to conduct these negotiations under arrest for three days. Among them, a member of the CC, Legros, was detained. After Legros was released, the lawyer who worked on his case informed Legros that Abetz wanted to meet with him to discuss the possibility of resuming publication of "L'Humanité." The party leadership authorized Legros and another member of the CC, Catelas, to meet with Abetz in the presence of a lawyer. This meeting took place but produced no results. From the context of the discussion between Abetz, Legros, and Catelas, it was absolutely clear that Abetz tried to capitalize on the Communist Party and its influence among the masses in order to promote the aggressive designs of the German occupiers.

Finally, the leadership of the French Communist Party asked us, through Duclos, for advice on how to act in case the general discontent of the masses issued into disturbances.

After acquainting themselves with the report by Duclos, members of the French Communist Party leadership Thorez, Marty, Rammette, and Raymond [Guyot] organized a meeting in the ECCI Secretariat and, after exchanging opinions, sent Duclos the following telegram:

"1. We consider the party line essentially correct.

"2. It is necessary to step up vigilance regarding the maneuvers of the occupiers. It was correct for the party to take steps to strive to legalize publication of its press, but the meeting with Abetz was a serious mistake which can compromise the party and its leadership.

"3. We consider it appropriate to encourage passive resistance by the broad masses to the occupiers in every form, but it is imperative to do so carefully, using illegal means, without overt propaganda, and not involving the party formally.

"While avoiding any premature action that might play into the hands of the occupiers, it is important to support open manifestations of popular discontent, provided such a movement is well prepared and organized and will be joined by broad masses, especially women.

"4. We consider the party line to organize friendly conversations between the population and German soldiers correct; in particular, we think it beneficial to involve women in such conversations who are properly instructed and trained for such a role.

"5. We recommend that the party corrects its formulation about observing the armistice; otherwise it could seem that the party endorses the terms of the armistice.

"6. We recommend no mention of General de Gaulle and no attack on England, in order not to play into the hand of Pétain and his protectors. While it is correct to conduct agitation in favor of the pact of friendship between France and the USSR, it is wrong to portray such a pact as a supplement to the German-Soviet pact. In this connection, there is no need to speak of European pacification.

"7. In general, the program of demands of the party is correct. However, by demanding payment of unemployment benefits and resumed work in the enterprises, you should not assist the occupiers to start up branches and enterprises whose output could be used to strengthen the occupiers militarily.

"8. It is essential to step up a mass campaign against utilizing resources and the territory of France to continue the war, [a campaign] for repatriating prisoners of war and refugees, for unimpeded exchange between the occupied and unoccupied territories of France. It is important to conduct a campaign under the slogan of mobilizing all the resources of the country to alleviate the destitution of the people and not to service the military needs of the occupiers. It is essential to sharpen the demand 'to make the rich pay.'

"9. We consider correct the tactical line on exposing the Pétain-Laval clique and thereby attacking the occupiers.

"10. We consider it appropriate to send Communists, men and women [alike], to gathering places in order to conduct agitation against the perpetrators of the disaster and especially the clique that is in power.

"11. It is important to stress, orally and in writing, that only the working class under the leadership of the Communist Party, by uniting all the toiling strata, is capable of saving France and securing its independence while struggling for socialism.

"12. One should not underestimate the danger of nationalist demagogy of the reactionaries who retain power, and the possibility of a strengthening of the fascist movement in France. Playing on the disasters and disillusionment of the masses, the reactionaries' demagogy may find a response among the unemployed and in particular among the middle classes, intelligentsia, and officers. Therefore, it is essential that the party does not content itself with general ideological work among these sectors but take in its hands the protection of their economic demands so as to attract the best part of these strata.

"13. It is essential to pay particular attention to the youth; it would be good to publish a special proclamation to the youth and to take organizational measures to [improve] the work with them.

"14. Your line of using all legal opportunities is correct, as long as the Communist Party's illegal organization is being strengthened and solidified. It is important to use only part of the old cadres for directing overt legal work of the party in different organizations (deputies, municipal councilors, trade union workers); the rest, the bulk of the old tested cadres, must conduct active work under underground conditions and observe the strictest rules of concealment."

* * *

From the latest reports, it is clear that the game of the German occupiers with the Communist Party continues and assumes forms that are dangerous to the party. After discussing this question with Comrades Thorez and Marty, we have worked out a more detailed and categorical directive to the leadership of the CP of France. Enclosed is the text of this directive.

With fraternal greetings,

(G. DIMITROV)

3 August 1940

Draft Directive to the CP of France

From the information on the situation in France obtained from different sources it is clear that the party is seriously threatened by the maneuvers of the occupiers. We consider it necessary to reiterate the necessity for strictest vigilance regarding the maneuvers of the occupiers and their French agents. These maneuvers will intensify and appear in many different forms as the economic collapse worsens, unemployment rises, poverty and hunger increase, winter approaches, the war continues, popular discontent grows, and the activities of the party grow and its role increases.

The occupiers realize that the party is the only unsullied, growing, organized political force that enjoys the confidence of the masses and has a real possibility to become a center of gravity for the people and a most important factor in raising the country. Therefore, the occupiers are maneuvering with the party with the following goals in mind:

1. To use the party as an instrument for creating a favorable attitude toward the occupiers within the masses, and thus to secure a solid rear to continue the war, to rebuild the economy of the country in the interests of the occupiers, and to shift the responsibility for the growing disasters associated with the occupation onto the party.

2. To use the growing influence of the party, which the occupiers are consciously exaggerating, as an argument for blackmailing and pressuring the Pétain-Laval clique in order to make them more pliable and obedient. *The occupiers want to frighten Pétain-Laval with the specter of Communism and*

a popular government in order to push them to make more concessions at France's expense. At the same time, they are trying to discredit the party by providing their agents with the argument that the party is supposedly cooperating with the occupiers.

3. They are trying to discredit the party, to isolate it from the masses, to corrupt it from the inside, to paralyze its activities, to demoralize and compromise part of its cadres, and to lure the other part out of the underground so it can be shadowed, in order to decapitate the party by way of some kind of provocation at an appropriate time.

It is precisely with such aims that Abetz and his associates are stepping up their feverish activity, the occupation authorities are persistently attempting to approach the party, test the waters, promote an insolent slogan of creating a popular government, and temporarily display a show of liberalism toward Communists.

We are extremely worried by this. The party is threatened by the greatest danger if it yields to the influence of the occupiers' maneuvers and if it does not demonstrate sufficient perspicacity, caution, and political tenacity, if it permits itself to be pushed into various meetings and negotiations with the occupation authorities.

In our view, it is an elementary axiom that the country's economic reconstruction and national revival are impossible on the basis of political conciliation, compromise, and solidarity with the occupiers.

Considering all the above, we propose that [the party] adhere to the following directives:

1. The party must categorically refute and condemn as treason any display of solidarity with the occupiers. It is essential to avoid [publishing] articles, [making] declarations, [conducting] negotiations, and [holding] meetings that could be interpreted as a display of solidarity with the occupiers or as approving or justifying their actions.

2. Limit relations with the occupation authorities, strictly and exclusively, to mere formal and administrative issues.

3. Continue efforts to secure the legalization of the workers' press and to utilize every legal opportunity to conduct political activity and propaganda. Nevertheless, it is essential that our legal press not be used in the interests of the propaganda and policy of the occupiers. If the newspaper "Ce Soir," with its prestige as a popular newspaper, will not be able to retain its character and its independence and will face the demand of the occupiers to serve as their mouthpiece, then it will be necessary immediately to discontinue its publication and to explain verbally to the masses the motives for this shutdown.

4. It is essential urgently to explain to all the leading party cadres the meaning of the maneuvers of the occupiers and to demand that all the party members redouble their vigilance and discipline.

5. It is important to personally alert renowned party parliamentarians and

journalists like Péri and others so that they resolutely refute any attempt to entice them into negotiations or joint discussions with the occupiers or their agents of tactical or other party issues. It is imperative to report the initiators of such attempts to the party leadership. The behavior of the lawyer Foisson leads [us] to think that he is an agent of the occupiers.

6. The strictest measures must immediately be taken, including expelling from the party and public exposure as traitors to the proletariat and the people, all those who turn out to be involved, directly or indirectly, in deals with the occupiers, become spreaders of their influence, or express, to any degree, solidarity with them. By acting in such a way, the party leadership will retain and increase its authority, and the party in general will strengthen and broaden its influence among the masses. It is absolutely inadmissible for the party to conciliate the occupiers, the renegades, and individuals responsible for the disasters and the present calamities that have occurred.

7. We are pleased to ascertain the fact that the members and cadres of the party in overwhelming majority retain their loyalty and observe discipline, and that the masses display confidence in the party. Nevertheless, it is important to remember that the strength of the party's influence among the masses and the strength of its ties with the masses are tested only when the masses follow the party and carry out its directives in difficult and critical moments. In this respect, our party has not yet achieved the desirable level of strengthening its organizations and strengthening its ties with the masses.

8. We inform the party leadership that Duclos is charged with the responsibility of personally securing the unconditional implementation of the above directives, and we propose that all the [party] leaders display a maximum of self-control, responsibility, and iron discipline, and demand the same from all party members.

G. Dim.

---

19 February 1941

In November 1940, as part of the exchanges arranged between the Soviet Union and Germany and its "allies," Hungary released Mátyás Rákosi, a veteran Communist who had been serving a life sentence in jail (even though he had been granted Soviet citizenship in 1934). Although Stalin typically wanted to be sure that Rákosi had no Trotskyite sympathies, Dimitrov was delighted by his arrival and was eager to put him to work at the Comintern.[17]

17. See TsPA (Sofia), f. 146, op. 2, a.e. 6.

It turned out that there was a skeleton in his closet that first needed to be cleared away. After his arrest in 1925 Rákosi had told the Hungarian police the names of the participants of a Communist underground congress and of the members of the party's (illegal) secretariat. This fact had been established by the Comintern's International Control Commission in 1926. But at this point Dimitrov and Manuilsky seemed eager to forgive—and to put Rákosi to work. Rákosi provided an "explanation" for his behavior; Manuilsky wrote Stalin about it on 29 January 1941; Dimitrov discussed it with members of the ECCI Presidium and with several Soviet Politburo members; and finally Dimitrov and Manuilsky sent Stalin the following letter, which sums up Rákosi's defense. On 26 February, Zhdanov informed Dimitrov that Stalin had agreed to the proposed resolution, and as of that date the ECCI Presidium and the Bureau of the ICC declared the case closed.

Document 33

Dimitrov and Manuilsky to Stalin, 19 February 1941, with enclosure. RTsKhIDNI, f. 495, op. 74, d. 107a, ll. 176–175. Original in Russian. Typewritten.

TO COMRADE STALIN

Dear Comrade Stalin,

Regarding the case of Com. Rákosi, with which you are familiar from the letter of Com. Manuilsky to you, we consider it appropriate for the ECCI Presidium and the ICC Bureau to pass the following resolution:

"The Presidium of the ECCI and the Bureau of the ICC, after studying the testimony that C. Rákosi gave during the preliminary investigation in 1925 and the related statement of C. Rákosi of 25 January 1941, state that by giving such testimony C. Rákosi committed a political mistake incompatible with behavior that the Communist International recommends to arrested Communists facing the class enemy.

"However, taking into consideration the brave conduct of C. Rákosi during the court-martial and the two trials that followed, as well as C. Rákosi's irreproachable behavior in prison for fifteen years, the Presidium of the ECCI and the Bureau of the ICC resolve:

"1. To take notice of the statement by C. Rákosi in which he recognizes his mistake.

"2. To consider the case of C. Rákosi's testimony closed and not requiring further review by the ICC.

"3. To use C. Rákosi as a member of the Executive Committee to work in the Comintern."

Com. Dimitrov acquainted the members of the ECCI Presidium and the International Control Commission, including Com. Shkiriatov, with the materials in the Rákosi case and his statement of 25 January 1941, as well as personally talked with C. Zhdanov and C. Andreev.

We request your directives regarding this question.

With fraternal greetings,

(G. DIMITROV)
(D. MANUILSKY)

19 February 1941. Enclosure: Statement by C. Rákosi of 25.1.41.
Sent in package No. 61 on 19/II/41.
Stern.

TO THE GENERAL SECRETARY OF THE ECCI
Com. DIMITROV

Dear Comrade,

A week ago, you informed me that in 1925 the ICC initiated an investigation regarding my behavior before the Hungarian police but finally deferred taking any decision until my release [from prison]. As I can see from the protocols, the case was initiated by Pyatnitsky and Angaretis, and the then representative of the CP of Hungary, Com. Szántó, protested the contents and the form of this accusation.

I was arrested, along with 100 other comrades, in September 1925 because of the agent-provocateur Ludwig Szamuely. Since this provocateur participated in the illegal party congress and was a secretary of the Komsomol, the police had most detailed information, and the rest came from those who were arrested, who were seized with a lot of materials, as well as in the course of interrogations. During the first days, I refused to give any statements; [then] I signed one protocol, only to prevent the discovery of a certain stock of arms. This protocol, however, contained only what the police had already known from the statements of the others under arrest. Before the court-martial, I renounced this protocol. Of course, I informed the CC CP of Hungary of this fact, since I sent them all the materials about the trial, and provided written and oral reports. The CC took my explanation and behavior after the trials in 1925 and 1926 into consideration, informed me that it was satisfied with my behavior, and made a corresponding public statement. Already in prison, I considered signing this protocol a mistake; for 15 years, I tried to . . . [18]

---

18. Page missing in the original document—Trans.

17 April 1941

There appear to have been few contacts between Dimitrov and
Stalin in the winter of 1940–41. One reason for this was that Dimitrov was absent on medical leave; another, harder to demonstrate,
may have been the declining presence and importance of the Comintern in Stalin's political perception. His preoccupations were elsewhere. After Molotov's pompous but unproductive visit to Berlin
in November 1940, stronger anti-German notes in Soviet and Communist Party pronouncements became detectable.[19] Most overtly,
when the German army attacked Yugoslavia and Greece in April
1941, Dimitrov, with Stalin's explicit approval, pronounced that although the imperialist character of the war as a whole remained the
same, Yugoslavia's and Greece's national defense efforts were
just.[20] This illustrated the confused and contradictory position
taken by Moscow: to the end, the Soviet leadership was eager to
avoid doing anything that might alarm the Germans or give them a
pretext to respond with hostility; on the other hand, it also needed
to mind both its domestic audiences and the Communist parties
abroad.

It would have been customary to issue the annual slogans in April
for the upcoming May Day celebration. On 9 April, Zhdanov told
Dimitrov that this time the Comintern had better not do so. As Dimitrov recorded it, Zhdanov said, "To make a thorough analysis
means to some extent to show your cards, to give your enemies
grounds for their undesirable use."[21] Instead, the Comintern ought
to send its sections abroad a set of directives. Accordingly, in the following days the ECCI Secretariat drafted a letter, which Dimitrov
forwarded to Stalin (with a copy to Zhdanov) on 17 April. More
explicitly than before, the ECCI gave the Communist parties in en-
emy-occupied countries the task of "mobilizing the masses against
the bourgeoisie and the occupation regime" while "directing their
main blow against those bourgeois groups who help the occupiers."
The next day Zhdanov telephoned Dimitrov with Stalin's comments, essentially approving the document with minor changes. It

19. See e.g., *KI*, p. 40.
20. See ibid., pp. 524–525.
21. TsPA [Sofia], f. 146, op. 2, a.e. 7.

was sent out the following day, after approval by the ECCI Secretariat.

Document 34

Dimitrov to Stalin, 17 April 1941, with enclosure. Letter: RTsKhIDNI, f. 495, op. 73, d. 69, l. 16; enclosure: f. 495, op. 18, d. 1330, ll. 226–230. Original in Russian. Typewritten.

TO COMRADE STALIN[22]

Dear Comrade Stalin,

Enclosed is a directive, worked out by us, to the Communist parties of capitalist countries regarding the celebration of May Day.

If there are no other instructions from you regarding this issue, the directive will be sent out in an appropriate form in the coming days.

With fraternal greetings,

(G. DIMITROV)

17 April 1941

Sent in package No. 132

TU <. . .>

Secret

DIRECTIVES TO THE COMMUNIST PARTIES OF CAPITALIST
COUNTRIES REGARDING THE CELEBRATION OF MAY DAY 1941

In view of the spread and exacerbation of the imperialist war, Communist parties must give the highest attention to the May Day campaign. Instead of a common proclamation by the Communist International, individual Communist parties must issue their own May Day proclamations. In their proclamations, just as in their conduct of the May Day campaign in general, the Communist parties must be creative, basing them on the particular situation in their own countries and [custom-tailoring] the tasks for the working class and toilers of their own countries that follow from them. For example, in the warring imperialist countries, it is necessary to issue the well-founded charges against the national bourgeoisie that plunged the people into the war for the sake of its own predatory interests, and to show that it is precisely the task of the working class with the toiling masses around it to lead the people out of the hell of this war. In the occupied countries, [it is necessary] to pointedly expose the betrayal by the bourgeoisie, which is to be blamed for the country's and the people's loss of national independence and for their submission to the foreign yoke, and to mobilize the masses against the bourgeoisie and the occupation regime by aiming the main strike against those groups of the bour-

22. A similar letter was also sent to Zhdanov. See RTsKhIDNI, f. 495, op. 73, d. 96, l. 17.

geoisie which serve as accessories to the occupiers. In the nonwarring capitalist countries, [it is necessary] to expose and attack the ruling cliques that are striving to draw the people into imperialist war. In the countries that are defending their independence from imperialist aggression, [it is necessary] to concentrate against the capitulationist groups and elements that are disrupting the defensive war, etc.

In every country it is important to formulate concrete demands in defense of the vital interests of the masses, to initiate the struggle against shifting the burden of war to the shoulders of the toilers, to strive to make the rich pay the costs of war, to oppose political reaction in defense of the democratic freedoms of the peoples. [It is necessary] to appeal to the younger generation and to women, who are especially suffering from the consequences of war.

As to the general international orientation, the Communist parties must be guided by the following propositions:

The war has become a world war. Neither of the two imperialist blocs is able to give the peoples the solution that would correspond to the interests of the masses and the cause of peace. On the contrary, as a result of the efforts of each side to preserve or establish their world dominance, the war continues to spread, the military operations involve ever new countries, and more peoples are losing their independence and freedom. The devastating character of the war is becoming more acute.

In recent months, the unification of the masses in the struggle against the imperialist war has made several important advances, for example, in England and in the United States (people's congresses against the war). In the occupied countries the resistance of the masses to the national oppression is becoming more evident. The peoples who became objects of aggression, like the Yugoslavs and the Greeks, are waging a just defensive war. The Chinese people continue their war for national liberation. The movement against colonial enslavement is gaining ground (India, Syria).

Under these conditions, the May Day campaign can and must become a very important step in the cause of unifying and mobilizing the forces of the working class and toilers to struggle against the imperialist war and against the capitalist cliques that are responsible for its prolongation and aggravation; to struggle against the enslavement of the masses by the military machine, against national oppression and colonial enslavement, to struggle for popular peace, a peace without enslaving other peoples, a peace on the basis of securing national freedom for every people, on the basis of fraternal collaboration among peoples. The imperialist war is the cause of imperialists; the people's peace must be the cause of the working class and the people.

It is important to especially emphasize the independent peace policy of the powerful Soviet Union, its actions on behalf of the peoples defending their national independence, and to call upon the toilers and peoples to rally around the country of socialism.

Document 34 *continued*

It is also important to express solidarity with the heroic struggle of the Chinese people, as well as with the just war of the Yugoslav and Greek peoples who have become victims of imperialist aggression.

It is important to stress that, contrary to the betrayal in some countries of the national interests of the peoples by their capitalist cliques, the working class is a consistent representative and defender of the interests and the future of the nation.

In the course of the May Day campaign, it is important to decisively attack social democracy that has betrayed the interests of the working class and the people, that is actively collaborating in establishing openly dictatorial antinational regimes in the occupied countries, and everywhere serving the interests of capitalism and working to spread the war. In order to fulfill its great historical mission, the working class must once and for all liberate itself from the influence and tutelage of the social-democratic traitors, establish the unity of its forces, and rally around the consistent revolutionary leadership, the Communist Party.

On May Day, Communists call on the masses to express their international solidarity in the struggle against war and reaction, to voice their demands to liberate those who fight against the imperialist war, the Spanish refugees and soldiers of the International Brigades in France, the prisoners of the bourgeoisie Browder, Thälmann, Prestes, and Ana Pauker, the trade union leaders Sémard and Zápotocký, the French deputies Billoux, Bonte, and others.

The forms for celebrating the May Day must be adapted to the situation in each particular country. It is extremely important to strive for a work stoppage on 1 May. It is equally important to extend our agitation to the soldiers at the front and in the rear.

It is necessary to struggle everywhere for the independent actions of the proletariat against the bourgeoisie on May Day. Wherever trade union manifestations are organized, the masses must participate in them with their own slogans. It is important to raise in each country the question of the class unity of trade unions and their defense against reaction.

The entire preparation and accomplishment of the May Day campaign must proceed under the slogan of unity and broad preparation of the forces of the working class and the toiling masses of the city and the countryside in a genuine popular front in the struggle for the prompt termination of the war and the establishment of a popular peace. In doing so, it is essential to rely on the forces of each people, on the genuine active internationalist proletarian solidarity and solidarity with the great country of socialism.

Inform us promptly about the progress of the May Day campaign.

18.4.41.

G. Dim[itrov]
Ercoli
Gottwald
Dolores

It was also at this time that Stalin for the first time seems to have mentioned the possibility of dissolving the Communist International.[23] But for the time being this option, casually dropped, was not pursued. What was far more urgent during the next two months were the rapidly multiplying signs that Germany was preparing for an invasion of the Soviet Union. In addition to the many reports that arrived through diplomatic, intelligence, and foreign channels, the Comintern received several indications from Tito in Yugoslavia: the Germans were recruiting "White Guard" Russian émigrés as instructors and parachutists, and German officers and men as well as Gestapo officials were talking about the coming German invasion.[24]

Similarly, Zhou Enlai reported from Chongqing that Chiang Kaishek was insisting that Germany was going to invade the Soviet Union on 21 June. Dimitrov wrote in his diary for that date: "Rumors of the impending attack are multiplying from all sides." But when Dimitrov called Molotov about this, he was evasive.[25]

Stalin did not want to hear about it.[26]

23. See below, Chapter 8.

24. RTsKhIDNI, f. 495, op. 184, vkhod. 1941, d. 7, ll. 99, 112, 116.

25. TsPA, f. 146, op. 2, a.e. 7.

26. On Stalin's reactions to the impending German invasion, see Alexander Dallin, "Stalin and the German Invasion," in Operation Barbarossa (Soviet Union, 1991, vol. 18, nos. 1–2), pp. 19–37. Dimitrov was present at Stalin's 5 May speech, which has been the key argument of those who assert that Stalin was planning an offensive move against Nazi Germany—a most implausible hypothesis. Dimitrov's version of Stalin's remarks is: "Our policy of peace and security is at the same time a policy of preparing for war. There is no defense without offense. The army must be educated in the spirit of an offensive. We must be prepared for war" (TsPA, f. 146, op. 2, a.e. 7). The idea that one should carry the war to the enemy's territory had been standard Soviet military doctrine for years. See in particular Cynthia A. Roberts, "Planning for War: The Red Army and the Catastrophe of 1941," Europe-Asia Studies, 1995, vol. 47, no. 8, pp. 1293–1326. Another vesion of Stalin's 5 May speech is in RTsKhIDNI, f. 558, op. 1, d. 3808, ll. 1–12.

CHAPTER SIX

The War Years

THE GERMAN INVASION of the Soviet Union, on 22 June 1941, was perhaps the greatest shock the Soviet Union had ever experienced, and it offered the greatest challenge. For the Comintern, the most immediate task following the invasion was yet another fundamental reversal of the whole strategic line: the Comintern now abandoned the argument that both sides in the war were imperialists, fighting an unjust fight. The new line demanded a return to the broadest possible united fronts and alliances—within and between countries—and the downplaying of all explicitly Communist and revolutionary goals.

As Dimitrov recorded in his diary, he was called to the Kremlin the day of the attack. Some ten Soviet leaders were assembled, discussing the German invasion. "They fell upon us, without making any claims, not demanding any negotiations, [Stalin said], they made a vile attack like bandits." As for the role of the Comintern, Stalin cautioned, "For now the Comintern must not appear openly. The parties everywhere will develop a movement in defense of the USSR. [We must] not raise the question of a socialist revolution. The Sov[iet] people are waging a patriotic war against fascist Germany. The task is to crush fascism, which has enslaved a number of peoples and is striving to enslave additional ones as well."[1]

1. TsPA (Sofia), f. 146, op. 1, a.e. 7; cited in "Iz 'Dnevnika' na Georgi Dimitrov ot godinite na Vtorata svetovni voina," *Letopisi*, 1992, nos. 9–10, p. 75.

For Dimitrov the coming days were bound to be devoted to fleshing out and implementing the new line. The same day, 22 June, Dimitrov reported to the ECCI Secretariat what the line would be. In essence the Communist parties in the capitalist world were to unconditionally support the Soviet Union against Germany, whereas those in the occupied countries must launch a national liberation movement, and within Germany an antifascist campaign, and all must proclaim that the Soviet Union was fighting a just, patriotic war against aggressive Germany.[2] And as usual the Secretariat loyally fell into line.

Dimitrov was prompt to recognize that with the German invasion the character of the war had changed. Now whatever helped the Soviet Union and speeded the defeat of its enemy would be the deciding factor in any policy choice. The ECCI Secretariat resolved to immediately revamp its entire work, to instruct the Communist parties to act in accordance with Dimitrov's remarks, and to empower a "troika" of Dimitrov, Manuilsky, and Ercoli (Palmiro Togliatti) to direct the work of the ECCI on a day-to-day basis.[3]

In the days that followed the Secretariat sent variants of the directives to the foreign parties that were adapted to the particular needs of each country.[4] In a typical sample, the French party was urged to cooperate with General de Gaulle's Free French movement, which it had earlier shunned. In addition, the directive stressed the "need to avoid depicting the German-Soviet conflict as a war between capitalist and socialist systems. For the Soviet Union it is a patriotic war against fascist barbarism. All the chatter about world revolution helps Hitler and impedes the international cohesion of all anti-Hitler forces."[5]

This dismissal of world revolution was no accident. In revealing remarks on 21 January 1940, during the Winter War, Stalin had told Dimitrov, "World revolution as a single act is nonsense. It takes place at different times in different countries. The actions of the Red

2. See "Iz vystupleniya na zasedanii Sekretariata IKKI 22 iyunya 1941 goda," in Georgi Dimitrov, *Izbrannye proizvedeniya* (Moscow: Politizdat, 1983), vol. 2, p. 390.

3. See RTsKhIDNI, f. 495, op. 18, d. 1335, ll. 3b, 1.

4. See RTsKhIDNI, f. 495, op. 18, d. 1335, ll. 1, 10, 17–18; op. 184, iskh. 1941, d. 4, l. 18.

5. RTsKhIDNI, f. 495, op. 184, iskh. 1941, d. 13, l. 12.

Army also serve the cause of world revolution."[6] It was characteristic of Stalin that he would dismiss the prospects of successful revolts by foreign Communist parties—he had been doing so for
twenty years. But this outlook also contributed to the downgrading
of the role and visibility of the Communist International. Now
when Dimitrov, identifying especially with the Bulgarian Communists, urged Soviet encouragement and support for their efforts,
Stalin refused, though subsequently there and elsewhere in German-
occupied Europe the Comintern and other Soviet agencies did
encourage partisan warfare.[7]

31 October 1941

In October the advance of the Nazi forces precipitated the evacuation of many Soviet party and government offices from Moscow.
Comintern staff and files were moved east to Ufa, in the Bashkir
Republic. (Dimitrov himself moved to Kuibyshev [Samara], where
the Soviet government had been evacuated.) In their new quarters,
Dimitrov and his staff worked increasingly closely with Soviet intelligence and military agencies, as their appeals abroad called for
partisan warfare behind the German lines. But Soviet wartime propaganda was focused on patriotic themes and slogans, and even to
Dimitrov the ritual vocabulary of proletarian internationalism now
appeared out of place. Hence Dimitrov's proposal in Document 35
to camouflage the Comintern's apparatus as an *"Institute for the
study of international questions."* Stalin did not reply in person, but
word passed back from the Kremlin that the Comintern in exile was
to be an administrative office of the ECCI, otherwise known as the
inscrutable "Institute No. 305."

---

6. TsPA (Sofia), f. 146, op. 1, a.e. 6; cited in "Iz 'Dnevnika,'" p. 52.
7. See RTsKhIDNI, f. 495, op. 74, d. 784, l. 5; op. 74, d. 84, ll. 13–16; TsPA
(Sofia), f. 146, op. 2, a.e. 8, 9, cited in "Iz 'Dnevnika,'" p. 77, and *Letopisi,* nos. 11–
12, p. 86.

Document 35

Dimitrov to Stalin, 31 October 1941. RTsKhIDNI, f. 495, op. 73, d. 112, l. 2. Original in Russian. Typewritten.

TO COMRADE STALIN

Dear Comrade STALIN,

With the transfer of the ECCI to Ufa, a number of questions have arisen regarding the legal status of our organization, the registration of its employees, how to provide them with various documents, certificates for food, and other [products], etc.

The question is whether it is expedient, in the present situation, to do all this under the banner of the Communist International, or whether it would be better for us to exist in Ufa <u>outwardly</u> as some other organization.

My personal opinion is that at this time we should not openly emphasize the [activities of the] Communist International. On the contrary, it would be politically more advantageous if all our practical work and ties with other organizations are organized and conducted formally under the auspices of a different firm, for example, <u>Institute for the study of international questions.</u>

I beg your advice and directive regarding this question.

With fraternal greetings,

(G. DIMITROV)

31 October 1941

5 May 1942

As the war progressed, Dimitrov's contacts with Stalin became sporadic—only in part because of the ECCI's exile to Ufa—although he continued to send information received from Communists abroad to the Kremlin. Increasingly, directives sent to Communist parties were coordinated in advance with other Soviet leaders, such as Molotov, Shcherbakov, Malenkov, and Andreyev. But occasionally, Dimitrov still turned to Stalin himself.

The Comintern's wartime tactics called for "close relations" with other groups and parties on the left. And yet, as always, suspicion and skepticism of the social democrats (which included the British Labour Party) remained paramount. There was always tension between the wish to use and the fear of being used by the alien partner. In May 1942 Harry Pollitt asked the Comintern for advice on behalf of the British Communist Party after being approached by

Harold Laski, chairman of the Labour Party, who was seeking to unify the international labor movement. Presumably this meant the Socialist and Communist Internationals, beginning with the British Labour Party and British Communist Party, along with the respective trade unions and analogous organizations in other countries. Despite the fact that on many occasions the Communists had urged such "unity," which would eliminate the profound division in the world labor movement, they also feared that such a move could mean the end of their organizational autonomy. Moreover, in Britain the Communists were much weaker than the Labourites. Interestingly, even in 1942, with the "benign" Harold Laski taking the initiative, Dimitrov remained profoundly suspicious of the idea, and he voices his skepticism in Document 36, a request for Stalin's approval of his cautious course of action. Not surprisingly, Stalin agreed. A notation on the document indicates that it was returned by Stalin, by implication approving Dimitrov's recommended course of action.

Document 36

Dimitrov to Stalin and Molotov, 5 May 1942. RTsKhIDNI, f. 495, op. 74, d. 52, ll. 24–26. Original in Russian. Typewritten.

TOP SECRET
  TO COMRADE STALIN
  TO COMRADE MOLOTOV
  Com. Harry Pollitt, on behalf of the CC of the Communist Party of England, is asking us for advice regarding the following question:
  A famous Labour Party theoretician, Professor Harold Laski, has recently suggested to the leadership of the Labour Party that they establish contact with the VKP(b) and discuss the question of the unification of the international workers' movement. Laski's suggestion was offered for discussion in a commission composed of Laski, Barbara Gould, Dalton, Walker, and Middleton. The commission considered it appropriate to ask Huysmans, Brouckère, and Albarda—former leaders of the Second International—for their point of view on this issue. They agreed with Laski's proposal but indicated the need to call a broader meeting that included representatives of other allied parties, who are now in England. This meeting was held. Representatives of Norway,

Document 36 *continued*

Czechoslovakia, and France approved the proposal, and the Norwegian representative suggested that the Labour Party retain the initiative on this question.

After this meeting, the Labour Party commission resolved to submit the following proposals to the Executive Committee of the Labour Party for consideration:

1. That the Executive Committee, at the coming annual conference of the Labour Party to be held on 25 May, ask the conference to sanction negotiations between the Labour Party and the VKP(b).

2. That representatives be elected from among the conference delegates to be sent to the USSR with the authority to initiate such negotiations.

The commission also resolved to recommend to the Executive Committee to submit this question for discussion at the conference only if these proposals are openly endorsed by the General Council of the trade unions and by the council of the Cooperative Party, considering that the trade unions had already reached an agreement with the Soviet trade unions.

In his conversation with C. Pollitt, Laski stated that there is an expectation in Labour Party circles that these proposals may lead to the convocation of a conference reminiscent of the <u>1922 Berlin conference</u>.

Com. Pollitt believes that Laski's suggestions are supported in the Labour Party because if they are adopted, the leaders of the Labour Party could [then] raise the idea of liquidating the English Communist Party. At the same time, [these suggestions] may lead to certain forms of common action for the Communist Party and the Labour Party. The Labour Party leaders also believe that the <u>potential decision by the VKP(b) would be automatically implemented by the Communist Party of England</u>.

Com. Pollitt asks [us] to advise him on this question, since a national conference of the English Communist Party will be held on 23 May.

We find this whole undertaking of Laski's to be suspect. Even if such an initiative was serious and sincere, in the current situation it is politically inappropriate and harmful.

Therefore, if we do not receive from you any instructions to the contrary, we plan to recommend to C. Pollitt that he and the CC of the CP of England do not assume any obligations toward the Labour Party in this regard, and do not submit this question for discussion in any form at their national conference on 23 May.

With fraternal greetings,

G. Dim[itrov]
(G. DIMITROV)

5 May 1942

20 May 1942, 30 July 1942, and 29 March 1943

Information about the Comintern's finances has typically been scant, although some evidence of its subsidies to foreign Communist parties came to light when the files became accessible in 1991. The Comintern's overall budget appears always to have been set by the Central Committee of the Communist Party of the Soviet Union; this included both its apparatus in Moscow and its activities abroad (including subsidies to foreign Communist parties). We can assume that during the war, funds, and especially hard foreign currency, were particularly scarce. Here Dimitrov seeks Stalin's help to support the Comintern's telegraph (news) agencies abroad, its publishing activities, travel, radio communication system, and subsidies to "illegal" foreign parties. When he received no reply, Dimitrov renewed his request two months later. The following March he submitted a new request: at the beginning of 1943 the CI had received an advance of $30,000, which had already been spent. Now he requested a monthly allocation of $25,000.

On 20 April 1943 the Secretariat of the Central Committee of the VKP(b) resolved to instruct Comrade Zverev, people's commissar of finances of the USSR, to open a credit line of $30,000 for the months of April and May 1943, for the use of the ECCI, in advance of approval of its 1943 budget.[8]

Documents 37, 38, and 39

Dimitrov to Stalin, 20 May 1942 and 30 July 1942, and Dimitrov to Stalin and others, 29 March 1943. RTsKhIDNI, f. 495, op. 73, d. 196, ll. 14, 20, 26–27. Original in Russian. Typewritten.

TO COMRADE STALIN

In 1941, 200,000 American dollars were allocated for our foreign spending.

During this period, 268,414 American dollars were spent. Using the funds of the French and Spanish Communist parties, as well as some reserve funds, we

---

8. It is idle to speculate whether the limitation to two months, through May 1943, foreshadowed thinking about terminating the Comintern altogether later that year.

managed to cover the deficit of 68,414 American dollars and to continue to cover the current expenses. However, these funds are running out, and in order to cover further expenses, a new allocation of hard currency is essential in 1942.

Before the end of this year we may need, according to approximate calculations, 355,000 American dollars, in particular:

1. For our telegraph agencies abroad (New York, Stockholm, London, Geneva, Mexico, Montevideo, Buenos Aires, Chile, etc.)	70,000 dol.
2. For publishing abroad	55,000 " "
3. For sending groups of staff workers abroad	50,000 " "
4. For communication centers abroad	70,000 " "
5. For direct support of illegal fraternal Communist parties	110,000 " "
Total	355,000 dol.

I request allocation of hard currency in the amount indicated.
With fraternal greetings,

(G. DIMITROV)

20 May 1942

TO COMRADE STALIN

Dear Comrade Stalin,

On 20 May we requested allocation of hard currency in the amount of 350,000 American dollars for 1942 in order to cover expenses related to our work abroad.

Since by now all the remaining assets of hard currency have been fully used up, we beg you to help hasten permission for hard currency being issued to us in an amount that you find appropriate, so that at least the most important work abroad is not suspended due to the lack of hard currency.

With fraternal greetings,

(G. DIMITROV)

30 July 1942

TO THE POLITBURO OF THE CC VKP(b)
To Comrade STALIN
To Comrade MOLOTOV

In order to cover the most essential hard currency expenses of the ECCI, the Secretariat is asking for a <u>monthly</u> allocation in the amount of 25,000 American dollars.

These monthly expenses are approximately as follows:

1. To maintain centers of communication abroad (including radio communications)	9,000 dol.
2. To pay for the telegraph information received from our foreign correspondents	8,000 dol.
3. To support the publication of the weekly antifascist journal	

"Die Welt" in Stockholm and of literature in the German language (for Germany, Norway, Denmark, and other countries)	4,300 dol.
4. To send the leaders of fraternal Communist parties to their countries	3,000 dol.
5. For other needs (equipment, foreign literature, etc.)	700 dol.
TOTAL	25,000 dol.

Early this year, we received an advance in the amount of 30,000 Am[erican] dollars, which we have already spent, and there is in fact a debt remaining that has to be paid off in the near future.

Therefore I entreat you to hasten the resolution of the hard currency problem for the ECCI.

GENERAL SECRETARY OF THE ECCI
(G. DIMITROV)

29 March 1943

3 December 1942

By December 1942 the tide of war was beginning to turn. American and British troops had landed in North Africa, and Germany had responded by seizing the balance of unoccupied France. The Soviet army launched a massive offensive which led, several months later, to the German catastrophe at Stalingrad. The Comintern was busy shaping and guiding the tasks of its member parties. Within two weeks of the German attack preparations began for sending several men to Poland to rebuild the Communist Party there that had been demolished on Moscow's orders (see Chapter 2). On 27 August 1941 Stalin gave Dimitrov instructions that he recorded as follows: "Better create a Workers' Party of Poland with a Com[munist] program: [Calling it] a Communist Party frightens not only the outsiders but even some of our people. At this stage the task is to struggle for national liberation."[9]

As Dimitrov developed the plan, the new workers' party was not to be formally affiliated with the Comintern (though it would of course be loyal to it). He had sent Stalin the draft program. Then the plane that was to take the Polish Communists to Poland crashed

9. TsPA (Sofia), f. 146, op. 1, a.e. 7, cited in "Iz 'Dnevnika,'" p. 78.

at the airport, so their departure was postponed from September to December.

On 5 January 1942 the new Polish Workers' Party was (illegally) established in Warsaw, headed by Marceli Nowotko. As instructed by Moscow, it began preparing for partisan warfare against the Germans. In a coded exchange with Dimitrov, Nowotko reported that summer on the party's progress, remarking that "the greatest difficulty is repressing the sectarian inclinations, especially among former members of the KPP [the prewar Communist Party of Poland], for whom every one who is not a Communist is an enemy." The Poles asked for arms, and Dimitrov arranged through the Soviet partisan headquarters to send them some captured German automatic weapons. In turn, military intelligence asked him to question the Poles about German troop deployment and transportation facilities. Dimitrov forwarded the reports to Stalin and other Soviet leaders.[10]

Dimitrov repeatedly warned the Poles to take especial care to ensure against exposure or infiltration. Nevertheless, one of the other Polish leaders, Bolesław Mołojec, radioed that on 28 November Nowotko had been seized and killed. The circumstances of his arrest and death remained obscure and controversial until on 7 January 1943, when four prominent Polish Communists, including Pawel Finder and Władysław Gomulka, informed Dimitrov in a coded message that they had decided to "liquidate" Mołojec as the man responsible for Nowotko's death, even though the evidence was circumstantial and remained somewhat clouded. The four declared themselves the new leadership of the Polish party, and after duly informing Stalin and other Soviet leaders, Dimitrov in effect accepted this action, although he questioned whether other means could not have been used to remove Mołojec.[11] Finder responded that there had been no other means and that in the meantime, Mołojec's brother had allegedly confessed to doing the killing at Bolesław's request.[12]

10. RTsKhIDNI, f. 495, op. 184, iskh. 1942, d. 3, ll. 13 and 45, and vkhod. 1942, d. 18, l. 60 and 176; and TsPA (Sofia), f. 146, op. 1, a.e. 7, cited in "Iz 'Dnevnika,'" pp. 59–60.

11. See RTsKhIDNI, f. 495, op. 184, iskh. 1942, d. 3, ll. 67 and 84; vkhod. 1942, d. 18, ll. 193, 196, 202; vkhod. 1943, d. 22, ll. 6–7; iskh. 1943, d. 3, l. 4; and TsPA (Sofia), f. 146, op. 1, a.e. 7, cited in "Iz 'Dnevnika.'"

12. See RTsKhIDNI, f. 495, op. 184, vkhod. 1943, d. 22, ll. 31, 52–53. See also

The Mołojec liquidation was by no means the only case of individual terror in the Polish underground.[13] At times Moscow was involved. Thus, on 6 August 1942, Dimitrov warned the Poles about "compromising" information he had allegedly received on Jan Izydorczyk, one of the few surviving members of the prewar Polish Communist leadership. And in 1943 the Finder party in Poland "liquidated" Leon Lukasz Lipski, a Polish Communist who in the late 1930s had protested the Comintern's dissolution of the Polish Communist Party.[14] Finder himself was arrested and killed by the Germans in November 1943.

The other major source of tension between Dimitrov and the Polish Communists concerned relations with the Polish government in exile in London and the Home Army, which was under its direction. Moscow urged the Communists in Poland to eschew such slogans as an appeal for the creation of a government of "workers and peasants" and instead to demand a truly democratic regime.

When the Germans broke the news of the Katyn massacre of Polish officers, blaming the atrocity on the Soviets, the Sikorski government in exile joined in the attacks on the Soviet government, in return for which Moscow broke off diplomatic relations. Dimitrov,

---

Jan de Weydenthal, *The Communists of Poland,* rev. ed. (Stanford: Hoover Institution Press, 1986), pp. 36–42; and Marjan Malinowski, *Geneza PPR* (Warsaw: Książka i Wiedza, 1972).

13. The name of one Bronisław [*sic*] Mołojec appears in other Comintern records. His wife, Romana Szyker, renounced him in November 1938 after she learned—erroneously—that he had perished while under arrest. In fact, he is allegedly one of eleven (out of 132 foreign Communists arrested) who was recruited by the NKVD and survived. See Arkadi Vaksberg, *Hôtel Lux* (Paris: Fayard, 1993), pp. 103–4. For some tantalizing details on the Nowotko-Mołojec affair, see also interview with Jakub Berman, in Teresa Torańska, *"Them"* (New York: Harper and Row, 1987), pp. 216 ff.

14. For Izydorczyk, see RTsKhIDNI, f. 495, op. 184, iskh. 1942, d. 3, l. 26. Leon Lipski had studied at the Lenin School in Moscow, worked for the Profintern, and apparently sought to reestablish the Polish Communist Party after its dissolution by the Comintern. Charged with having been an agent-provocateur, he was arrested by the NKVD in Bialystok in 1940. Evidently he formed a Communist group that was insubordinate to Moscow. In June 1943 the Polish Workers' Party leadership informed Moscow that he was heading up diversionary activities and soon afterward reported that it had "decided to liquidate" Lukasz Lipski and that "the decision has already been carried out" (Dimitrov to Stalin, Molotov, Shcherbakov, and Merkulov, 9 July 1943, in RTsKhIDNI, f. 495, op. 184, vkhod. 1943, d. 22, l. 333). Both Lipski's brothers, active Communists, had been liquidated in the Soviet Union before the war.

keeping Stalin informed, urged the Polish Communists to mount a massive propaganda campaign in defense of the Soviets and against the Nazi charges.[15]

Dimitrov and his staff maintained similarly active contact, by encrypted messages, with other Communist parties abroad, notably the French, Belgian, and Dutch, as well as with the Bulgarian and Finnish comrades. Even more than previously, these exchanges concerned questions relating to the anti-German resistance movement; in many instances, they were closely coordinated with Soviet military intelligence. Still, broader political questions were also part of the agenda, as is illustrated by the following document.

A commission consisting of "Ercoli" (Palmiro Togliatti), Maurice Thorez, André Marty, Dmitry Manuilsky, and Dimitrov produced a set of directives for the French and Italian Communists which were adopted by the ECCI Secretariat on 1 December 1942. Two days later Dimitrov sent them to Stalin, who approved them on 5 December.

Document 40

Dimitrov to Stalin, 3 December 1942, with enclosures. Letter: RTsKhIDNI, f. 495, op. 74, d. 528, l. 1; enclosures: ll. 3–10. Original in Russian. Typewritten.

TO COMRADE STALIN

I am sending you two documents regarding the line and the immediate tasks of the Communist Party of France and the Communist Party of Italy relevant to the new situation created by the events in North Africa and in France, and by the offensive of the Red Army against the German-fascist hordes.

The documents were drafted in conjunction with Cc. Thorez, Marty, and Ercoli.

15. See RTsKhIDNI, f.495, op. 184, iskh. 1943, d. 9, ll. 47–46, 62, 64, 66–65, and vkhod. 1943, d. 22, l. 289; see also "Perepiska General'nogo sekretarya IKKI G. M. Dimitrova s rukovodstvom Pol'skoi rabochei partii (1942–1943)," in *Novaya i noveishaya istoriya*, 1964, no. 5, p. 122. Not until fifty years later did Moscow finally admit Soviet responsibility for the execution of more than 10,000 Polish army officers at Katyn. For the Soviet documents from the Presidential Archive, officially transmitted to Poland in 1992, see *Katyn: Dokumenty ludobojstwa. Dokumenty i materiały archiwalne przekazane Polsce 14 pazdziernika 1992 r.* (Warsaw, 1992) [English ed., *Katyn* (Warsaw: Institute of Political Studies, 1993)].

Document 40 *continued*

It would be very helpful for our work if you could find the time to receive me regarding these and some other questions, which I beg you to do.

If, however, this is impossible due to the extreme lack of time on your part, I request your directives concerning whether and what changes are needed in these documents, so that we can consider them before the actual implementation of the outlined course and the immediate tasks of both Communist parties.

With fraternal greetings,

(G. DIMITROV)

3 December 1942

I. The new situation in France and the outlook

1. The landing of the Americans in North Africa, the occupation of all of France by German troops, the heroic act of the officers and sailors of the Toulon fleet, who blew up their ships to forestall capture by Hitler, all this has created a new situation in France, the main elements of which are the following:

a) the violation of the armistice by Hitler, his banditlike occupation of the entire country, the unbridled pillage in the formerly unoccupied zone;

b) the failure of the so-called policy of collaboration, the bankruptcy of the Vichy regime, the disintegration of the Vichy gang;

c) the increase in popular hatred of the occupiers and traitors, the broadening of the base of the national front of struggle for the liberation of France;

d) the opportunity to organize a new French anti-Hitler army;

e) France as the most proximate theater of military operations against Hitler Germany, that is, the early prospect of the rebellion of the French people in connection with the growing tensions inside the country and with the opening of a second front in Europe.

2. This new situation in France, in connection with the turn in the war (the offensive of the Soviet troops at Stalingrad and on the central part of the Soviet-German front, the African campaign, and the taking of the initiative by the Allies) opens extremely favorable prospects for a quick solution of the basic task of the French people—liberating France from the occupiers.

II. Concrete tasks

1. First of all, it is essential to strengthen the national front and attract all the French who want to struggle against Hitler in earnest, regardless of former political and other disagreements. The sacrifice of the Toulon officers, who went down with their ships, clearly demonstrates that even people who until the very last moment were under the influence of Vichy can participate in the national front of struggle against the Hitlerite occupiers. Only obvious traitors exclude themselves from the national front —Laval, Doriot, Déat, and their accomplices, who must all be exterminated.

The Communist Party must strive to unite all the national forces and to organize them through various committees of the national front. For this purpose, the Communist Party must cooperate with de Gaulle and his supporters and support the other elements in France and North Africa that are joining the struggle against Hitler.

2. Simultaneously, the party must work to create a leadership in North Africa that would be capable of organizing immediate military actions with the Allies to defeat the Italian-German forces in Bizerte, Tunis, et al.

The Communist Party supports all the efforts and measures aimed at using North Africa as a base for the creation of a genuine national French army that will serve the cause of liberating France.

In North Africa, the Communist Party demands: the restoration of democratic liberties, the liberation of the incarcerated patriots and antifascists, a purge of the army, police, and organs of administration of all the remnants of the fifth column, the disarming and disbanding of Hitlerite groups (Doriotists, the Laval legion, etc.) and the arrest of their leaders.

The Communist Party also demands equal rights for all those living in the Maghreb—Arabs, Berbers, and French—without regard for color or race, since these measures will provoke enthusiasm among the people and will secure true mobilization of all the resources of French Africa for the war against Hitler.

3. It is essential to approach the task of the actual preparation of the popular uprising to liberate France from a new angle, not as mere propaganda but as a practical task: to ceaselessly disorganize the forces of the enemy, which are weakened by their dispersal throughout the entire territory of the country; to disorganize the lines of transportation of the occupiers, raiding Hitlerite stocks and columns, engaging in sabotage, organizing subversive acts, disrupting the system of requisitions and the transfer of workers to Germany, organizing strikes and demonstrations and various other military actions, in particular, stepping up the partisan movement against the occupiers. All these activities will weaken, demoralize, and disintegrate the occupation troops, will raise the fighting capacity of the masses, will raise their readiness for sacrifice, will hasten and secure the general uprising for the liberation of France.

4. In the course of [this] struggle, it is essential to organize the francs-tireurs [partisans], to create new units of francs-tireurs which, being connected with one another, will form the nucleus of a new national army in France; to organize the arming of the patriots—de Gaullists, Communists, and other antifascists—by capturing arms from the enemy; to involve veterans, officers, and petty officers who are ready to follow the example of Toulon in partisan units, in order to improve the military education of the partisans.

It is important to capitalize on the forced demobilization of the French army in Toulon and other parts of formerly unoccupied France. [It is necessary to ensure] that patriotic soldiers and officers come over to the ranks of francs-tireurs with their weapons, organize military actions against the occupiers and the traitors of Vichy, and take actions to liberate soldiers, officers, and hostages arrested by the Germans.

5. [It is important] to energetically demand that the officers and sailors of the Alexandrian and Antillan fleets, who have been aroused by the drama of Toulon, place their ships in the service of the liberation of France.

6. The tasks that the new situation is presenting to the working class and the people of France, in particular, the preparation of the popular rebellion, can be assured by the strengthening of the party, of its iron discipline and fighting spirit, of its capacity to struggle and lead while protecting itself from the provocations of the enemy, of its varied ties to the masses in the city and countryside, at enterprises, in the army, in partisan units, [among] young people, women, etc.

7. These propositions must serve for the orientation of the leadership of the Communist Party and for the radio transmissions of "Radio France."

1 December 1942

Situation in Italy and the Immediate Tasks of the Italian Communist Party

1. The defeat of the Italo-German armies in Africa, the Anglo-American offensive in the Mediterranean area, and the offensive of the Red Army have created an entirely new situation for Italy. The question of Italy quitting the war becomes real and concrete. Italy has already partially become a theater of military operations (bombing) and is facing the possibility of military operations on Italian territory in connection with the opening of the second front in Europe. The Italian people are facing a question of life or death. To continue the war makes no sense for Italy, since it means total destruction, devastation of the country, unprecedented disaster. The task of everyone who wants to save the country is to take Italy out of the war as soon as possible.

2. The main obstacle to quitting the war for Italy is the Mussolini government, which, having made the country Hitler's vassal, is now turning it into a defensive bulwark of Hitler Germany. To overthrow the Mussolini government is the concrete and immediate task not only of the antifascist forces but also of all those who reject the fascist policy of war, [the task] of the entire people. The government Italy needs is a government of peace, a government which, supported by the people, is capable of taking necessary and urgent steps to cease military operations and to conclude a peace in order to save the country from economic destruction and famine, and to restore popular liberties, which are the necessary condition for the participation of the masses in saving the country from the catastrophe. The overthrow of the Mussolini government and the creation of a government of peace can result only from a popular uprising against fascist tyranny for freedom and peace. That is the goal of all the existing oppositional forces, and this goal must be kept in mind in determining concrete and urgent tasks.

3. These tasks can be reduced to the following:

a) The further rebuilding and strengthening of Communist Party organizations in all regions and, most important, in the large industrial centers, their expansion and transformation into genuine fighting organizations linked to the masses, remains the first and major task.

b) It is important to strengthen the already existing bloc of the leftist antifascist forces (Communists, socialists, democrats), by reforming it into a permanent organization (joint committees of action) in the center, in the city, in the countryside, at the enterprises.

c) In order to hasten the rapprochement of all the forces opposing the military policy of Mussolini (left antifascists, Catholics, monarchists, oppositional fascists), to coordinate their efforts and to organize a common action of the entire people to expel the Mussolini government, to end the war, and to establish peace, it is essential to conduct intensive work to create a national front relying on a network of committees of action, which should be organized throughout the population and especially among workers and peasants, in the army, in the navy, in fascist organizations, in the state apparatus, etc. The task of the committees of action of the national front is to organize and lead the people in the active struggle against the Mussolini regime and its military plans, [to organize and lead the people] to mass sabotage and to the creation of partisan units to conduct military operations against the Hitlerites and the fascist militia, aiming at an uprising to overthrow the fascist government.

4. As a political platform for which the national front must struggle, the following measures should be proposed:

• immediately to rupture the military alliance with Hitler; to recall all the Italian troops from the USSR, the Balkans, and France; to cease military operations in Africa and propose an armistice with the Anglo-American armies; to open peace negotiations with the powers of the Anglo-Soviet-American coalition;

• to discontinue all food supplies to the Germans; to abolish wartime taxes; [to introduce] freedom of trade for peasants; to requisition food stocks hidden by large speculators; to confiscate excessive war profits and the property of Germans and their agents;

• to reestablish constitutional freedoms: freedom of the press, unions, religion; to abolish racist laws; to liberate all the citizens incarcerated because of their struggle against fascist tyranny and against the war;

• to disband the fascist militia, to purge the army and the state apparatus of the cabal that led the country to bankruptcy and to vassal dependency on the foreigner; to prosecute those responsible for the military defeats and the economic devastation of the country;

• to create conditions that will let the people take the fate of their country into their own hands and create a free Italy.

5. In order to facilitate the overthrow of the Mussolini war government by accelerated preparation for the popular uprising against the fascist tyranny, it is necessary, in particular, to pay attention to the following tasks:

a) disorganization and liquidation of the positions that Hitlerite Germany now holds in Italy, which permit it to control the country and manipulate it. This must be achieved by means of mass sabotage of the military, economic, and political machine of the Germans (airports, coastal defenses, barracks, police, economic control, etc.), as well as through the appropriate work among the German soldiers;

b) disorganization of the fascist camp, since the majority of the elements who until now were blindly following the Mussolini government can and must be attracted to the struggle to save the country from catastrophe.

c) It is impossible to overthrow Mussolini without the active participation of a part of the army. In view of this, it is important to establish an organizational tie between the army and the forces of popular opposition. Within the army itself, a broad movement must be organized to support a rift with Germany and peace, to sabotage the military plans of Mussolini, to urge disobedience to the fascist government, to create a government of peace.

1 December 1942

CHAPTER SEVEN

Yugoslavia in World War II

WITH THE COMINTERN'S BLESSINGS, Josip Broz Tito had been made general secretary of the Communist Party of Yugoslavia (CPY) in 1937 after the purge of his predecessor Milan Gorkić. Under the pseudonym "Walter," he had been active in the Balkans and western Europe for some years. He had returned to Yugoslavia, illegally, well before the war, but the Communist movement there had remained without broad support. In fact, when the German army occupied Yugoslavia in April 1941, the Yugoslav Communists took an overtly anti-Nazi position at a time when Moscow was still at peace with Germany and was insisting that relations between the two powers were good.[1] After the German attack on the Soviet Union, contacts between the Yugoslav Communists and the Soviet authorities became sporadic and were initially limited to brief radio messages handled by the Comintern's Code Section. For all intents and purposes, the CPY and its partisans were functioning on their own.

1. On the other hand, Dimitrov, after consulting Molotov, advised Tito on 30 March to refrain from public demonstrations and clashes with the authorities (RTsKhIDNI, f. 495, op. 74, d. 599, l. 8; and op. 184, vkhod. 1941, d. 7, l. 82). For Tito's report to the Comintern on conditions in Yugoslavia in May 1941, see Tito, *Vojna djela* (Beograd: Vojno delo, 1961), vol. 1, pp. 11–20.

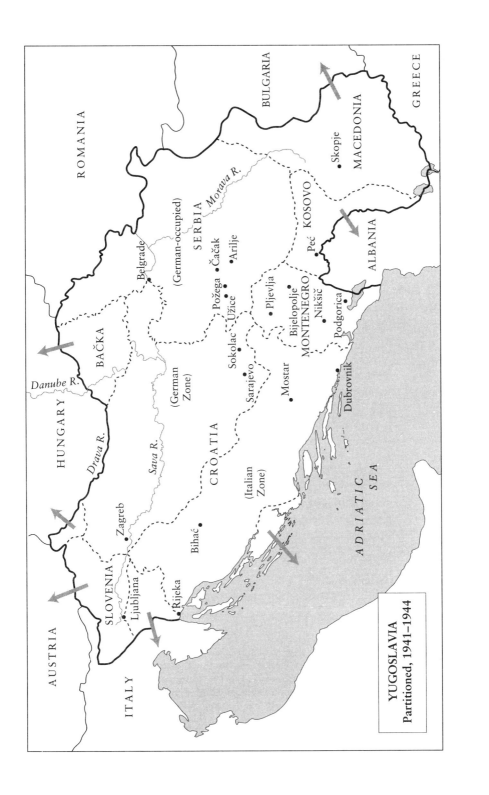

YUGOSLAVIA
Partitioned, 1941–1944

Under German and Italian occupation, Yugoslavia was carved up: Croatia was declared an independent state under Ante Pavelić; Hungary, Albania (itself occupied by Italy in 1939), Bulgaria, and Germany (Austria) each received territory adjoining their own lands; Montenegro was occupied by Italy, which annexed much of the Dalmatian coast; and German-occupied Serbia was placed under a puppet regime headed by Milan Nedić.

On 7 July 1941 a Serbian partisan unit began an armed uprising against the occupiers on a local scale. On 13 July fighting broke out in Montenegro. On 4 August the Central Committee of the Communist Party of Yugoslavia (or a group acting in its name) radioed Dimitrov, "Numerous partisan detachments are active in the country in accordance with the plan of the CPY. Their basic task is to destroy transportation, military objects, and military supplies and to spread panic among the enemy. Railroads and telegraph and telephone networks are constantly being destroyed. The partisan detachments have annihilated two battalions of Croatian troops and have shot down three German planes. The party has successfully organized an uprising in Montenegro. All the towns are in our hands." Though he may have suspected some exaggeration, Dimitrov ordered copies of this message distributed to Stalin, Molotov, Malenkov, Beria, and Zhukov.[2]

It is striking how little the Soviet leadership appears to have known either about the partisans, Communist and otherwise, or about Tito (or rather the pseudonymous "Walter"), even though he had worked at the ECCI in Moscow, been a delegate to the Seventh Comintern Congress, been appointed CPY general secretary with Moscow's full approval, and returned to Yugoslavia with the knowledge of the Comintern.[3]

Indeed, the situation soon proved to be a complex one, with rival

2. RTsKhIDNI, f. 495, op. 184, vkhod. 1941, d. 7, ll. 149, 150, 153.

3. In reply to a request from Dimitrov dated 13 December 1941, the partisans wired Moscow biographical information on Tito and other leaders of the partisan movement. On 27 February 1942 Dimitrov forwarded this and other data in the files of the ECCI Cadre Section to Stalin and Molotov (RTsKhIDNI, f. 495, op. 184, vkhod. 1942, d. 4, l. 135; op. 74, d. 555, ll. 1–5). On 8 May he forwarded further information on the partisan commanders (RTsKhIDNI, f. 495, op. 184, d. 4, l. 2); and as late as 22 November 1943 he sent Stalin, Molotov, and Shcherbakov detailed biographical information on Tito (RTsKhIDNI, f. 495, op. 74, d. 603, ll. 3–8).

fighting units—not always under the disciplined command of their nominal leaders—and diverse priorities and loyalties. The major outside powers on the Allied side, Great Britain and the Soviet Union, were each torn between at least two conflicting courses of action for occupied Yugoslavia.[4] Tito, as a loyal Communist and as (he hoped) a matter of self-interest, sought to keep in touch with the Comintern, originally by means of a secret radio installation. It soon became apparent that there were significant differences in perception between Moscow and the Yugoslav partisans.

12 September 1941

An early problem arose as a consequence of a message received on 31 July in which Tito asked Dimitrov: "Will you be able to send to Serbia by airplane from the USSR arms, ammunition, and several military specialists? If the answer is yes, we will inform you of location and security of landing." The partisans were at the time in difficult straits. Dimitrov promptly sent copies of this message to Stalin, Molotov, Malenkov, Beria, and Zhukov, after replacing "Walter's" signature with "Central Committee of the CP of Yugoslavia."[5] On 1 August he sent Tito an acknowledgment, saying that the Soviets were exploring the feasibility of complying with Tito's request and promising an early response.[6]

Tito's request came when the USSR was suffering massive defeats, and the Soviet leaders had no sympathy for diverting even small amounts of scarce resources from their own struggle. On 8 September, Dimitrov spoke to Molotov about Tito's request and received the decision, "This is now impossible. We have tremendous needs ourselves. There are great losses to be made up." But Dimitrov was clearly not satisfied. On 12 September he met with Major General Panfilov, of the Intelligence Section of the Red Army General Staff, who thought it would be possible to fly a Douglas aircraft with arms and military supplies to Yugoslavia. After this con-

---

4. Perhaps the best overall account of the issues involved, well informed and balanced in its judgments, is Walter R. Roberts, *Tito, Mihailović and the Allies, 1941–1945* (New Brunswick, N.J.: Rutgers University Press, 1973).

5. RTsKhIDNI, f. 495, op. 184, vkhod. 1941, d. 7, l. 149.

6. RTsKhIDNI, f. 495, op. 184, iskh. 1941, d. 11, l. 61.

versation Dimitrov—an ardent advocate of the partisans—sent Stalin the letter printed below. Evidently his request was turned down, and on 26 September he regretfully informed Tito, "For now it is technically impossible to organize the supply of arms. Use all possible means to supply yourselves within the country."[7]

It is curious that Dimitrov early on emerged as an advocate of the Yugoslav partisans—partly, one may surmise, because they were fellow southern Slavs, in part because they were the only force in Nazi-occupied Europe actually waging a fight, and also, perhaps, because "Walter" had been his man earlier on. Indeed, Dimitrov's (by no means uncritical) advocacy of the Yugoslav cause represents one of the few instances in which even in his dealings with Stalin and Molotov, he shed the cloak of neutral bureaucratic objectivity he otherwise liked to don.

Document 41

Dimitrov to Stalin, 12 September 1941. RTsKhIDNI, f. 495, op. 74, d. 599, ll. 10–11. Original in Russian. Typewritten.

<u>Top secret</u>
<u>Personal</u>
TO COMRADE STALIN

Several days ago, the CC of the Communist Party of Yugoslavia informed us that the partisan movement in Serbia increasingly takes the form of a popular uprising. The Germans are holding only the large cities. The partisans are creating popular committees as the organs of power. The major hindrance to the popular uprising is the lack of arms. Capturing arms from the Germans and gendarmes is a slow process. The CC is asking for help with arms from here. If this is possible, the CC will inform us where and when to drop them.

The question evidently concerns a rather small amount of arms, which would be dropped from a plane.

As far as I could find out, it is actually entirely possible to drop, from a Douglas plane in an indicated location, 150–200 machine guns, 500 revolvers, and a certain number of cartridges, grenades, and explosives.

If this were done, it could help our Serb comrades to at least disrupt more successfully the German lines of transportation between Zagreb, Belgrade,

7. RTsKhIDNI, f. 495, op. 184, iskh. 1941, d. 8, l. 81.

Document 41 *continued*

and Sofia during the transfer of troops and war matériel toward the Bulgarian ports on the Black Sea and to the Turkish border, as well as communications between Salonika, Serbian Macedonia, and Belgrade. It will help them capture arms from the local stocks for the partisan units.

Assuming that such a small amount of arms could be allocated despite the tremendous needs of our front, I request your positive decision on this question.

With fraternal greetings,

(G. DIMITROV)

12 September 1941

---

1 December 1941

On 4 October, Colonel Dragun, acting head of Section 5 of General Staff Intelligence (*Razvedupravlenie*), directed a letter to the ECCI, requesting that "Comrade Walter be asked about convenient and secure landing places for airplanes and for dropping parachutists at the end of October or early November 1941." The ECCI dragged its feet; it wasn't until 4 November that Dimitrov radioed "Walter": "Between 15 and 20 November a plane will be sent to you with people and some matériel. Inform us where to drop people and equipment and land the plane. Take measures for reliable reception. We are awaiting urgent reply." The coded message cited below, ostensibly received from Yugoslavia on 1 December, actually came from two telegrams: the first paragraph was in a telegram of 27 October (received or decoded 15 November), the second was received and decoded on 1 December.[8] Deciphering was evidently handled rather imperfectly by the ECCI section evacuated to Ufa. As best we can tell, the drop never took place.

8. RTsKhIDNI, f. 495, op. 184, vkhod. 1941, d. 7, ll. 198, 199.

Document 42

Dimitrov to Stalin, Molotov, and Beria, 1 December 1941. RTsKhIDNI, f. 495, op. 73, d. 112, l. 29. Original in Russian. Typewritten.

To Comrades STALIN, MOLOTOV, BERIA

On 1 December 1941 we received the following coded telegram from Yugoslavia:

"TO DIMITROV. In the liberated territory of Yugoslaviá we have three good airfields and about three million liters of gasoline. The first airfield is at Arilje near Užice. The second in Užitka Požega. The third is Sokolac in Bosnia near Sarajevo and Zvornik, 40 kilometers from Sarajevo toward Vlasenica.

"The Užitka Požega airfield is prepared for landing airplanes. At night, there is a lighted T sign and three large lights in the mountains. During the day, a red star, if there is snow, otherwise a white star.

"Arilje and Sokolac airfields are for landing people and matériel. When your planes fire two red rockets and one green, our response will be the same.

"We urgently ask you to send automatic weapons and ammunition, or we will not be able to hold out much longer.

"FOR THE PARTISAN HEADQUARTERS—WALTER."

(Secretary of the CP of Yugoslavia)

6 and 17 December 1941

A more serious political issue concerned the nature of the Serb Chetnik organization led by Colonel Dragoljub (Draža) Mihailović and Tito's relations with it. There were different Chetnik groups, but gradually the Mihailović staff assumed central command. They were easily recognized by the Yugoslav government in exile in London as "their" army in the homeland, and the colonel was made commander-in-chief. In fact his position was difficult, as was the strategy he pursued. In brief, while the raison d'être of his force was to fight the occupants, actually Mihailović soon became primarily concerned with his domestic rivals—and above all, of course, Tito's partisans. It took some time for the British, who who helped support him, to realize that he was scarcely fighting the Germans; that he—or more demonstrably, his subordinates—was prepared to make deals with the occupying Italian forces; and that his central concern was keeping the Communists from gaining control of the country by the end of the war, which he trusted the Allies would win.[9]

Initially, Moscow appeared somewhat ignorant of political conditions in Yugoslavia, and both the Kremlin's and the Comintern's instinct in the situation, as elsewhere in the periods of broad "antifascist" alliances, was to advocate (or better, order) close cooperation with other, non-Communist antifascist forces. That meant a Tito-Mihailović alliance (not unlike the one between Mao Zedong and Chiang Kai-shek that the Comintern had advocated in China). From the outset Tito was suspicious of the idea, though he met with Mihailović at least twice in 1941. On 21 November and again on 28 November, Dimitrov asked Tito about the Chetniks and Mihailović ("What measures are you taking to create a united leadership of the movement against the occupants?").[10] Tito's reply is the message cited in the following document. Apparently, the ECCI had not managed to decode part of Tito's message. It was deciphered on 17 December and promptly sent ahead.

Document 43

Dimitrov to Stalin and Molotov, 6 December 1941, and Dimitrov to Stalin, Molotov, Beria, and Malenkov, 17 December 1941. Letter of 6 December: RTsKhIDNI, f. 495, op. 74, d. 599, l. 13; of 17 December: l. 15; op. 184, vkhod. 1941, d. 7, l. 202. Original in Russian. Typewritten.

To Cc. STALIN, MOLOTOV

In reply to my inquiry regarding the relations between the headquarters of the partisans and the leader of the Chetniks, Colonel Mihailović, I received the following coded telegram from the CC CP of Yugoslavia, dated 2 December 1941:

"Your information about Colonel Mihailović as a liberator is false. With our consent, he organized the Chetniks on the territory liberated by us, but on 1 November, he stabbed us in the back by turning them against us."

DIMITROV

6.XII.41.

9. On the Chetniks, see also Jozo Tomasevich, *The Chetniks* (Stanford: Stanford University Press, 1975).

10. RTsKhIDNI, f. 495, op. 184, iskh. 1941, d. 11, l. 101.

Document 43 *continued*

To Cc. STALIN, MOLOTOV, BERIA, MALENKOV

I forward a coded telegram received from Walter from Yugoslavia, dated 4.12.41.[11]

"We possess all the documents relevant to the Mihailović treason. Our attempts to persuade him to struggle against the Germans failed. When he attacked us from behind, we smashed his units. He retains only gendarmes and policemen who are severely terrorizing the partisans and their families. We have to struggle against the occupiers and various Chetniks in Serbia and against the Ustashes in Croatia. Our partisan troops (more than 100 thousand) have been defeating all the enemies. Our military factory in Užice already has a lot of raw material; nevertheless, we have not been able to start the necessary production. We urgently need your help."

(DIMITROV)

17.12.41.

15 January 1942

On 12 January, Tito sent Dimitrov the following message, which was received three days later and promptly forwarded to Stalin and other Soviet leaders.[12] It is not clear what previous understanding with Mihailović Tito is referring to, since he had earlier told Moscow that Mihailović had betrayed him and the Chetniks were fighting the partisans, but they had been all but annihilated. Nedić headed the Serbian puppet government set up by the Germans.

11. Tito's original telegram had been dated 2 December, but the decoded telegram was dated 4 December.
12. Molotov, Voroshilov, Beria, Malenkov, Shcherbakov, and Andreyev.

Document 44

Dimitrov to Stalin and others, 15 January 1942. RTsKhIDNI, f. 495, op. 184, vkhod. 1942, d. 4, l. 4. Original in Russian. Typewritten.

In accordance with the resolution of C. Dimitrov
[the telegram] was forwarded through Sazonov
to Cc. Stalin, Molotov, Voroshilov, Beria, Malenkov, Shcherbakov, Andreyev

No. 9
12 January 1942
15 January 1942
In[coming] no. 32
Sp[ecial] nos. 8–12.
TO DIMITROV

Last October, an Anglo-Yugoslav mission, composed of the English Captain Hudson and the Yugoslav Majors Lalatović and Ostoić with a radio transmitter, was transported by submarine to Montenegro on their way to Mihailović. Immediately after their arrival, Mihailović started to systematically break our old agreement and prepare an open attack on us. On behalf of the British government, Captain Hudson demanded in November that we disband the partisans and unconditionally submit ourselves to the leadership of Mihailović. Hudson declared that the English government would demand that the USSR government make us fulfill the demand of the English.

On 1 November, Mihailović withdrew his units from the front and attacked our troops from the rear. Within 15 days we defeated Mihailović; he capitulated and agreed to cease hostilities between us. We have documents about the contacts of Mihailović and Nedić. Mihailović's aide, Major Dangić, made several trips to Belgrade to negotiate with Nedić. In December, Dangić entered into an alliance with Nedić to fight against us in Bosnia; Nedić was supposed to supply them with arms.

A radio operator for the English mission, Dravićević, defected to our side and gave us a number of secret telegrams from the English government that demonstrate that the directives from London are not aimed at supporting the people's liberation war.

WALTER

We suggested to Walter that he turn over texts of the secret telegrams from the English government to us.

5 and 6 March 1942

On 4 March, Dimitrov received a message from Tito reporting that a second proletarian brigade had been created and had already begun to fight the Italians and the Chetniks. The next day Dimitrov sent Tito the following message, with copies to Stalin and other Soviet leaders.

Document 45

Dimitrov to Stalin and others, 5 and 6 March 1942. RTsKhIDNI, f. 495, op. 184, vkhod. 1942, d. 5, l. 302. Original in Russian. Typewritten.

To Cc. STALIN, MOLOTOV, BERIA, SHCHERBAKOV[13]

On 5 December 1941, the Serb fascist newspaper "Novo Vreme," [published] in Belgrade, printed the following: "The English have invented a front on the western Morava River and claimed Draža Mihailović as commander-in-chief of the Yugoslav units, despite the fact that everybody knows that in the western Morava River Valley, particularly in the towns of Čačak and Užice, there are two Communist strongholds and that the people of Draža Mihailović, feeling their Serb national duty, have adhered to the government of General Nedić and his units fighting against the Communists."

This information refers to General Mihailović, praised by the English and appointed by the Yugoslav government in London as war minister of Yugoslavia. It confirms the information sent to us by the Yugoslav comrades about the traitorous role of Mihailović's Chetniks.

DIMITROV

* * *

Top secret
Copy no. *8*
In[coming] no. *294*
Spec[ial] no. *41–44*

Decoded telegram[14]

In connection with the latest news from Yugoslavia, we sent Walter the following telegram:

---

13. In the margin, handwritten by Dimitrov:
Send via Sazonov. 5.3.42. GD.
14. In the upper left corner, a stamp:
Making copies prohibited. To be returned to the ShO ECCI [*Shifroval'nyi otdel*: Encryption Department—Trans.]. From Ufa. 6 March 1942.

Document 45 *continued*

"A review of your information gives the impression that you yourself, by some of your actions, give reason for the supporters of England and the Yugoslav government to suspect that the partisan movement is acquiring a Communist character and is aiming at the Sovietization of Yugoslavia. For example, why was it necessary to form a special proletarian brigade? Today the main task is to unite all the anti-Hitler elements in order to defeat the occupiers and to achieve national liberation. How to explain the fact that England's supporters manage to create armed units against the partisan forces? Is it really the case that, besides Communists and [their] sympathizers, there are no other Yugoslav patriots with whom you could fight jointly against the occupiers? It is hard to imagine that London and the Yugoslav government support the occupiers. There must be a big misunderstanding. We are asking you to seriously review your tactics and activities, to check whether you, on your side, are doing everything possible to create a genuine unified national front of all the enemies of Hitler and Mussolini in Yugoslavia to accomplish the main task—expelling impudent occupiers and enslavers from your country—and if not, take urgent measures and inform us."

Dimitrov

Printed 8 copies.
1 and 2—to C. Stalin
3—to C. Molotov
4—to C. Voroshilov
5—to C. Beria
6—to C. Malenkov
7—to C. Andreyev
8—to C. Shcherbakov

28 April 1942

In less than two months Dimitrov had changed his tune with regard to the Tito-Mihailović relationship. Now he was emboldened to raise a more fundamental policy question with Stalin. Until now Dimitrov, and evidently also Stalin (and therefore Molotov), had favored a united-front policy in Yugoslavia. There had been some concern when Tito reported that the Chetniks had attacked the partisans from the rear on 1 November 1941. Later that month the British, at the request of the Yugoslav government in London, had sought Soviet help to convince Tito to accept Mihailović as commander-in-chief; a similar request was made by the Chetniks in the field. Tito indignantly refused. In the following months it became apparent that no deal between the two forces was possible. As Dimitrov reported to Stalin, Tito had evidently provided enough "documentary" proof (in fact, some of his assertions proved to be vast exaggerations) to persuade first Dimitrov and then his Soviet masters to change their minds.[15]

Document 46

Dimitrov to Stalin, 28 April 1942. RTsKhIDNI, f. 495, op. 74, d. 595, ll. 20–21. Original in Russian. Typewritten.

Top secret
TO COMRADE STALIN
Dear Comrade Stalin,

According to information from reliable sources in Yugoslavia, there are great opportunities to develop the partisan movement into a genuine popular war against the occupiers. Using these possibilities might lead to rather significant results from the point of view of the common struggle against Hitler Germany. First, it would tie up some important German and Italian armed forces from other fronts; second, it would create another serious obstacle in the attempts of Tsar Boris to send the Bulgarian army to our front; third, it would help the Turks offer stronger resistance to Hitler.

In the meantime, one of the major obstacles that hinders the stepping up of the partisan war in Yugoslavia is clearly the behavior of the English and the Yugoslav government in London. They probably do not like the fact that the bulk of the partisan forces are under the leadership of pro-Soviet elements and not English agents. That is why they not only fail to support the partisan war in Yugoslavia but hinder it by all possible means. They promote Colonel Draža Mihailović in the press and on the radio as leader of the partisan army, while in fact insignificant and corrupt units of this Mihailović meanly attack units of the partisan army from the back who are struggling against the enemy. They

15. Although it was some time before Moscow publicly attacked the Chetniks and praised the partisans, in March 1942 one of Dimitrov's key assistants, Boris Ponomarev, published an article in *Pravda* and another (under the pseudonym "B. Voinich") in the Comintern journal, stressing that it was possible to wage partisan warfare behind the German lines because of close ties to the local population (B. Voinich, "Boyevoi primer Yugoslavii," *Kommunisticheskii Internatsional*, 1942, nos. 3–4, pp. 25–35, and B. Ponomarev, "Yugoslaviya v ogne partizanskoi voiny," *Pravda*, 23 March 1942).

Document 46 *continued*

wage no war against the occupiers and their Nedićevite flunkies. The general headquarters of the partisan army, on the basis of captured original documents, even accuses Mihailović of acting together with Nedić and the Italians against the Yugoslav partisans.

Due to the importance of this part of the common front against the fascist armies, which could become a significant part of the so-called second front, I think that it is important to take possible measures to clarify the question of the attitude of the English and the Yugoslav government toward the partisan war in Yugoslavia and to strive to eliminate the existing obstacles on their side.

I also beg you to receive me in order to get your advice and directives regarding the behavior of our Yugoslav comrades, who are playing an outstanding role in the General Staff of the partisan army, given the current situation in Yugoslavia.

With fraternal greetings,

(G. DIMITROV)

28 April 1942

There is no evidence that Stalin did in fact receive Dimitrov, as he requested, but Dimitrov evidently consulted someone—probably Molotov—about Yugoslav policy.

4 June 1942

Two issues continued to dominate relations between Moscow and the Yugoslav partisans: the partisans' demand for Soviet arms and ammunition, and their increasingly bitter conflict with the Chetniks. On 24 May, Dimitrov received a message from Tito reporting that the situation in Montenegro had become critical: both the Italian troops and Mihailović's Chetniks were attacking the partisans. Speaking of the exhaustion of his men and the lack of ammunition, Tito claimed, "The whole people curse the Yugoslav government in London, which helps the occupants through Draža Mihailović. On all sides I am asked by fighters and people, 'Why does the Soviet Union not send us help, at least some automatic weapons?'" Tito requested that Moscow try to pressure the government in exile, "Can something not be done in London against such a treacherous policy of the Yugoslav government?" On 31 May, Tito again reported to Dimitrov, "All the Chetniks in Yugoslavia, and especially

Draža Mihailović, are fighting with the occupiers against our people's liberation forces. . . . We are profoundly convinced that the Yugoslav government in London is also complicitous in this. . . . A few days ago we issued an appeal against the Chetniks and the Yugoslav government in London. . . . Please give us your opinion."[16]

Dimitrov sent Tito the two messages enclosed with his letter to Stalin, whom he in turn sought to persuade that some action was called for. It seems clear that Dimitrov's advice to Tito followed a high-level decision in Moscow, probably Molotov's.

Document 47

Dimitrov to Stalin and Molotov, 4 June 1942, with enclosures. RTsKhIDNI, f. 495, op. 74, d. 595, l. 22; enclosures in op. 74, d. 595, ll. 23–25. Original in Russian. Typewritten.

TO COMRADE STALIN
TO COMRADE MOLOTOV
In response to C. Walter's recent telegrams from Yugoslavia, we have sent him the two enclosed telegrams.

The question of the attitude of the Yugoslav government in London toward the partisan war in Yugoslavia remains unclear and unsettled. In the meantime, the so-called Chetniks of Draža Mihailović, along with the Nedić puppet government and the occupiers, are waging battles against the units of the people's liberation partisan army with open support from London.

I would think that since the Yugoslav government and the British have a treaty with us about struggling against fascist Germany, we ought to find an opportunity to indicate to them, in an appropriate form and in the interest of our common cause, the inadmissibility of such behavior and the necessity of securing a satisfactory settlement in the relations between the Yugoslav government and the partisan army [that is] struggling heroically in Yugoslavia.

With fraternal greetings,

(G. DIMITROV)

4 June 1942

TO WALTER

1. It is necessary, of course, to expose the treacherous actions of the Chetniks to the people in a concrete, documented, and persuasive manner. However, at present it would be politically [more] appropriate to do this in the form of an

---

16. RTsKhIDNI, f. 495, op. 184, iskh. 1942, d. 4, ll. 171–170.

appeal to the Yugoslav government, stressing that the struggling Yugoslav patriots are rightfully expecting support from it, not its permitting some individuals, on its behalf, to stab the popular-liberation partisan army in the back at the time when it is fighting hordes of invaders. This means to expose but not yet to attack the government directly.

2. It is necessary to launch a broad campaign against the accomplices of the invaders, based on the necessity of a united struggle of Serbs, Croats, Montenegrins, and Slovenes against the common enemy. This campaign should be waged so as to divide rather than unite all the Chetniks to oppose the partisans' struggle. In this regard, your tactical line should be to win over some of the Chetniks, neutralize others, and mercilessly destroy the most malicious of them.

3. It is very important to organize actions (with leaflets, etc.) by prominent public and political figures of Yugoslavia, along with the actions on behalf of the general headquarters and of specific partisan headquarters, against the accomplices of the occupiers and in support of the people's liberation partisan army, in support of the militant unity of [all] Yugoslav patriots, regardless of different political convictions and former foreign policy orientation (pro-Soviet or pro-English).

4. You should strive to organize a national committee of support for the Yugoslav people's struggle for liberation, composed of prominent patriotic Serb, Croat, Montenegrin, and Slovene figures. [This committee should] promote, in the country and abroad, the political platform of struggle of the people's liberation partisan army.

Please discuss our recommendations and let us know your thinking as well as the concrete actions you will undertake in this direction.

DIMITROV

1.6.42.

TO WALTER

As we informed you earlier, you unfortunately cannot expect to receive ammunition and automatic weapons from us in the very near future, for reasons that you can understand. The major reason is the impossibility of shipment. Therefore, it is essential that you use most rationally and to the extent possible all the existing possibilities (including the smallest and the most difficult ones) of local self-supply. Thus, despite the damned difficulties, continue to conduct the war of liberation, hold on, and repel the enemy's attacks until external help becomes available.

DIMITROV

2.6.42.

At this point, Moscow radio began publicizing Tito's charge that the Chetniks were collaborating with the enemy, leading the Western Allies to demand clarification or evidence from the Soviet government. On 7 August, Moscow gave the British a document detailing the alleged collaboration of the Chetniks with the Italian forces and occasionally with Nedić against the partisans, but it took some months for British policy to shift from full support of Mihailović to establishing closer links with Tito's forces. (The United States was virtually absent from the scene.) At the same time Soviet policy remained equivocal. In August 1942 Moscow consented to raising the Royal Yugoslav legation in Moscow to the rank of an embassy. Because of its recognition of the exile regime (and because of the Western Allies) Moscow also pressed Tito not to consider the Antifascist Council of National Liberation (AVNOJ), launched in Bihać (in November 1942), a government; although Tito professed to accept this advice, his command increasingly came to recognize the council as Yugoslavia's highest authority.

22 May 1943

Even more galling to the partisans was the fact that Moscow in effect ignored their insistent requests—some rather pathetic—for military and humanitarian aid. Dimitrov fell back on contrived technical reasons to explain why even in 1942–43, when the war was turning more in favor of the Allies, the Soviet Union could not provide the much-needed assistance to the comrades in Yugoslavia.[17] Indeed, several years later, after the break between the Soviet and Yugoslav Communist leaderships, Moša Pijade, a leading Titoist "theorist" who had himself experienced the long and futile wait for Soviet airdrops during the war, wrote a bitter (and well-documented) condemnation of Moscow. His pamphlet *About the Legend That the Yugoslav Uprising Owed Its Existence to Soviet*

17. In response to one of Tito's requests, Dimitrov, who was probably frustrated himself, explained: "I have repeatedly discussed with Iosif Vissarionovich [Stalin] the ways and means of providing help [for you]. Regrettably, to this day it has not been possible to find a positive solution because of the insuperable technical and transportation difficulties. We have not ceased our efforts to find realistic possibilities to send aid. As soon as these possibilities are found, we will do what is needed" (10 February 1943, in RTsKhIDNI, f. 495, op. 184, iskh. 1943, d. 5, l. 76).

Assistance (1950), for the first time revealed documents from the Yugoslav archives—some of them the same materials that are published in this chapter from the Soviet files. Insofar as the identical documents are concerned, this process fully validates those published at the time.

Pijade's point was to refute the later Cominform—Soviet—charges that Yugoslavia owed its liberation from the Nazis to help "from without" (as did the rest of Eastern Europe) rather than from within. Although he slighted the challenges the Soviet Union faced—the country was on the brink of catastrophe under the German onslaught in 1941—and the technical problems of providing the partisans with military assistance from behind the Soviet lines, Pijade does present a picture of a Soviet leadership whose concerns and priorities conformed far more with the standards of *sacro egoismo* than with those of proletarian internationalism. Indeed, in this perspective Soviet wartime policy—whatever the Western media may have said at the time—provided more evidence of Moscow's lack of regard for foreign Communist movements. This had always been true of Stalin, but it intensified after 1935, and soon brought about the dissolution of the Comintern.

Not surprisingly, this argument is also in tune with the charges of Soviet betrayal voiced by Spanish Communists and Chinese, Vietnamese, and Cuban comrades later on. The other side of the argument was naturally the claim that the Soviet Union was practicing responsible statesmanship: Moscow needed to balance a great variety of ties and commitments—although these included a healthy dose of self-interest. This attitude was mirrored in the saying popular in Bolshevik ranks in the early 1930s that "one tractor is worth more than ten foreign Communists." But the "objective" difficulties the Soviets faced hardly sufficed to defuse the bitterness that the Titoist leadership felt about their Russian comrades. There is little doubt that these attitudes were part of the backdrop for the Soviet-Yugoslav rift in 1948.

Document 48

Dimitrov to Stalin, 22 May 1943. RTsKhIDNI, f. 495, op. 74, d. 595, l. 29. Original in Russian. Typewritten.

To Comrade STALIN

I received today the following encoded telegram from C. Walter (Yugoslavia):

"It is necessary to ask the English to bomb Sarajevo, where 300 planes are located, and Zagreb, where there are 700 planes. It is also necessary to bomb the cities of Pljevlja, Mostar, Peč, Bijelopolje, Nikšić, and Podgorica."

(G. DIMITROV)

22 May 1943

24 May 1943

Tito's message, cited in Dimitrov's letter below, was sent on 22 May and received the next day. On 26 May, Stalin received Dimitrov and approved the proposed reply, in which Dimitrov advised Tito, "It would be sensible for the time being not to send your own military representative to Cairo, explaining that all military people suitable for this task are busy with the direct organization of defense against the new attack of the Italo-German armed forces against the partisan army. However, indicate that you will send your military representative at the first opportunity."[18]

Document 49

Dimitrov to Stalin, 24 May 1943. RTsKhIDNI, f. 495, op. 74, d. 595, l. 30. Original in Russian. Typewritten.

To Comrade STALIN

Today I received the following coded telegram from C. Walter (Yugoslavia):

"The English promised to send, in the coming days, 1,500 kilograms of med-

18. *Georgi Dimitrov Dnevnik (9 Mart 1933–6 Fevruari 1949)* (Georgi Dimitrov: Diary [9 March 1933–6 February 1949]) (Sofia: Sofia University St. Climent of Ohrid Press, 1997), p. 376.

Document 49 *continued*

ical supplies and are promising to provide arms, if necessary. They further demand that we send our military representative to headquarters in Cairo. We request your opinion on this question as soon as possible."

To my mind, we should recommend that Walter reject the proposal to send the military representative to Cairo under the pretext that all military specialists suitable for this mission are busy directly organizing the repulsion of the new offensive of the Italo-German armed forces against the partisan army.

I request your directives on this matter.

(G. DIMITROV)

24 May 1943

On 24 May, Tito sent another message that was forwarded, after decoding, to Stalin, Molotov, Voroshilov, Beria, Vasilevsky, Ilichev, and Golovin. In it Tito reported the imminent arrival of an Allied "delegate" from Cairo and asked that a Soviet army representative be sent out at the earliest possible moment A Soviet military mission did not in fact arrive in Yugoslavia until February 1944.[19]

19. See RTsKhIDNI, f. 495, op. 74, d. 595, l. 31.

CHAPTER EIGHT

Dissolution

IT WAS IN THE PERIOD of the Nazi-Soviet Pact that the possibility of dissolving the Communist International was first discussed with some seriousness. Milovan Djilas, a Yugoslav Communist who was close to Dimitrov during the war (and later became a prominent anti-Stalinist), reports that Dimitrov told him "how the idea first arose to dissolve the Comintern. It was at the time the Baltic states were annexed by the Soviet Union [mid-1940]. It was apparent even then that the main power in the spread of Communism was the Soviet Union, and that therefore all forces had to gather around it. The dissolution itself had been postponed because of the international situation, to avoid giving the impression that it was being done under pressure from the Germans, with whom relations were not bad at the time."[1] The matter clearly remained on Stalin's mind, however, as he was paying less and less attention to the International.

We now know that on 20 April 1941, at a closed dinner at the Bolshoi Theater, Stalin made some rather unexpected remarks as he raised his glass in a toast for Dimitrov. Referring to the fact that the

1. Milovan Djilas, *Conversations with Stalin* (New York: Harcourt, Brace, 1962), p. 33; see also pp. 80–81.

American Communists had disaffiliated from the Comintern in order to avoid prosecution under the Voorhis Act (although they remained in Moscow's good graces),[2] Stalin (according to Dimitrov) declared,

> Dimitrov is losing his parties. That's not bad. On the contrary, it would be good to make the Com[munist] parties entirely independent instead of being sections of the CI. They must be transformed into national Com. parties under various names—Labor Party, Marxist Party, etc. The name doesn't matter. What is important is that they take root in their own people and concentrate on their own special tasks. The situation and the tasks vary greatly from country to country, for instance in England and Germany, they are not at all the same. When the Com. parties get stronger in this fashion, then you'll reestablish their international organization.

Stalin continued:

> The [First] International was created in the days of Marx in anticipation of an early world revolution. The Comintern was created in the days of Lenin in a similar period. At present the national tasks for each country move into the forefront. But the status of Com. parties as sections of an international organization, subordinate to the Executive of the CI, is an obstacle. . . . Don't hold on to what was yesterday. Strictly take into account the newly created circumstances. . . . From the point of view of departmental interests [of the Comintern] this is perhaps unpleasant, but those are not the interests that must prevail! Under present conditions, membership in the Comintern makes it easier for the bourgeoisie to persecute the Com. parties and accomplish its plan to isolate them from the masses in their own countries, while it hinders the Com. parties' independent development and task-solving as national parties.[3]

Although for the time being this bombshell, so casually dropped, had no further repercussions, Dimitrov took the suggestion seriously enough to discuss it with Dmitry Manuilsky and Andrei

2. The Voorhis Act, passed by the U.S. Congress in 1940, required organizations subject to foreign control to register and provide detailed information about their officers, activities, and finances. In response the CPUSA in an emergency convention disaffiliated from the Comintern. See Harvey Klehr, *The Heyday of American Communism* (New York: Basic, 1984), pp. 408–409.

3. TsPA (Sofia), f. 146, op. 2, a.e. 7.

Zhdanov as well as with Comintern representatives Palmiro Togliatti and Maurice Thorez. Without noticeably questioning the idea
of dissolution, he tried to envisage some of the organizational, ideological, and political problems such an action would cause and remained worried about the "multitude of unclear and difficult questions" that would arise in such a case. But with the outbreak of war,
the issue remained moot for another two years.

11 May 1943

The matter came up again—a bit unexpectedly for Dimitrov and his
staff—in the spring of 1943. As Dimitrov noted in his diary, "They
have come to the conclusion that the Comintern as the directing center for the Com[munist] parties under the existing circumstances is
an obstacle to the indep[endent] development of the Com. parties
and to the fulfillment of their special tasks."[4] The immediate decision was transmitted on 8 May to Dimitrov and Manuilsky in a
meeting with Molotov, who informed them that is was necessary to
dissolve the whole organization and asked them to prepare the documents needed for this purpose.

In the days that followed Dimitrov and Manuilsky unhesitatingly
prepared the draft resolution for the Presidium of the ECCI, dissolving the organization that had symbolized world communism
and to which they had devoted many years of their lives. On 11 May
they sent the draft (Document 50) to Stalin, who received them that
evening together with Molotov and approved the draft. The four of
them decided to adopt the resolution at a meeting of the Presidium
of the ECCI as a proposal that would go to the national sections—
the member organizations—for approval, and then to publish it.
There was no mention of convening a world congress for the occasion. Dimitrov and Georgy Malenkov were charged with drafting a
proposal concerning how contact with foreign Communist parties
was to be maintained in the future. Stalin remarked, "Experience
has shown that one must not have an intern[ational] directing center for all countries. This became clear under Marx, under Lenin,
and now again. Possibly one ought to shift to regional clusters, e.g.,

4. TsPA (Sofia), f. 146, op. 1, a.e. 11.

South America, the United States and Canada, some European countries, etc., but one must not rush with this."[5]

Document 50

Dimitrov and Manuilsky to Stalin and Molotov, 11 May 1943, with enclosed draft resolution of the ECCI Presidium. RTsKhIDNI, f. 495, op. 73, d. 174, ll. 9–12. Original in Russian. Type-written.

TO COMRADE STALIN
TO COMRADE MOLOTOV
We are sending you the draft resolution of the ECCI Presidium on the dissolution of the Communist International. We request your directives.

> **G. Dimitrov**   G. DIMITROV
> **D. Manuilsky**   D. MANUILSKY

11 May 1943

Top secret
RESOLUTION OF THE PRESIDIUM OF THE ECCI
(Draft)

The historic role of the Communist International, founded in 1919 as a result of the political collapse of the overwhelming majority of the old prewar workers' parties, was to protect Marxist teaching from vulgarization and distortion by opportunist elements in the workers' movement, to contribute to the unification of the vanguard of workers in a number of countries in genuine workers' parties, to help them mobilize the masses of toilers to protect their economic interests and political rights, and to struggle against fascism and the predatory war launched by it. The Communist International early on exposed the real meaning of the "anti-Comintern pact" as a tool in the preparation of war by the Hitlerites. Long before the war [broke out], [the CI] had exposed the foul subversive work of the Hitlerites in other countries that was masked by their phrases about the supposed intervention of the Comintern in the internal affairs of those countries.

But long before the war it was becoming clear that as the internal and international situation of certain countries was becoming more complex, the resolution of the problems of the workers' movement in each individual country would meet with insurmountable obstacles.

5. TsPA (Sofia), f. 146, op. 1, a.e. 11. The pertinent excerpts from Dimitrov's diary are also quoted in Grant Adibekov, *Kominform i poslevoennaya Evropa 1947–1956 gg.* (Moscow: Rossiia Molodaya, 1994), pp. 6–9.

ПОСТАНОВЛЕНИЕ ПРЕЗИДИУМА ИККИ

(Проект)

Историческая роль Коммунистического Интернационала, образовавшегося в 1919 г. в итоге политического крушения подавляющего большинства старых довоенных рабочих партий, состояла в том, что он отстоял учение марксизма от опошления и извращения его оппортунистическими элементами рабочего движения, содействовал сплочению в ряде стран авангарда передовых рабочих в подлинные рабочие партии, помогал им мобилизовывать массы трудящихся для защиты своих экономических интересов и политических прав, для борьбы против фашизма и подготовляемой им грабительской войны. Коммунистический Интернационал своевременно раскрыл подлинное значение "антикоминтерновского пакта", как орудия в подготовке гитлеровцами войны. Он неустанно разоблачал задолго до войны гнусную подрывную работу гитлеровцев в чужих государствах, маскируемую их криками о мнимом вмешательстве Коминтерна во внутренние дела этих государств.

Но еще задолго до войны все более становилось ясным, что по мере усложнения как внутренней, так и международной обстановки отдельных стран, решение задач рабочего движения каждой отдельной страны каким-либо международным центром будет встречать непреодолимые препятствия.

Своеобразие исторических путей развития различных стран, особенности их общественного уклада, различие в уровне и темпах развития производительных сил, различие в степени сознательности и организованности рабочих, путей развития рабочего движения, обусловили и разные задачи, стоящие перед рабочим классом отдельных стран.

Весь ход событий за истекшие четверть века и накопленный КИ опыт убедительно показали, что организационная форма об"единения рабочих, избранная Первым Конгрессом

DOCUMENT 50. First page of the draft resolution of the ECCI Presidium on the dissolution of the Communist International enclosed in Dimitrov and Manuilsky to Stalin and Molotov, 11 May 1943

The specific historical paths of development of different countries, peculiarities of their social systems, differences in the level and pace of development of their productive forces, differences in the level of consciousness and organization of the workers and of the forms of development of the workers' movement in turn shaped the different tasks facing the working class of individual countries.

All the events of the past quarter-century and the accumulated experience of the Comintern have clearly shown that the organizational form of uniting the workers chosen by the First Congress of the Comintern, which corresponded to the needs of the initial period of the revival of the workers' movement, became outdated as this movement grew and its tasks in individual countries became more complicated, and it became a hindrance to the further strengthening of the national workers' parties.

The world war unleashed by the Hitlerites exacerbated further the difference in the situation of individual countries, by creating a deep divide between the countries that became spreaders of the Hitlerite tyranny and the freedom-loving peoples who have united in a powerful anti-Hitler coalition. Although the main task of the workers, toilers, and all honest people in the countries of the Hitlerite bloc is to contribute in all possible ways to the defeat of this bloc by undermining the Hitler military machine from within, to contribute to the overthrow of the governments responsible for the war, in the countries allied against Hitler the sacred duty of the broad masses, and in particular of progressive workers, is to give all possible support to the military effort of the governments of these countries for the sake of the prompt defeat of the Hitlerite bloc and protecting the commonwealth of nations based on their equal rights.

At the same time, the war for liberation against the Hitler tyranny waged by the freedom-loving peoples, which set in motion wide popular masses who are uniting, regardless of their nationality, party affiliation, or religion, into a powerful anti-Hitler coalition, has clearly demonstrated that the national upsurge and the struggle of the masses, who are organized statewide, have outgrown the organizational framework of the CI. [The war] has demonstrated that this powerful mobilization of the masses can best contribute to the earliest possible victory over the enemy with the best results through the vanguard of the workers' movement in each individual country, in accordance with the best historical traditions of the national-liberation struggle of each given country.

The Seventh CI Congress, which took place in 1935, taking into consideration changes that took place both in the international situation and in the workers' movement that required more flexibility and independence for its sections to resolve the tasks facing them, has already stressed the importance for the Executive Committee of the Comintern, while resolving all questions of the workers' movement, to "proceed from the specific conditions and peculiarities of each country and to avoid, as a rule, direct interference in the internal organizational affairs of the Communist parties."

The CI was guided by similar considerations when it considered and approved the November 1940 decision of the Communist Party of the USA to withdraw from the Communist International.

Guided by the teachings of the founders of Marxism-Leninism, Communists have never been supporters of organizational fetishism, have always subordinated organizational structure and methods of work of the workers' movement to the vital political interests of the workers' movement as a whole, to the particularities of the specific historical situation, and to the tasks that directly derive from this situation. They remember the example of the great Marx, who united the vanguard workers in the ranks of the International Workingmen's Association and, after the First International had accomplished its historical mission by creating a basis for development of the workers' parties in Europe and America, dissolved the First International, since that form of organization no longer corresponded to the new level of the workers' movement.

Starting from these considerations and taking into account the growth and political maturity of the Communist parties and their leadership in the individual counties, the Presidium of the ECCI, having no chance of convoking a Congress of the CI in the situation of world war, submits the following proposal for ratification by its sections:

To dissolve the Communist International as the leading center of the international workers' movement and to relieve its sections of the obligations ensuing from the statutes and decisions of the CI congresses.

The Presidium of the ECCI calls on all the supporters of the CI to concentrate their forces on the fullest support of and active participation in the war for liberation waged by the peoples and states of the anti-Hitler coalition for the earliest possible defeat of the deadly enemy of the toilers—German fascism and its allies and vassals.

Only the complete victory over this rabid enemy of mankind will make possible a new upsurge of the workers' movement, the rebuilding and expansion of the economic and political gains of the working class, the consolidation of the cause of freedom and peace among nations, thus achieving such social and international relations that the resurrection of fascism and the recurrence of its predatory wars would be impossible.

14 May 1943

On 12 May, Dimitrov acquainted the Comintern officials one by one with the draft.[6] The meeting of the ECCI Presidium was set for the following day. Before it began Stalin directed Dimitrov to submit the resolution for discussion and give members of the Presidium two or three days to introduce changes, but not to send it abroad for the time being. "We must avoid giving the impression that we are simply evicting the leading for[eign] comrades." Document 51 contains the protocol of that Presidium meeting. Stalin also directed Dimitrov to organize the publication of four newspapers—in German, Romanian, Italian, and Hungarian, the languages in which Moscow could appeal to prisoners of war and Axis troops facing the Red Army—which could be new venues of operation for some of the foreign Communists, and also to set up national antifascist committees in which they could work.[7]

Document 51

Dimitrov to Stalin and Molotov, 14 May 1943, with protocol of the ECCI Presidium, 13 May 1943. Letter: RTsKhIDNI, f. 495, op. 73, d. 174, l. 22; enclosure: f. 495, op. 18, d. 1340, ll. 78–84. Original in Russian. Typewritten. The cover letter of 14 May is missing from its file.

PROTOCOL (B) No. 823 OF THE CLOSED SESSION OF THE PRESIDIUM
OF THE ECCI of 13 MAY 1943
PRESENT
1) Members of the Presidium: Dimitrov, Manuilsky, Pieck, Marty, Thorez, Koplenig, Kolarov; 2) Members and candidate members of the ECCI: Dolores Ibárruri, Rákosi, Ulbricht, Šverma, Wolf; 3) Representatives of the parties: Pauker (Romanian Communist Party), Vlasov (Yugoslav Communist Party), Lehtinen (Finnish Communist Party); 4) Interpreters: Stepanov and Fürnberg.

HEARD
§1604. Draft resolution of the Presidium of the ECCI concerning the disso-

6. These officials were André Marty, Maurice Thorez, Dolores Ibárruri, Wilhelm Pieck, Walter Ulbricht, Johann Koplenig, Mátyás Rákosi, Jan Šverma, Ana Pauker, Inkeri Lehtinen, Veljko Vlahović, Vasil Kolarov, and Mihály Farkas.
7. TsPA (Sofia), f. 146, op. 1, a.e. 11.

lution of the Communist International as the leading center of the international workers' movement.

RESOLVED

Chairman Dimitrov, opening the meeting, outlines and explains in detail the essence of the draft [resolution] submitted for discussion by the Presidium of the ECCI. He stresses that the document brought to the attention of the members of the Presidium of the ECCI is only a draft to be freely discussed and corrected if any of the Presidium members would like to introduce such corrections into the draft resolution. At issue is not a formal move but the actual dissolution of the Communist International as the leading center of the international movement. The proposal submitted for discussion is extremely important and weighty. Therefore, each member of the Presidium of the ECCI must seriously and carefully think it over, weigh the pros and cons, all the considerations and arguments, realistically appraise whether this move is politically appropriate and opportune. After the exchange of opinions at this meeting, if the proposed draft is unanimously accepted as a working draft, members of the Presidium will have two or three days to work on their corrections, amendments, and changes.

Manuilsky suggests that the discussion of the issue be conducted in the following terms: a) whether it is politically appropriate to dissolve the Comintern; b) whether the correct timing has been chosen for this move; c) whether the proposal to dissolve the Comintern is sufficiently substantiated in the draft resolution; d) what changes and amendments need to be made to the draft.

Rákosi: It is not easy to dissolve the CI, but it is a correct step. For Lenin, too, it was hard to replace grain requisitioning with a food tax, but he chose to do it in the interests of the revolution. The draft resolution complies with this requirement. Nevertheless, we ought to add to the draft the motives of proletarian solidarity in order to make it clear to our people abroad. We must think today about how we are going to crush the arguments of the elements hostile to us who will try to use the dissolution of the Comintern for anti-Soviet purposes.

Thorez: I fully agree with the draft. We Communists failed to defeat social democracy or to block the fascists from coming to power in some countries. Communists also failed to prevent the fascists from unleashing a predatory war. The old form of the international association of workers has outlived itself. Already before the war, the French party was growing because of the application of the popular-front policy. Today in France, after its occupation by the Hitlerites, a base for a broad national front has been created. This movement is more far-reaching than the organizational frame of the CI. I consider that the timing of the dissolution is also good. The Red Army is gaining victories. Hitler Germany has been beaten in Africa. Under these conditions, it will be difficult for anybody to treat the dissolution of the Comintern as a retreat. As a French Communist, I welcome this step also because it will contribute to the growth of the national anti-Hitler front in France.

Wolf: The decision to dissolve the Comintern is necessary and correct, although I am anguished by the thought that the organization that brought me up is being dissolved. However, in politics, political reason determines decisions, not emotions. The decision to dissolve the Comintern derives not from our weakness but from our strength. The parties have grown and matured. With this step, we will help the parties, especially a party like the one in England, to grow faster. This decision will boost the feeling of responsibility of the Communist parties to their working class and their people. It is important to remember that the enemy will portray our decision as a maneuver, as a merely formal decision, and therefore, we will have to implement this decision firmly and consistently in order to cut the ground from under the agitation of the hostile elements.

Pieck says that when Dimitrov acquainted him yesterday with the draft resolution, he at first expressed doubts about the need to dissolve the Comintern at that particular moment. It is clear to everyone now that Germany has lost the war and at first it seemed to him that under the circumstances, with great shocks impending in Germany, the Comintern should not be dissolved. However, after having carefully thought over the proposal, he considers it absolutely correct, appropriate, and necessary. But he thinks that it is hard to say whether all the parties are mature enough to be able to solve all their tasks independently. In his opinion, some form of ideological support to the German party from the more experienced Soviet friends is necessary.

Kolarov announces that he is the oldest member of the ECCI, but he votes for the dissolution of the Comintern without any hesitation because it has long ceased to be a real leading organ. It ceased to be [the leading organ] because the situation has changed. There is the USSR, a new factor of such a great force that the Comintern looks archaic. The Comintern was created at a time of revolutionary upheaval, but expectations of rapid revolution were disappointed. The development took a somewhat different course. The USSR became the bulwark of all the aspirations of the toilers. Naturally, the role of the Comintern started to fade. Communism did not get weaker as a result but rather became a great force. Today other bourgeois states must create military blocs with the state that incarnates this Communism.

Kolarov believes that the reference to the example of the First International should be specified in the draft. As is known, the liquidation of the First International came as a result of the defeat of the Paris Commune, but today the situation is quite different.

In conclusion, Kolarov thinks that regional associations of Communist parties are possible, like, for example, the Balkan Federation.

Dolores fully supports the dissolution of the Comintern. One should not cling to organizational forms that have outlived themselves. Today there is no doubt that the Comintern has become a hindrance to the further development of the parties. If we want the parties to grow, we must educate them to be independent and responsible. The existence of the Comintern played a great role in educating the parties. Through this transmittor, the Comintern, [they] absorbed the spirit of Bolshevism, the spirit of the flexible and wise strategy of Lenin-Stalin.

Šverma: Yesterday, when I was reading the draft, my heart was heavy. I grew up in the Comintern, my entire life was with the Comintern. But this is an emotion. And the political decision proposed in the draft is the only possible and wise one. I think that we are liquidating the Comintern because we are closer to socialism than in 1918–19. It is not impossible that the announcement of the liquidation of the Comintern may cause certain vacillations abroad, especially among the illegal parties. However, confidence in the Soviet Union is so great that these vacillations will rapidly be overcome. Šverma thinks that in Czechoslovakia the dissolution of the Comintern will create the basis for a unified mass party, where Communists can have decisive influence.

Marty fully agrees with the decision proposed in the draft. He also agrees with the arguments justifying this step. However, he believes that it is necessary to consider Kolarov's observation regarding [mentioning] the First International in the final text of the resolution. He thinks that the dissolution of the Comintern is determined by the fact that the Comintern's existence creates many inconveniences and provides few advantages. Some comrades are concerned that the dissolution of the Comintern could weaken internationalist feelings. This concern is unfounded. The international prestige of the USSR is enormous. The battles and victories of the Red Army are the real basis for this internationalism.

Pauker fully supports the draft. She calls attention to the fact that Communists have not yet realized that a new era [is at hand] and are measuring current events from the prewar point of view. Like Marty, she is not afraid that internationalist feelings can suffer, since there is the Soviet Union. In conclusion, she argues against Kolarov's idea about the creation of a Balkan Federation because the Balkans are torn apart by the war into different camps with specific and different tasks facing them.

Vlasov believes that the dissolution of the Comintern will facilitate the situation of the Yugoslav insurgents accused by the reaction of being "agents of Moscow." He completely agrees with the draft.

Koplenig considers the decision about the dissolution of the Comintern politically correct and timely. However, this decision will be useful only if there are no halfhearted measures, if it is made clear that this is not a formal dissolution but a real one. He considers it useful, in the course of the subsequent explanatory work, to explain more about the positive work done by the Comintern during the quarter of a century of its existence than appears in the resolution.

Ulbricht agrees with the draft but says that it is necessary to legalize some functions of the Comintern, which have played and will play a positive role in everyday antifascist work.

Document 51 *continued*

Lehtinen declares her agreement with the draft.

In conclusion, Dimitrov states that all the participants of the meeting have unanimously accepted the discussed draft as a working draft and suggests that members of the Presidium think over the draft and formulate their corrections. The deadline for submission of possible corrections is 17 May 1943. This proposal is unanimously approved.

G. Dim[itrov]

---

18 and 22 May 1943

On 18 May, Dimitrov forwarded to Stalin and Molotov the protocol of the second session of the Presidium of the ECCI held on 17 May that had been devoted to the revised text of the dissolution resolution; he also sent the protocol of the editorial commission which met on 18 May. On 19 May the resolution was again discussed in Stalin's office by Molotov, Voroshilov, Beria, Malenkov, Mikoyan, and Dimitrov. Clearly to lift the onus for the dissolution from the CPSU, Stalin proposed deleting the last paragraph, adding that the question of dissolution had been raised by a number of sections of the CI during the war, and stressing that Marx had dissolved the First International because it was necessary to create national parties.

The following day Dimitrov reconvened the editorial committee and explained Stalin's and Molotov's "proposed" changes, which were readily adopted. The whole resolution was thereupon signed by the members of the ECCI Presidium and the representatives of several Communist parties. (No Chinese Communists took part.) Dimitrov retroactively dated the document "Moscow, 15 May 1943."[8]

8. RTsKhIDNI, f. 495, op. 18, d. 1340, l. 104. The text with the changes introduced by Dimitrov on the basis of Stalin's comments of 19 May is in f. 495, op. 73, d. 174, ll. 2–7. On the arguments surrounding the dissolution, see also Alfred Burmeister (pseud. of Wanda Pampuch), *Dissolution and Aftermath of the Comintern* (New York: Research Program on the USSR, 1955), and Enrique Castro Delgado, *J'ai perdu la foi à Moscou* (Paris: Gallimard, 1950), p. 219ff. On the dissolution at the Comintern school, see Wolfgang Leonhard, *Child of the Revolution*; (Chicago: Regnery, 1958). The resolution appeared in English in the Communist *World News and Views*, May 29, 1943, and is reprinted in Jane Degras, ed., *The Communist International, 1919–1943: Documents*, vol. 3 (London: RIIA, 1965), 476–479.

The resolution was translated into several languages and at Dimitrov's request was sent in code by radio to the Communist parties abroad on 21 May. That same day, at a meeting of the Politburo in Stalin's office that included Dimitrov and Manuilsky, Molotov read the resolution, which was unanimously adopted by the Politburo. It was published in *Pravda* on 22 May. During the Politburo discussion, Stalin remarked,

> When we created the CI and thought we could direct the movement in all countries, we were overestimating our forces. That was our error. The further existence of the CI would discredit the idea of the international, something we do not wish to see. . . . There is also another motive for the dissolution of the CI which is not mentioned in the resolution. And that is the fact that the CPs that belong in the CI are falsely accused of being the agents of a foreign state, and this hinders their work among the masses. By dissolving the CI we are knocking this ace out of the enemies' hand.[9]

The "enemies" presumably included the "bourgeois" states and parties abroad, several of whom were allies of the USSR.

Documents 52 and 53

Dimitrov to Stalin and Molotov, 18 May 1943, and Dimitrov to Stalin and Malenkov, 22 May 1943, with enclosures. Letter, 18 May: RTsKhIDNI, f. 495, op. 73, d. 174, l. 48; enclosures: f. 495, op. 18, d. 1340, ll. 89–98, and op. 73, d. 174, ll. 28–33; letter and enclosures, 22 May: f. 495, op. 73, d. 174, ll. 50–55. Originals in Russian. Typewritten.

To Comrade STALIN
To Comrade MOLOTOV
I am sending you the protocol of the second closed meeting of the Presidium of the ECCI regarding the question of the dissolution of the Comintern.
I am also sending you the protocol of the editorial commission selected by the Presidium of the ECCI. Enclosed is the text of the draft resolution with the passages that have been altered marked in red pencil.

---

9. TsPA (Sofia), f. 146, op. 2, a.e. 11.

Товарищу СТАЛИНУ.

Товарищу МОЛОТОВУ.

Направляю Вам протокол второго закрытого заседания Президиума ИККИ по вопросу о роспуске Коминтерна.

Направляю также протокол выбранной Президиумом ИККИ редакционной комиссии. Прилагаю при этом текст проекта постановления с отмеченными красным карандашом местами, подвергшимися изменению.

По ВЧ осведомил т.т.Эрколи, Куусинева и Готвальда /членов Президиума, находящихся в СССР, но вне Москвы/ о содержании проекта постановления Президиума. Все они выразили свое полное согласие с предложением о роспуске Коминтерна.

Прошу Ваших дальнейших указаний.

/Г.ДИМИТРОВ/

18 мая 1943 г.

DOCUMENT 52. Dimitrov to Stalin and Molotov, 18 May 1943, with first and last pages of the protocol of the ECCI Presidium, 17 May 1943

ПРОТОКОЛ /Б/ № 825

ЗАКРЫТОГО ЗАСЕДАНИЯ ПРЕЗИДИУМА ИККИ от 17 мая 1943 г.

Присутствовали: 1) Члены Президиума -
Димитров, Мануильский, Пик, Марти, Торес,
Коплениг, Коларов; 2) Члены и кандидаты
ИККИ - Долорес Ибаррури, Ракоши, Ульбрихт,
Шверма, Вольф; 3) Представители партий -
Паукер (румынской компартии), Власов (югос-
лавской компартии); 4) Переводчики - Сте-
панов и Фюренберг.

(Отсутствует Лехтинен).

СЛУШАЛИ:	ПОСТАНОВИЛИ:
1.	1.

§ 1606. Обсуждение проекта постановления о роспуске Коминтерна.

Председательствующий Димитров, откры-
вая заседание, предлагает присутствующим
высказаться, желают ли они добавить какие-
либо новые соображения, помимо высказанных
на предыдущем заседании Президиума ИККИ,
по вопросу о роспуске Коминтерна.

Ввиду того, что присутствующие счи-
тают дискуссию по этому вопросу исчерпан-
ной, Димитров предлагает перейти к чтению
проекта постановления по абзацам с тем,
чтобы участники заседания имели возможность
вносить поправки к проекту, если они этого
пожелают.

а) Дискуссия вокруг 3-го абзаца стр.1
проекта постановления, гласящего:

"Своеобразие исторических путей развития различных стран, особенности их общественного уклада, различие в уровне и
темпах развития производительных сил, различие в степени сознательности и органи-

К настоящему Постановлению присоединяются следующие
представители коммунистических партий:

БИАНКО (Италии), ДОЛОРЕС ИБАРРУРИ (Испании),
ЛЕХТИНЕН (Финляндии), ПАУКЕР (Румынии), РАКОШИ
(Венгрии).

Москва — ⬛⬛. 15 мая 1943г

I called by VCh[10] Cc. Ercoli, Kuusinen, and Gottwald (members of the Presidium who are in the USSR but outside of Moscow) and informed them about the contents of the draft resolution of the Presidium. They all expressed their full agreement with the proposal to dissolve the Comintern.

I await your further directives.

(G. DIMITROV)

18 May 1943

PROTOCOL (B) No. 825
OF THE CLOSED MEETING OF THE PRESIDIUM OF THE ECCI
of 17 MAY 1943

PRESENT

1) Members of the Presidium: Dimitrov, Manuilsky, Pieck, Marty, Thorez, Koplenig, Kolarov; 2) Members and candidate members of the ECCI: Dolores Ibárruri, Rákosi, Ulbricht, Šverma, Wolf; 3) Representatives of the parties: Pauker (Romanian Communist Party), Vlasov (Yugoslav Communist Party); 4) Interpreters: Stepanov and Fürnberg. (Lehtinen absent).

HEARD

I.

§1606. Discussion of the draft resolution on the dissolution of the Comintern.

RESOLVED

I.

Chair Dimitrov, opening the meeting, offers to give the floor to those present if they have any new considerations besides the ones mentioned at the previous meeting of the Presidium of the ECCI.

Since all those present consider the discussion on this question completed, Dimitrov suggests proceeding with the reading of the draft resolution paragraph by paragraph so that the participants can make such corrections in the draft as they wish.

a) Discussion of page 1, paragraph 3, of the draft resolution, which reads:

"The specific historical paths of development of different countries, peculiarities of their social systems, differences in the level and pace of development of their productive forces, differences in the level of consciousness and organization of the workers and of the forms of development of the workers' movement in turn shaped the different tasks facing the working class of individual countries."

Rákosi thinks that the motives for the dissolution of the Comintern outlined in this paragraph of the resolution, based on the particularities of different

10. Russian abbreviation for *vysoko-chastotnyi,* "high-frequency [communication device]," a type of telephone line used by the government for secret communications.—Trans.

countries and differences in the workers' movement, are not temporary but permanent factors that will remain after the war under any conditions. "Do we not block the way," asks Rákosi, "for our rebuilding of an international association of workers in this or that form in the future?" Rákosi, without suggesting an amendment, asks for clarification of this point of the draft resolution.

Kolarov thinks that Rákosi's fears are unfounded. When conditions are created for such forms of the international association of workers, forms of association that will correspond better than the Comintern to the specific conditions of the political situation, we will find persuasive reasons for reestablishing the international links in the workers' movement, taking into account the particularities of individual countries and differences in the workers' movement under all conditions.

Thorez thinks that if this paragraph is taken out, the chief justification for the dissolution of the Comintern will disappear. It cannot be omitted in the resolution or weakened by conditioning stipulations.

Dolores is convinced that a form of the international workers' association will be found when conditions are ripe, and the motives mentioned in the paragraph "on the particularities of different countries" will no longer be a hindrance to the establishment of an international association but will only require a careful approach to the particularities of the workers' movement in each country and shaping the tactics of this movement after analysis of the particular situation in a given country.

Dimitrov, summing up the discussion of the question raised by Rákosi, emphasizes that it is unlikely that after the war there will be the need for such a centralized international organization as the Comintern. In his opinion, a new form of the international association of workers, if it is at all necessary, can be created only on the basis of recognizing the specifics of the situation in individual countries and differences in the workers' movement. Therefore, the 3rd paragraph of our resolution is not a hindrance to such association.

Rákosi says that he is satisfied with the clarification.

b) Amendment to page 2, paragraph 1, of the draft resolution, which reads:

"The world war unleashed by the Hitlerites exacerbated further the difference in the situation of individual countries, by creating a deep divide between the countries that became spreaders of the Hitlerite tyranny and the freedom-loving peoples who have united in a powerful anti-Hitler coalition. Although the main task of the workers, toilers, and all honest people in the countries of the Hitlerite bloc is to contribute in all possible ways to the defeat of this bloc by undermining the Hitler military machine from within, to contribute to the overthrow of the governments responsible for the war, in the countries allied against Hitler the sacred duty of the broad masses, and in particular of progressive workers, is to give all possible support to the military effort of the governments of these countries for the sake of the prompt defeat of the Hitlerite bloc and protecting the commonwealth of nations based on their equal rights."

Dimitrov asks the participants of the meeting whether they deem it necessary to supplement this point of the draft resolution with a short paragraph characterizing the specific situation in the countries occupied by the Hitlerites and the specific tasks facing the working class and broad popular masses there.

"In some countries of this type," says Dimitrov, "there are no national governments or there are puppet governments that carry out the will of the occupiers. The masses in these countries cannot use the state apparatus in the war against Hitler Germany. Here the task is to mount an armed struggle against the occupiers which would turn into a national-liberation war." Dimitrov asks what the representatives of the occupied countries, in particular Marty, Thorez (French), and Šverma (Czech), think about it.

Thorez and Šverma support Dimitrov's suggestion and propose to create an appropriate addition for the final text of the resolution. Participants of the meeting agree with Thorez and Šverma.

> *Kolarov, Pieck*

c) Amendment of Dolores to the 2nd paragraph on page 3 of the draft resolution that reads:

"Guided by the teachings of the founders of Marxism-Leninism, Communists have never been supporters of organizational fetishism, have always subordinated organizational structure and methods of work of the workers' movement to the vital political interests of the workers' movement as a whole, to the particularities of the specific historical situation, and to the tasks that directly derive from this situation."

Dolores, in this paragraph of the draft resolution, suggests replacing the words "Communists have never been supporters of organizational fetishism" with "Communists have never been supporters of a frozen form of organization, set once and forever." The motives for her amendment are the following: there is no such word as "organizational fetishism" in the Spanish language and [political] vocabulary. And this is no accident, since Spaniards have never been famous for a predisposition toward efficient organization. If we introduce the term in Spain and in the countries of Latin America, it will be interpreted as disregard of organization, which conforms to the Spanish character. Why do it if the same idea can be expressed with different words?

Ulbricht objects to Dolores' amendment saying that it may create the impression that we are not dissolving the Comintern, but merely replacing it with another, camouflaged, organization. Second, the "Outline History of the VKP(b)," known in Spain and in the Latin American countries as well, refers to "organizational fetishism," and has produced no confusion. On the contrary, studying the "Outline History of the VKP(b)" encourages Spaniards' disposition to organization. We Germans, says Ulbricht, have no doubts about "organizational fetishism."

> *Thorez is opposed*

Marty supports Dolores' amendment and declares that it is here that we have

Documents 52 and 53 *continued*

to consider the particularities of such a country as Spain and not measure Spaniards with the German yardstick. "You in Germany," says Marty sharply, "cannot even urinate without organization. In Latin and Roman countries the situation is different."

Dimitrov suggests taking Dolores' amendment into account in the final editing of the resolution; there are no objections.

d) Amendment by Kolarov to the same 2nd paragraph on page 3 of the draft resolution, which reads:

"They [i.e., the Communists] remember the example of the great Marx, who united the vanguard workers in the ranks of the International Workingmen's Association and, after the First International had accomplished its historical mission by creating a basis for development of the workers' parties in Europe and America, dissolved the First International, since that form of organization no longer corresponded to the new level of the workers' movement."

Kolarov reverts to his suggestion, made at the previous meeting of the ECCI Presidium, that it is necessary to specify or amend this passage in the draft resolution in order to avoid false analogies, which may raise doubts about the correctness of the argument. Since the liquidation of the First International was prefaced by the defeat of the Paris Commune, it is essential to demonstrate that the current situation is entirely different and that it is not the reactionary forces that are gaining the victory but the progressive forces of the world.

Rákosi objects to Kolarov's proposal. "For our supporters," says Rákosi, "reference to Marx's example is the most convincing argument. We are not writing a history treatise about the objective conditions that had led to the dissolution of the First International, but a political document supported by the example of our teacher Marx."

<. . .>

Dimitrov is also opposed to Kolarov's suggestion, stressing that Marx and Engels, in their political speeches, always indicated that the dissolution of the First International resulted from the urgent need to create mass parties on a national basis in the individual countries. Kolarov is afraid that our people make an error in interpreting the resolution. This can be prevented by [publishing] a clearly written article warning against drawing direct parallels between the two different historical periods in the development of the workers' movement.

Kolarov's suggestion is rejected unanimously.

There are no other amendments.

Dimitrov suggests electing an editorial commission to formulate the amendments that is composed of Dimitrov, Dolores, Manuilsky, Pieck, Thorez. The Presidium approves the composition of the commission.

II.

§1607. Discussion of the question of how to implement the resolution of the Presidium.

II.

Dimitrov says that there are two major alternatives for implementing the resolution:

The first alternative: The Presidium of the ECCI, after the final adoption of the resolution, informs the CI sections of it by publishing it in the press, over the signature of the members of the Presidium present here, as a proposal requiring approval by the sections of the Comintern. Declarations of the CI sections approving the Presidium's proposal will be considered the final decision to dissolve the CI. In this case, it might be necessary to warn the sections in advance so that it will not come as a surprise to them.

The second alternative: The Presidium of the ECCI, after having voted on the resolution as its own proposal, forwards it to the sections with which it has telegraph communication: France, England, China, Belgium, Holland, Yugoslavia, Poland, Sweden, and Latin America. After receiving their answers, [the Presidium] publishes it in the press as a decision adopted and approved by the sections.

Dimitrov asks the participants of the meeting to express their opinion of which alternative is preferable or to suggest another means.

Wolf supports the first alternative. This assures a maximum of democratism and openness in resolving such an important question as the dissolution of the Comintern. At the same time, this alternative guarantees maximum political effect, whereas the second alternative has the disadvantage that the enemy can publish our decision before we do.

Wolf's opinion is supported by Thorez, Dolores, Kolarov, and Koplenig, who stress that the "illegal manner" suggested by the second alternative carries the risk that the resolution will be used by the enemy before it actually reaches the sections of the CI. Moreover, in the present circumstances, when most of the CI sections are illegal, it is impossible to make a broad announcement or call meetings to discuss the proposals. Decisions will be made by the CCs of the parties and by the underground leadership. Therefore, publishing the resolution in the press as a proposal by the Presidium of the ECCI is the most expedient method to secure openness and democratism.

Dimitrov puts the question to the vote. The Presidium of the ECCI unanimously pronounces in favor of the first alternative.

Manuilsky thinks it expedient, in case the resolution of the Presidium of the ECCI is published as a proposal to be approved by the sections of the CI, to publish along with it declarations of approval of the resolution by the members of the Executive Committee of the Comintern and representatives of the Communist parties who are now in Moscow. The suggestion is adopted.

G. Dim[itrov]

The following representatives of Communist parties subscribe to this resolution:

Documents 52 and 53 *continued*

BIANCO (Italy), DOLORES IBÁRRURI (Spain), LEHTINEN (Finland), PAUKER (Romania), RÁKOSI (Hungary).

Moscow, 15 May 1943

G. Dim[itrov]
W. Pieck
A. Marty
Gottwald
Dolores Ibárruri
Koplenig
Thorez
D. Manuilsky
Rákosi
V. Kolarov
Lehtinen
Bianco, B.
Ercoli
Ana Pauker

PROTOCOL
OF THE MEETING OF THE EDITORIAL COMMISSION
ON THE DRAFT RESOLUTION
18 MAY 1943

Present: Dimitrov, Dolores, Manuilsky, Pieck, Thorez.

The Commission unanimously resolved:

1) To amend the end of the second paragraph on page 2:

"At the same time, one should not forget that the individual countries supporting the anti-Hitler coalition have their particular tasks. For example, in the countries occupied by the Hitlerites that had lost their status as independent countries, the major task of the vanguard workers and broad popular masses is to step up the armed struggle, which will turn into a war for national liberation against Hitler Germany."

2) To alter the beginning of the third paragraph on page 3:

"Guided by the teachings of the founders of Marxism-Leninism, Communists have never been supporters of preserving organizational forms that have outlived themselves: they have always subordinated organizational structure and methods of work of the workers' movement to the vital political interests of the workers' movement as a whole, to the particularities of the specific historical situation, and to the tasks that directly derive from this situation."

3) To introduce the following change at the end of the first paragraph on page 4:

"The Presidium of the ECCI, having no chance of convoking a Congress of the CI in the situation of world war, submits the following proposal for ratification by the sections of the CI."

G. Dim[itrov]

To Comrade STALIN

To Comrade MALENKOV

At the closed meeting of the Presidium of the ECCI on 19 May, a number of questions pertaining to the resolution on the dissolution of the Communist International were discussed.

I am sending you the enclosed protocol of this meeting.

(G. DIMITROV)

22 May 1943

PROTOCOL (B) No. 826

OF THE CLOSED MEETING OF THE PRESIDIUM

OF THE ECCI OF 19 MAY 1943

PRESENT

1) Members of the Presidium: Dimitrov, Manuilsky, Pieck, Marty, Thorez, Koplenig, Kolarov; 2) Members and candidate members of the ECCI: Dolores Ibárruri, Rákosi, Ulbricht, Šverma, Wolf; 3) Representatives of the parties: Pauker (Romanian Communist Party), Lehtinen (Finnish Communist Party), Vlasov (Yugoslav Communist Party); 4) Interpreters: Stepanov and Fürnberg.

HEARD

§1608. On the organizational questions pertaining to the dissolution of the Comintern.

RESOLVED

Chair Dimitrov suggests that the Presidium discuss how to deal with the most important functions of the Comintern so as not to harm the cause of war with the Hitlerite bandits. Among these functions are:

a) national radio broadcasting

b) connections with fraternal parties

c) the "Supress"[11] Agency

d) the cadres of the Communist parties in the USSR

e) the party school in the USSR for these cadres

f) publishing house for foreign-language literature

g) the archive of the Comintern and individual parties

h) the library.

Dimitrov suggests discussing these questions in the order indicated by him.

a) national radio broadcasting

Pieck considers it necessary to preserve national radio broadcasting, since this broadcasting, unlike Soviet foreign-language broadcasts, is based on conditions in the corresponding countries and the particular tasks facing the masses in these countries in their struggle against fascism. Soviet broadcasts are incapable of either posing or resolving such tasks the way national radio

---

11. The Soviet Union Press Agency.

broadcasting is. Pi	eck asserts, based on information from the country, that in Germany they listen to the programs of the national radio broadcasting and make use of them.

Thorez argues in favor of retaining the national radio broadcasting, based on the following considerations: it provides correct information and political orientation for antifascist activists in the country and, to some extent, serves as an organizing center for the antifascist movement. At the same time, given the lack of coordination and disjunction among illegal party organizations in France, national radio broadcasting serves as their consolidating center. In Soviet radio broadcasts it is impossible to transmit to the partisans, for instance, such important advice as how to make explosives. Thorez stresses the achievements of the French national radio broadcasting: a series of campaigns which led to mass actions, forced the London radio to assume a favorable position toward the partisan movement in France, etc.

Marty supports Thorez. Soviet radio is hampered by the USSR's diplomatic relations; the illegal national radio can speak more openly.

Kolarov sides with the previous speakers, adding that liquidating the national radio broadcasting now when the end of the war is approaching, would be a blow to the entire work against Hitler Germany. Why should we liquidate the illegal Bulgarian radio station when there are four illegal radio stations in London broadcasting to Bulgaria? The Bulgarian government itself has illegal radio stations to conduct anti-Soviet propaganda. Programs of our station "Khristo Botev" are being transcribed by our comrades in Bulgaria and distributed in the form of leaflets. They serve to orient our party, other antifascist organizations, and the masses.

Dolores, Mihal, Rákosi, and all others, except for Manuilsky, support the previous comrades.

Manuilsky points out that keeping the national radio broadcasting going may undermine the political effect of the dissolution of the CI. It may be interpreted as restructuring the Comintern to continue illegally.

Dimitrov, in conclusion, emphasizes that Manuilsky's considerations merit serious attention, but in this case they are not decisive. Operating the national radio broadcasting could indeed be interpreted as restructuring the Comintern to continue illegally if it had been created after the dissolution of the Comintern; but it has been in existence for more than a year and a half and has a non-Communist, all-national character in the struggle against fascism. It is also important to remember that in almost every warring country there are illegal national radio stations. In his opinion, there are no obstacles to the continuation of the work of the national radio broadcasting to the countries at war with the USSR, and a way can always be found to avoid the danger regarding the occupied countries allied with us, which Manuilsky pointed out in his remarks.

b) connections with fraternal parties

Dimitrov points out that in the USSR there are the following foreign bureaus of fraternal Communist parties:

Germany: Pieck, Florin, Ulbricht, Ackerman.

Spain: Dolores Ibárruri, Hernández, Anton, Uribes.

France: Thorez, Marty, Rammette.

Austria: Koplenig, Fürnberg, Wieden, Schilling.

Czechoslovakia: Gottwald, Šverma, Kopecký, Bruno Keller, Slánský.

Italy: Ercoli, Bianco, Garlandi.

Bulgaria: Dimitrov, Kolarov, Belov, Chervenkov.

Hungary: Rákosi, Gerö, Révai, Weinberger.

Finland: Kuusinen, Lehtinen, Taimi, Äikiä.

Romania: Pauker.

All those present, Pieck, Kolarov, Thorez, and the others, speak about the necessity of retaining ties between the foreign bureaus and their parties, with the help of the existing apparatus; otherwise the enemy may be able to create hostile leadership in the countries in order to disorganize the Communist movement.

c) the "Supress" Agency

All those present argue in favor of retaining the agency. At Dimitrov's suggestion, the question is passed for [final] decision to the CC VKP(b).

d) registration of the cadres of Communist parties in the USSR

Their registration must be done in the CC VKP(b).

Questions of material support must continue to be dealt with by MOPR.

e) the party school for foreign cadres in the USSR

Complete the current session. Pass the question about the future of the school to the CC VKP(b).

f) publishing house for foreign-language literature

It must be under the control and supervision of the CC VKP(b).

g) the "Communist International" magazine

To discontinue the publication of the magazine after publishing the forthcoming issue.

To raise a question with the CC VKP(b) about launching a new magazine, "International Politics" or "International Information."

h) the archive of the Comintern and the individual parties

To be transferred for preservation by the CC VKP(b), with the possibility for the foreign bureaus of the various Communist parties to access their party archives.

i) the library

The Presidium considers it appropriate to transfer it to the Marx-Engels Institute and to make this proposal to the CC VKP(b).

(G.DIMITROV)

31 May 1943

The resolutions or messages of a number of foreign Communist parties approving the dissolution of the Comintern were published, in full or in excerpts, in the journal *Kommunisticheskii Internatsional* (1943).[12] Additional parties advised the ECCI of their approval during the following days. On 5 June, Dimitrov wrote Stalin and Molotov that twenty-nine replies concerning the dissolution, all positive, had been received from foreign Communist parties, out of a total of forty-one. He was planning to hold a meeting of the ECCI Presidium on 8 June to adopt the text of a communiqué for publication before the opening of the annual Labour Party conference in England on 13 June. He was also planning to name a liquidation commission to dispose of the assets of the Comintern by 1 August.[13]

On 7 June, Dimitrov forwarded to Stalin and Molotov the draft of a communiqué listing the parties that had approved the dissolution of the Comintern and declaring that as of 10 June the ECCI would cease to function, and appointing a commission consisting of Dimitrov, Manuilsky, Pieck, and Ercoli to dispose of the Comintern's files, personnel, and property; Konstantin Sukharev, an ECCI administrator, was named as its secretary.[14] Stalin approved the communiqué that night, and on 8 June the ECCI Presidium followed suit and approved the communiqué. The communiqué was published on 10 June.

Document 54

Dimitrov to Stalin and Molotov, 31 May 1943. RTsKhIDNI, f. 495, op. 73, d. 174, l. 57. Original in Russian. Typewritten.

TO COMRADE STALIN
TO COMRADE MOLOTOV
I am sending you the communications received so far from the Communist parties of England, France, China, Sweden, Switzerland, Yugoslavia, Syria

---

12. *Kommunisticheskii Internatsional,* 1943, nos. 5–6, pp. 12–25.
13. RTsKhIDNI, f. 495, op. 73, d. 174, ll. 58–59, and op. 18, d. 1340, l. 175.
14. RTsKhIDNI, f. 495, op. 73, d. 174, ll. 62–65.

and Lebanon, Australia, Argentina, Chile, Cuba, and Colombia, approving the proposal of the Presidium [of the ECCI] to dissolve the Communist International.

The leading comrades of the Mexican, Uruguayan, and Canadian Communist parties have also expressed their support of the proposal of the Presidium, but the resolutions of their parties have not been received as yet.

In addition to these communications, there are resolutions (approving the proposal of the Presidium) from the Communist parties of Germany, Austria, Italy, Hungary, Romania, Finland, Czechoslovakia, Spain, and Bulgaria, whose political leaders are in Moscow.

We have not yet had any word from the Polish Workers' Party nor from the Communist parties of Belgium, Holland, Denmark, Norway, Greece, Egypt, Turkey, Japan, India, and a number of smaller parties in Latin America who will hardly be able to inform us of their decisions in time.

In the coming days, we expect to receive communications from a number of other countries. I think that after [they arrive] we could publish the communiqué on the approval of the proposals of the Presidium of the Comintern's Executive Committee by the overwhelming majority of Communist parties that have been able to communicate their decision.

(G. DIMITROV)

31 May 1943

Why did Stalin press for the dissolution and its announcement at this particular time? One hypothesis sees the action as congruent with other "national" Soviet gestures adopted at this time, such as stressing patriotic themes in wartime propaganda, reestablishing the Moscow Patriarchate, promoting Stalin to Soviet marshal, and the adoption of a new Soviet national anthem that followed soon afterward. After all, the idea had been in Stalin's mind even before the war. (We can dismiss the assertion found in some American media and among some pundits that the Comintern was not actually dissolved: the dissolution was only a fake to deceive the West.)

Another hypothesis—not necessarily in conflict with the first— ties the timing to a visit to Moscow of U.S. Ambassador Joseph E. Davies. Molotov had been informed of his forthcoming visit in April; and Moscow might have known through its own intelligence channels that among the questions Davies was apt to raise was the fate of the Comintern. Molotov and then Stalin received him on

20 May.[15] That day Stalin asked Dimitrov over the phone whether the announcement of the resolution of the ECCI Presidium could be given to the press: "We ought to rush with the publication."[16] Dimitrov replied that the announcement could not be published until the member parties had received the resolution. The two settled on 22 May as the date for the public announcement.

The connection with the Davies visit is strongly suggestive but not fully established. No doubt Moscow was eager to make its gesture at a key moment, a time when plans were shaping up for the first face-to-face meeting of the Big Three, which took place at Tehran later that year. Davies acknowledged the dissolution in his conversations with Soviet leaders, but there is no suggestion in any available sources that he had raised the issue with them beforehand, let alone that his actions influenced their decision.[17]

15. See V. L. Mal'kov, "Missiya Dzh. Devisa v Moskvu v mae 1943 g.," *Novaya i noveishaya istoriya*, 1985, no. 1, pp. 96–97.

16. TsPA (Sofia), f. 146, op. 1, a.e. 11.

17. In fact, Davies' instructions were to stick to a single issue—to schedule a personal meeting between Roosevelt and Stalin at an early date. See the Soviet archival materials in Ministerstvo inostrannykh del SSSR, *Sovetsko-amerikanskie otnosheniya vo vremya Velikoi Otechestvennoi voiny 1941–1945* (Moscow: Politizdat, 1984), vol. 1, pp. 312, 314–315, 323, 326; and American materials in *Foreign Relations of the United States*, vol. 3: *1943* (Washington, D.C.: GPO, 1963), pp. 503, 529, 533. Davies told the State Department that the previous autumn Soviet Ambassador Maxim Litvinov had assured him that the Soviet government had nothing to do with the Comintern and that "therefore" Davies believed (in all naïveté) that it might be possible to convince the Soviet Union that "it would be advantageous to liquidate the Comintern" in its own interest. The far less naive Cordell Hull made a similar point to Edward Beneš on 18 May. In London, Soviet Ambassador Maisky insisted soon afterward that the dissolution had been decided on before the Davies visit, and that the question had been under discussion the previous Christmas. It is not clear whether Maisky was in a position to know or whether he was telling the truth.

CHAPTER NINE

After the Comintern, 1943–1945

AS A RESULT of the dissolution of the Communist International, in 1943 Georgi Dimitrov ceased to be the nominal director of the world Communist movement. With the creation of the new Department of International Information (OMI) within the staff of the Central Committee of the CPSU, Manuilsky and Dimitrov both became second-level Soviet functionaries, serving under department head (and secretary of the CC) Aleksandr Shcherbakov. In December 1943 Dimitrov was promoted to department head. Although the change must have been galling, Dimitrov showed no resentment or disappointment. True, he was a Soviet citizen. He had looked and deferred to Stalin on all significant decisions during his tenure at the Comintern. He had always conveyed the impression that he was a thoroughly loyal bureaucrat. And yet the change of status was bound to be seen by him (and others around him) as a comedown. Although he continued to deal with the questions that had preoccupied him in the preceding years, he was now also enmeshed in the apparat of Soviet foreign policy, plain and simple.

On some questions, he continued to go "out of channels" directly to Stalin—primarily concerning problems arising out of previous Comintern affairs or issues related to Soviet-Bulgarian relations. And typically, Stalin's replies came even more infreqently or were more curt than previously; sometimes he would answer through associates like Molotov, Zhdanov, and now also Poskrebyshev.

But some of the Comintern's functions had not entirely disappeared. The successor to the Comintern was named more precisely at a meeting in Stalin's office on 12 June 1943 (in the presence of Molotov, Beria, Shcherbakov, and Dimitrov). Here the decision to set up the new Department of International Information was formalized—but the new department was not to be publicized. In effect, it took over the remaining functions of the former Comintern, including liaison with foreign parties, illegal radio broadcasts, the foreign-language publishing house, and the direction of "antifascist" committees. Dimitrov asked the foreign parties to "continue to send information in the same way as heretofore."[1]

As ever, one sensitive issue that remained concerned the Polish Communists. As part of the process of reestablishing the Communist organization in Poland, Dimitrov and Manuilsky had drafted a resolution even before the German troops were forced out that established a Central Bureau of Communists of Poland. They negotiated with both Molotov and some of the Polish Communists in Moscow about its function and put together a list of proposed members. On 24 January 1944 Dimitrov sent Stalin the relevant documents and the following day received a resolution of the CPSU Central Committee confirming his proposals. From start to finish, the establishment process was entirely a Soviet operation.[2]

Another preoccupation was the future of the German Communist Party. The German Communists had always been strongly represented in the Comintern, and what the proper policy was for them to pursue, especially in the Hitler years, had often been difficult to decide. During the war, as the number of German prisoners of war in Soviet hands grew, Moscow was eager to mount a broad campaign of indoctrination and organization that would reach far beyond the membership of the KPD. In December 1942, when it first appeared that the tide of war might turn, the Central Committee of

1. TsPA (Sofia), f. 146, op. 2, a.e. 11.
2. RTsKhIDNI, f. 495, op. 74, d. 441, ll. 12–15. The five persons Dimitrov recommended as members of the new Polish Central Bureau were Aleksandr Zawadzski, Stanislaw Radkiewicz, Karol Swierczewski, Wanda Wasilewska, and Jakub Berman.

the CPSU decided to approve a conference of prisoners of war, with obvious propaganda purposes. It similarly approved the creation of a Free Germany Committee.[3] No comparable committees of, or for, Hungarian, Romanian, or Italian prisoners of war were ever formed, perhaps out of concern over the response of the Western powers; nor were suitable and prominent "cadres" identified for such committees. In the following months preparatory work went forward under the overall direction of the ECCI Secretariat.[4]

The meeting in Stalin's office that established the OMI also approved the creation of the Free Germany Committee, which was launched at a conference in Moscow on 12–13 July 1943 with an appeal to the German army and the German people. The committee, with the participation of both prominent prisoners of war and Communist refugees, also began publishing its own paper, *Freies Deutschland*. The committee was active for two years, mostly under military auspices, but at the end of the war its status and future needed to be reviewed. Moreover, when the exiles returned to Germany, reestablishing the German Communist Party was bound to be a priority task.

On 6 June 1945 Dimitrov and several leading German Communists reviewed the draft of an appeal by the (Soviet-based) Central Committee of the KPD and sent it on to Stalin for his approval.[5] Stalin and Molotov received Dimitrov the next day, and Stalin proposed an emendation: that it would be wrong to introduce the Soviet system into Germany at that moment, that Germany needed an antifascist democratic parliamentary regime, and that the KPD wanted to form a bloc of antifascist parties on a common platform. The next day Dimitrov and his German associates edited the text in accordance with Stalin's instructions and sent it back to Stalin, who approved it that evening. It was published on 12 June under a Berlin byline and signed by fifteen leading German Communists.[6]

3. See Presidential Archive (APRF), f. 3, op. 20, d. 79, ll. 78–79.
4. See RTsKhIDNI, f. 495, op. 74, d. 155, l. 107.
5. RTsKhIDNI, f. 17, op. 128, d. 716, l. 53.
6. RTsKhIDNI, f. 17, op. 128, d. 716, ll. 54, 72–81. Dimitrov also served as a source of information on foreign "cadres." Thus on 2 April 1945 Stalin requested a list of Austrian Communists and prisoners of war to be dispatched to the Third Ukrainian Front (entering Austria). Dimitrov promptly sent a list headed by Johann Koplenig, a Comintern veteran and secretary general of the KPÖ, and Ernst Fischer

Meanwhile, now that the war was over the Free Germany Com-mittee had lost its raison d'être, and, prompted by Dimitrov, chair-man Erich Weinert proposed on 21 September 1945 that it dissolve itself (as well the Union of German Officers).[7] On 30 October the CPSU Politburo adopted a resolution and approved the text of the decision to be announced by the Germans, who met on 2 Novem-ber and carried out the dissolution as ordered.[8]

Meanwhile, the American Communists were to experience a rude shock. The April 1945 issue of *Cahiers du communisme,* the offi-cial publication of the Communist Party of France, contained a lengthy article by Jacques Duclos called "On the Dissolution of the American Communist Party."[9] Duclos was an old associate of Dimitrov's and during the war had remained in France to direct the Resistance. The article's significance lay in the fact that it was a high-level attack on American party leader Earl Browder and "Browder-ism," the line being pursued by American Communists that Moscow now viewed as impermissible revisionism. The article assailed the dissolution of the CPUSA, which had taken place in 1944, and its replacement by a "political association"—something that ran counter to Bolshevik practice and instruction. Browder's alleged inference from the Tehran Summit Conference of 1943 that capitalism and socialism were finding ways to coexist and even col-laborate was branded as un-Marxist. "By transforming the Tehran declaration of the Allied governments, which is a document of a diplomatic character, into a political platform of class peace in the United States in the postwar period, the American communists are . . . sowing dangerous opportunist illusions." If the implication was

(Peter Wieden), another KPÖ representative to the ECCI (RTsKhIDNI, f. 495, op. 74, d. 25, ll. 1–2). On 10 August, after the USSR had declared war on Japan, Dimitrov and Boris Ponomarev, his assistant at the OMI, recommended a Japanese Communist, Okano (Sandzo Nosaka), for a prominent position in the new (post-war) Japan. A member of the ECCI Presidium since 1933, Okano had been in China during the Sino-Japanese War and later served as first secretary and chairman of the Communist Party of Japan. (RTsKhIDNI, f. 17, op. 128, d. 718, ll. 93–97.)

    7. RTsKhIDNI, f. 17, op. 128, d. 839, ll. 137–140.

    8. RTsKhIDNI, f. 17, op. 162, d. 37, ll. 156, 172. On Soviet policy and behav-ior in the Eastern Zone of Germany, see Norman M. Naimark, *The Russians in Ger-many* (Cambridge: Harvard University Press, 1995).

    9. Jacques Duclos, "A propos de la dissolution du P.C.A.," *Cahiers du commu-nisme,* nouvelle serie, no. 6 (April 1945); English trans. in *Daily Worker* (New York), May 24, 1945.

an impending return to a period of "class versus class," this was news indeed. Friends and foes alike soon concluded that the attack, even after the dissolution of the Comintern, could hardly have been written on French initiative. Indeed, the article was viewed—correctly, it appears—as a signal of a "hardening" Soviet line toward the Western allies and toward the sloppy faith in convergence that Browderism seemed to reflect.

Dimitrov sent Stalin and Molotov a copy of the Duclos article on 28 May, remarking only that the Soviet party press had planned to reprint it after it was published in Paris. The Soviet archives, however, indicate a far more extensive Soviet involvement in the piece. It had evidently been drafted in the new OMI, part, as we have seen, of the Central Committee of the Soviet Communist Party. This new information corresponds to earlier surmises that some of the material in the Duclos article had been available abroad only to Dimitrov and his staff in Moscow.[10] The OMI then sent the article to the so-called Institute No. 205, a successor agency of the ECCI apparatus, to be translated into French. On 19 January 1945, Bedřich Geminder, who directed the press and information services of the Comintern and its successor agencies, returned both the original (Russian) draft and the French translation to "Comrade Shuklin," who headed the OMI secretariat, where it was decided to publish it in the name of Jacques Duclos, clearly to avoid giving the impression that Moscow was telling American Communists what to do and what not to do. (It is not clear why the article took from January to April to get to Paris for publication.)[11] Indeed, in response to Dimitrov's note it was evidently decided not to publish the piece at all in *Pravda* or *Bol'shevik;* but it was run in Russian in a classified Soviet party bulletin.[12]

10. See Joseph R. Starobin, *American Communism in Crisis, 1943–1957* (Harvard University Press, 1972), pp. 81–83. Chapter 4 has a good discussion of the effect of the Duclos article on the American Communists.

11. The significance of the dating of the original lies in the controversy over the origins of the Cold War. It is sometimes alleged that Soviet policy began to change in response to a hardening American policy after the death of Franklin D. Roosevelt on 12 April 1945. The Duclos article has been cited in support of this argument. The date of the Russian original and translation disposes of this use of the evidence—indeed, the article was drafted even before the Yalta conference.

12. Dimitrov to Stalin and Molotov, 28 May 1945, with enclosures, in RTsKhIDNI, f. 17, op. 128, d. 716, l. 51, and d. 754, ll. 95–98ob.

О КОММУНИСТИЧЕСКОЙ ПОЛИТИЧЕСКОЙ АССОЦИАЦИИ США

состоявшемся 20 мая 1944 г. в Нью-Йорке коммунистической партии Америки было принято решение о роспуске компартии США и о создании Коммунистической политической ассоциации США.

Причины роспуска компартии Америки и принятия «нового курса» в работе американских коммунистов изложены в официальных документах КП и в ряде выступлений бывшего генерального секретаря коммунистической партии Америки Браудера.

В речи, посвященной итогам Тегеранской конференции и политическому положению США, 12 декабря 1943 г. в Бриджпорте, опубликованной в журнале «Коммунист» в январе 1944 г., Браудер впервые обосновал необходимость изменения курса американской компартии.

Главным пунктом в обосновании изменения линии американской компартии для Браудера, по его заявлению, послужила Тегеранская конференция. Однако, правильно подчеркивая значение Тегеранской конференции для победы в войне с фашистской Германией, Браудер сделал из решений конференции целый ряд неверных, немарксистских выводов и по сути дела построил целую концепцию, неправильно определяющую пути общественного развития вообще и, в первую очередь, общественного развития США.

Браудер заявил, что в Тегеране капитализм и социализм начали находить путь к мирному сосуществованию и сотрудничеству в рамках одного мира, что тегеранское соглашение о совместной политике предполагает и совместные усилия в сведении к минимуму или к полному устранению методов насильственной борьбы в разрешении внутренних вопросов каждой страны в отдельности.

«Тегеранская декларация,— указывал Браудер в своей речи,— это единственная надежда на продолжение цивилизации в нашу эпоху. Вот почему я могу принять, поддержать и поверить в Тегеранскую декларацию, сделав ее исходным пунктом всех моих соображений насчет проблем нашей страны и всего мира».

Исходя из решений Тегеранской конференции, Браудер делает политические выводы в отношении проблем всего мира и, особенно, в отношении внутреннего положения США. Ряд этих выводов свидетельствует о том, что основные вопросы внутренней жизни США должны будут разрешаться в дальнейшем путем реформ, так как «неограниченная внутренняя борьба угрожает международному единству, установленному в Тегеране».

Тегеранское соглашение, по мнению Браудера, означает, что бо́льшая часть Европы, лежащей к западу от Советского Союза, вероятно, будет восстановлена на буржуазно-демократической базе, а не на фашистско-капиталистической или на советской базе.

«Но это будет такая капиталистическая база,— говорил Браудер,— которая обуславливается принципом полного демократического права на самоопределение для каждой нации, права, обеспечивающего полную свободу мнений внутри каждого государства всем прогрессивным и созидательным силам, не терпящего никаких помех в деле развития демократии и социального прогресса, в соответствии с различными желаниями народов. Это сулит Европе перспективу доведения до минимума и даже до полной ликвидации угрозы гражданской войны после мировой войны».

Значение Тегеранской конференции конкретно для Америки,— указывает Браудер,— означает перспективу обеспечения непосредственно после войны расширенного производства, предоставления всем работы, перспективу укрепления демократии в рамках нынешней системы, создание широкого национального единства на многие годы, но не перспективу перехода к социализму, к которому американский народ не подготовлен.

«Мы можем поставить своей целью,— говорил Браудер на пленуме ЦК компартии 4 января 1944 г.— либо осуществление политики Тегерана, либо же задачу немедленного перехода США к социалистической системе. Не ясно ли, что мы не можем добиваться того и другого. Первая перспектива, несмотря на многочисленные трудности, определенно находится в пределах практически осуществимого. Вторая перспектива является по меньшей мере сомнительной, в особенности, если учесть, что наиболее прогрессивная часть рабочего движения Америки не обладает даже теми гуманными социалистическими идеями, какие свойственны лейбористской партии Англии. Следовательно, политика марксистов в США должна заключаться в том, чтобы со всей реальностью считаться с перспективой послевоенной капиталистической реконструкции США, оценивать все планы, исходя из этой перспективы, и активно сотрудничать с наиболее демократическим и прогрессивным большинством в стране, добиваясь национального единства, достаточно широкого и эффективного для осуществления политики Тегерана».

First page of the proof for О КОММУНИСТИЧЕСКОЙ ПОЛИТИЧЕСКОЙ АССОЦИАЦИИ США (On the Communist Political Association of the United States), an article that was published in БЮЛЛЕТЕНЬ БЮРО ИНФОРМАЦИИ ЦК ВКП(б): ВОПРОСЫ ВНЕШНЕЙ ПОЛИТИКИ (Bulletin of the information bureau of the CC VKP[b]: Issues of foreign policy), January 1945. Several pages of the article proof have hand corrections, one of which is visible here. (From Harvey Klehr, John Earl Haynes, and Kyrill M. Anderson, eds., *The Soviet World of American Communism* [New Haven: Yale University Press, 1998], p. 102.)

The impact of the Duclos article was considerable. Within a few months, Browder and his deputies had been ousted, the CPUSA was reinstated, and the habit of taking the signals from abroad once again prevailed among American Communists.

Dimitrov was also active in the Balkans. He had an understandable concern for problems relating to his native Bulgaria and, as we have seen, to Yugoslavia. In turn, the traditionally pro-Russian Bulgaria, though an Axis member, sought to avoid fighting the Soviet Union in the war.[13] When the regime in Sofia collapsed in September 1944 and the Red Army approached in its westward drive, Dimitrov advised Stalin that the Muraviev government, which had taken over, was not good enough; he was banking on—and urged Soviet assistance for—the Communist-sponsored Fatherland Front. This group did indeed easily come to power in Bulgaria, and Dimitrov informed Stalin and Molotov about the personalities and background of the new regime, forwarding a report prepared for him by Dimitur Ganev, a member of the Bulgarian Communist leadership.[14]

If Dimitrov's position and advocacy on Bulgarian internal affairs were fairly predictable, Balkan international problems were more challenging. During World War II Germany had let Bulgaria occupy the (previously Yugoslav) Macedonia as well as (Greek) Thrace. If now both Yugoslavia and Bulgaria wound up as "fraternal" members of the Soviet bloc, what would their future relationship be? Leaving aside their rivalry over Macedonia, Tito wanted to make Bulgaria another member of the South Slav Federation, with the same status as Croatia or Slovenia. The Bulgarian Communists, insofar as they had any affinity for their fellow Slavs to the west, favored a confederation, or federation, in which Bulgaria and Yugoslavia were equal members. Stalin, though he wasn't very clear

13. For a background on Bulgarian politics, see Nissan Oren, *Revolution Administered: Agrarianism and Communism in Bulgaria* (Baltimore: Johns Hopkins University Press, 1973), and Marshall Lee Miller, *Bulgaria During the Second World War* (Stanford: Stanford University Press, 1975).

14. RTsKhIDNI, f. 495, op. 74, d. 95, ll. 7–14; f. 17, op. 128, d. 3, ll. 12–14. Among the people Dimitrov recommended was Nikola Petkov, a prominent agrarian leader who was friendly to the Soviet Union. Two years later, when Dimitrov was back in Sofia as head of the government, Petkov was sentenced to death on ludicrous charges in a Soviet-style trial. Dimitrov insisted that the sentence be carried out.

about it, favored—here and everywhere else—dividing his clients, the better to control them. The issue, explosive though it was, did not erupt until several years later. Meanwhile, in December 1944 the Yugoslav and Bulgarian Communist leaderships agreed on a draft treaty of alliance, which Dimitrov sent to Stalin and Molotov for comment. The draft included an explicit commitment to form a federal union and provided for a settlement of the Macedonian question.[15]

But the agreement was left in limbo inasmuch as the relationship between Tito's National Committee and the Yugoslav government in exile in London remained to be worked out. In April 1945, after the Yalta accord, a Soviet-Yugoslav friendship treaty was signed in Moscow. Stalin received Dimitrov and Tito and they agreed that diplomatic relations would be restored between Yugoslavia and Bulgaria and that everyone would work toward a Yugoslav-Bulgarian federation. In fact, of course, no such union ever came about.

The other issue concerning the postwar borders enmeshed Yugoslavia and Italy over the port city of Trieste and its hinterland, Venezia Giulia. A complicated and protracted issue, the conflict touched Dimitrov's OMI only insofar as the Italian Communists used the organization to transmit their views to Stalin in 1945. For the Communist Party of Italy the issue was a source of considerable embarrassment: as a "national" Italian party it did not wish to advocate the cession of Italian territory; as a matter of "proletarian solidarity" it did not wish to cross swords with the Yugoslav comrades. As a result, both "Ercoli" and Giuseppe di Vittorio (a veteran member of the PCI political leadership) went out of their way to assure Stalin that they would do whatever Moscow told them to. Yet they strongly disagreed with Tito's policy and behavior in the matter even if in the end they sought to weasel on the whole issue.[16]

Still Dimitrov recommended that Stalin support the Yugoslav claim, and Stalin agreed: presumably, acquiring Trieste for the

15. RTsKhIDNI, f. 495, op. 74, d. 599, ll. 86–90. See the essays by Leonid Ia. Gibianskii, "The Soviet-Yugoslav Conflict and the Soviet Bloc," Vesselin Dimitrov, "Revolution Released: Stalin, the Bulgarian Communist Party and the Establishment of the Cominform," and R. Craig Nation, "A Balkan Union?" in Francesca Gori and Silvio Pons, eds., The Soviet Union and Europe in the Cold War, 1943–53 (London: Macmillan, 1996).

16. RTsKhIDNI, f. 17, op. 128, d. 716, ll. 45–47, 88–92.

emerging Soviet orbit was more valuable than helping or humoring the PCI; moreover, the Yugoslavs had fought on the Soviet side while the Italians had not. In any event, it took years to settle the Trieste question; after the Stalin-Tito split, the Soviets played a subordinate role, and Dimitrov had no hand in the matter.[17] More generally, the transformation of Eastern Europe that the Soviet defeat of Germany ushered in did not offer a palpable role for the OMI or Dimitrov. There may be truth to one scholar's conclusion that in 1945 "the hero of Leipzig was all but a broken man."[18]

By the second half of 1945 Dimitrov's attention was again focused on Bulgaria, which was undergoing an unprecedented transformation into a Communist-ruled state and thus becoming an attractive prospect—and after all his native habitat—for the long-term exile. On 3 November, Dimitrov sent Stalin a letter thanking him for having given him the opportunity to work under Stalin's direct guidance for so many years; he had learned a good deal from Stalin, and he appreciated having enjoyed Stalin's confidence. "Of course I will continue to make every effort to justify your confidence. But I beg you to give me the opportunity, in the future as well, to call on your exceptionally needed valuable advice."[19] On 4 November he flew to Sofia, where he soon became head of the Bulgarian Communist Party and, a year later, prime minister of Bulgaria.[20] He held those two positions until his death in 1949.

17. On the relations between the PCI and the Yugoslav Communists, see Eric R. Terzuolo, *Red Adriatic* (Boulder, Colo.: Westview Press, 1985).

18. Oren, *Revolution*, p. 109.

19. TsPA (Sofia), f. 146, op. 2, a.e. 66, l. 132.

20. Ironically, Dimitrov's relations with Stalin seemed to deteriorate during the years he represented Bulgaria, which became increasingly a Soviet dependency. Retrospectively, Stalin spared no words in criticizing Dimitrov for his role as the Comintern's secretary general. Aleksandar Ranković, a leading Yugoslav Communist official, recorded his impressions of a dinner at Stalin's villa: "The main topic during the supper was the foundation of the Cominform. What struck me was the sharpness, almost the malice with which Stalin spoke about the work of the Third International, shooting his darts at Dimitrov. As he did so, old Dimitrov grew so red and was obviously so uncomfortable that the rest of us squirmed." Above all, Stalin sought to prevent the South Slav, or more broadly Balkan, alliance or confederation of Bulgaria and its neighbors that was being discussed in 1946–48. The Yugoslavs had reason to think that Stalin was seeking to split the Yugoslavs from the Bulgarians. Cf. Milovan Djilas, *Conversations with Stalin* (New York: Harcourt, Brace, 1962), pp. 74–86; and Vladimir Dedijer, *Tito Speaks* (London: Weidenfeld and Nicolson, 1953), pp. 284–285.

Biographical Notes

Abakumov, Viktor Semenovich (1894–1954): USSR minister of state security, 1946–51; arrested and shot, 1954.

Abetz, Otto (1903–58): German ambassador to Paris, 1940–44.

Ackermann, Anton (Eugen Hanisch) (1905–73): active in KPD, on ECCI staff and with Red Army Political Administration, 1940–43; in East Germany, in SED leadership, from 1945.

Andreyev, Andrei Andreyevich (1895–1971): member of CPSU Central Control Commission, 1920–61; member of CPSU Politburo, 1932–52.

Anton, Francisco Sanz (1909–76): candidate member of PCE Politburo, 1937–39; in ECCI 1940–43.

Azaña y Diaz, Manuel (1880–1940): Spanish prime minister, 1931–33; president of Spain, 1936–39.

Beria, Lavrenti Pavlovich (1899–1953): member of CPSU CC from 1934; candidate member of CPSU Politburo from 1935; full member of Politburo from 1946; head of NKVD, 1938–45; arrested and shot, 1953.

Berman, Jakub (1901–84): member of ECCI staff, 1941–43; member of Polish party Politburo, 1944–56.

Billoux, François (1903–?): member of PCF CC, from 1926; member of PCF Politburo, 1937–40; under arrest in France, 1940–43; minister under Charles de Gaulle, 1944–47; secretary of PCF CC, 1954–56.

Blum, Léon (1872–1950): leader of SFIO; prime minister of France, 1936–37 and March–April 1938.

Bo Gu [Po Ku] (Chin Panghsien) (1907–46): general secretary of CCP, 1931–35; later section head of CCP CC.

Bonnet, Georges (1889–1973): French foreign minister, 1937–38.

Bonte, Florimond: prominent French Communist.

Brouckère, Louis de (1870–1951): Belgian socialist, representative to League of Nations.

Browder, Earl (1891–1973): general secretary of CPUSA, 1930–44; candidate member of ECCI Presidium, 1931–40; member of ECCI Politsecretariat, 1933–35; chairman of Communist Political Organization, 1944–45; ousted from CPUSA, 1945.

Bukharin, Nikolai Ivanovich (1888–1938): member of CPSU Politburo, 1924–29; member of ECCI and its Presidium, 1919–29; editor-in-chief of *Izvestia*, 1934–37; arrested 1937, sentenced to death 1938.

Cachin, Marcel (1869–1958): leader of PCF; member of ECCI from 1924; member of ICC of Comintern, 1924–35; member of ECCI Presidium, 1935–43.

Chamberlain, Neville (1869–1940): British prime minister, 1937–40.

Chautemps, Camille (1885–1963): Radical Party leader in France; premier of France, 1933–34, 1937–38; vice premier in Pétain government, 1940.

Checa, Pedro (1910–42): member of PCE CC from 1932, member of PCE Politburo from 1935; emigrated to France, Mexico, 1939.

Chiang Kai-shek (1887–1975): head of Guomindang (Kuomintang) and Chinese Nationalist government from 1927.

Chicherin, Georgy Vasilievich (1872–1936): Soviet people's commissar for foreign affairs, 1918–30.

Codovilla, Vittorio (also Victorio Codovila, pseuds. Luis, Medina) (1894–1970): member Argentine CP CC, from 1921; general secretary of Argentine CP from 1941; candidate member of ECCI Presidium, 1926–28; secretary of South American Bureau of ECCI, 1928–30; ECCI representative to PCE, 1932–37.

Cogniot, Georges (1901–78): member of PCF CC from 1931; representative of PCF to ECCI, 1936–37; editor-in-chief of *L'Humanité*, 1937–49.

Comorera, Juan (1895–?): general secretary of United Socialist Party of Catalonia (PSUC), 1936–49; excluded from PCE, 1949.

Daladier, Edouard (1884–1970): member of various French cabinets as prime minister, minister of foreign affairs, war minister in 1930s.

Davies, Joseph E. (1876–1958): U.S. ambassador to USSR, 1936–38.

Déat, Marcel (1894–1955): dissident French socialist turned pacifist then pro-fascist; collaborated with Germans during the Occupation.

Decaux, Jules: student at MLS (pseud. Forcy), 1931–33; PCF representative at ECCI, 1930–38; under arrest in France, 1940–43.

Delbos, Yvon (1885–1956): French Radical Party leader; foreign minister of France, 1936–37; member of Resistance, 1940–43.

Diaz, José (1894–1942): from 1932 general secretary of PCE; from 1935 member of ECCI; 1939–42 on ECCI Secretariat.

Di Vittorio, Giuseppe (pseud. Mario Nicoletti) (1892–1957): member of PCI Politburo, later directorate, from 1931; commissar of International Brigade in Spain, 1936–37; vice president of World Trade Union Federation, after 1945.

Doriot, Jacques (1898–1945): member of PCF CC, 1924–34; alternate member of ECCI, 1924–34; expelled from PCF, 1934; became fascist, fought with Germans on Soviet front; killed, 1945.

Dragun, Colonel: headed 5th Section of Intelligence Administration (*Razvedupr*) of the Red Army General Staff in 1941.

Duclos, Jacques (pseud. Yves) (1896–1975): member of PCF Politburo and Secretariat from 1931; candidate member of ECCI Presidium, 1932; member of ECCI from 1935; PCF representative to Cominform, 1947–49; secretary general of PCF, 1950.

Ercoli. *See* Togliatti, Palmiro.

Fang Lin (Deng Fa [Teng Fa]) (1906–46): member of CCP CC from 1930; member of Politburo from 1931; member of CCP delegation to ECCI, 1936–37; CCP representative in Xinjiang, 1938.

Farkas, Mihaly (pseuds. Michal, Wolf) (1904–65): active in KIM and ECCI; candidate member of ECCI, 1935–1943; headed political police in Hungary after 1945, later defense minister; expelled from party, 1956.

Finder, Pawel (1904–44): Polish Communist leader who parachuted into occupied Poland; secretary of Polish Workers' Party from November 1942; arrested 1943; killed 1944.

Fischer, Ernst (pseud. Peter Wieden) (1899–1972): editor of journal *Communist International* from 1938; member of KPÖ CC; excluded 1969.

Flandin, Pierre-Etienne (1889–1958): French politician, minister, and collaborator with Vichy government.

Florin, Wilhelm (1894–1944): member of KPD CC from 1924; member of ECCI Presidium from 1933; in Moscow from 1935; member of ECCI Secretariat from 1935.

Foissin, Robert: French lawyer close to PCF and Soviet causes; excluded from PCF, 1940.

Frachon, Benoît: (1893–1975): in PCF CC from 1926; member of PCF Politburo from 1928; candidate member of ECCI, 1928–43; active in CGT and in wartime resistance.

Franco, Francisco (1892–1975): chief of Spanish insurgent movement, 1936; dictator and generalissimo of Spain, 1939–75.

Fürnberg, Friedl (1902–78): member of KPÖ CC from 1924; at ECCI from 1937; member of KPÖ Politburo from 1948.

Geminder, Bedřich (pseud. G. Friedrich) (1901–52): worked for Comintern in

1920s, in Moscow from 1934; a secretary of Czechoslovak CP CC, 1945–51; shot in 1952.

Gerö, Ernö (pseud. Pedro) (1898–1980): on ECCI staff from 1927; ECCI representative in Spain, 1936–37; Manuilsky's secretary, 1939–45; in Hungarian government after 1945; general secretary of Hungarian Labor Party, 1956; excluded from party, 1962.

Giral y Pereira, José (1880–1962): minister, later prime minister in Spanish Republican government.

Gomulka, Władysław (1905–82): active in Polish CP in 1920s and 1930s; secretary of Polish Workers' Party, 1942; general secretary of Polish Workers' Party, 1943–48; vice president of Lublin government, 1944; at founding meeting of Cominform, 1947; eased out of Polish CP leadership, arrested, 1948–53; secretary general of Polish CP, 1956–70.

Gorkić, Milan (né Josip Cizinski) (1904–37): secretary general, Yugoslav CP, 1932–37; candidate member of ECCI, 1935; arrested and purged, 1937.

Gottwald, Klement (1896–1953): member of Czechoslovak CP CC from 1925; member of ECCI from 1928, then Presidium, and Secretariat until 1943; prime minister, president of Czechoslovakia from 1945.

Guyot, Raymond (1903–86): secretary general of KIM, 1935; alternate member of ECCI Presidium, 1935–43; member PCF Politburo from 1945 on.

Henrykowski, Henryk (né Saul Amsterdam) (1898–1937): candidate member of Polish CP Politburo, 1930–36; arrested in Moscow, shot, 1937.

Hernández, Jésus (1907–?): member of PCE Politburo from 1932; Spanish minister of education in Largo Caballero and Negrín governments from 1936; PCE representative to ECCI, 1939; later split with Comintern, moved to Mexico.

Humbert-Droz, Jules (1891–1971): founder of Swiss CP; member of ECCI Orgburo, Secretariat, Presidium in 1920s; headed Latin Secretariat; ousted from ECCI as Bukharinite; political secretary of Swiss CP until ousted from party in 1943.

Huysmans, Camille (1871–1968): Belgian socialist; chair of Executive of Socialist Labor International, 1940–44.

Ibárruri, Dolores (1895–1989): member of PCE Politburo from 1932; member of ECCI, 1935–43; secretary of ECCI from 1939; general secretary, then chair, PCE, 1942–60.

Izydorczyk, Jan (1900–1974): Polish Communist activist, survivor of 1937 purge.

Kaganovich, Lazar Moiseevich (1893–1991): member of CPSU Politburo, 1930–57; people's commissar of transportation, heavy industry, etc.; ousted from party, 1961.

Kalganov, ?: Soviet major general stationed in Yan'an.

Kalinin, Mikhail Ivanovich (1875–1946): member of CPSU Politburo from 1926; chairman of Central Executive Committee, Russian Republic, later of Presidium of Supreme Soviet of USSR from 1919.

Kamenev, Lev Borisovich (1883–1936): leading Bolshevik; member of CPSU Politburo from 1919; member of ECCI from 1924, candidate member of ECCI Presidium; arrested 1935; sentenced and executed in first major purge trial, 1936.

Knorin, Wilhelm (1890–1938): Latvian revolutionary; later led Belarus CP; member of ECCI Secretariat; candidate member of ECCI Presidium, 1931–35; arrested, 1937; shot, 1938.

Kolarov, Vasil (1877–1950): secretary of Bulgarian CP CC, 1919; member of ECCI Presidium, Secretariat from 1922; Bulgarian minister of foreign affairs, 1947; Bulgarian prime minister, 1949.

Koplenig, Johann (1891–1968): secretary of KPÖ from 1924; member of ECCI from 1928; member of ECCI Presidium, 1935.

Kun, Béla (1886–1939): head of Hungarian Soviet Republic, 1919; member of ECCI Presidium, 1921; in key positions at ECCI until 1935; arrested, repressed, 1937.

Kuusinen, Otto Wilhelm (1881–1964): member of ECCI and its Presidium from 1921; over many years headed various sections and secretariats; head of Finnish puppet government, 1939–40; chair of Karelo-Finnish Republic of USSR, 1940–56; member of CPSU CC from 1941; member of CPSU CC Presidium, 1952–53, 1957–64; secretary of CPSU CC, 1957.

Largo Caballero, Francisco (1869–1946): president of Spanish Socialist Labor Party, 1932–35; prime minister and war minister of Spanish Republican government, September 1936–May 1937.

Laski, Harold (1893–1950): prominent British political scientist and chairman of Labour Party.

Laval, Pierre (1883–1945): leading member of French cabinets in the 1930s, later prominent in the Vichy government.

Legros. *See* Maurice Tréant.

Lehtinen, Inkeri (1906–?): Finnish militant, on staff of ECCI, 1940–43.

Lenski, Julian (né Leszczynski) (1889–1937): general secretary of Polish CP and member of ECCI Presidium from 1929; arrested, shot 1937.

Lin Biao [Lin Piao] (1907–71): army commander in Long March, 1934–35; CCP representative at ECCI, 1938–42; member of CCP CC from 1945; member of CCP CC Politburo from 1955; minister of defense of People's Republic of China from 1959, designated Mao's successor; purged in 1971.

Lipski, Leon Lukasz (1902–43): Polish activist, worked in Profintern, after dissolution of Polish CP sought to organize dissident group; killed in June 1943, evidently by pro-Moscow elements.

Litvinov, Maksim Maksimovich (1876–1951) member of CPSU CC, 1934–41; Soviet commissar of foreign affairs, 1930–39; Soviet ambassador to United States, 1941–43.

Liu Shaoqi [Liu Shao-ch'i] (1898–1969): member of CCP from 1921; member of CCP CC from 1927; member of CCP CC Politburo from 1931; secretary of CCP CC from 1943.

Longo, Luigi (pseud. Luigi Gallo) (1900–1980): member of PCI CC from 1921; member of PCI Politburo from 1951; candidate member of ECCI Presidium, 1932–33; general inspector of International Brigades in Spain, 1936–39; interned in France, extradited to Italy, deported; partisan leader, 1943–45; deputy general secretary, PCI, from 1946; general secretary, PCI, 1964–72.

Lozovsky, Solomon (Aleksandr) (pseud. of Samuil Abramovich Dridzo) (1878–1952): general secretary of Profintern, 1921–37; Soviet deputy minister of foreign affairs, 1939–46; member of ECCI Presidium, 1926–35; candidate member of ECCI Politsecretariat, 1926–27, 1929–35; candidate member of ECCI Presidium, 1935–43; arrested 1949, died in prison.

Luis. *See* Codovilla, Vittorio.

Malenkov, Georgy Maksimilianovich (1902–88): on CPSU CC staff from 1925; candidate member of Poliburo, 1941; member of Politburo, from 1946 until 1957; one of Stalin's successors, 1953–55; ousted from CPSU, 1961.

Manuilsky, Dmitry Zakharovich (1883–1959): member of CPSU CC, 1923–52; member of ECCI and its Presidium from 1924; member of ECCI Secretariat from 1926; de facto head of Comintern, 1929–33; deputy chair of council of ministers, minister of foreign affairs of Ukrainian SSR, 1944–53.

Marty, André (1886–1956): member of PCF Politburo from 1931; PCF representative to ECCI from 1932; commander of International Brigades in Spain, 1936–38; member of ECCI Presidium and Secretariat, 1935–43; ousted from PCF, 1953.

Mif, Pavel (1901–39): prorector of Communist University of Toilers of the East, 1926–28; rector of Communist University of Toilers of the East, 1928–37; deputy head of Eastern secretariat of ECCI, victim of purge.

Mihailović, Draža (Dragoljub) (1893–1946): commander of Serbian chetniks; minister of war of Yugoslav government in exile, 1942–45; killed, 1946.

Mikoyan, Anastas Ivanovich (1895–1978): member of CPSU Politburo, minister of foreign trade, food industry, supply, 1935–66; chairman, Presidium of Supreme Soviet USSR, 1964–65.

Mineff, Stojan (pseuds. Moreno, Stepanov) (1891–1959): Bulgarian CP delegate to two Comintern congresses; headed Roman (Latin) Ländersekretariat from 1926; illegally in Latin America and China; in Stalin's personal secretariat, 1927–29; Comintern representative to PCE, 1936–39; assistant to Manuilsky.

Mołojec, Bronisław (pseud. Edward): Polish Communist militant, apparently killed in 1942.

Molotov, Viacheslav Mikhailovich (Skriabin) (1890–1986): member of CPSU Politburo, 1921–57; chairman of Sovnarkom (Council of People's Commissars), 1930–34; member of ECCI Presidium, 1928–31; first deputy chair of ECCI Presidium, 1941–45; foreign commissar/minister of USSR, 1939–49, 1953–57; excluded from CPSU, 1957–83.

Nedić, Milan (1877–1946): head of "government" of German-occupied Serbia, 1941–44; arrested as war criminal, committed suicide, 1946.

Negrín Lopez, Juan (1894–1956): prime minister and defense minister of Spanish Republic, May 1937–March 1938.

Nosaka, Sandzo (pseud. Okano) (1892–1993): member of ECCI Presidium from 1933; first secretary of Japan CP, 1955–58; chairman of Japan CP CC from 1958; excluded from Japan CP, 1992.

Nowotko, Marceli (1893–1942): Polish Communist leader, organizer of Polish Workers' Party in underground; killed, 1942.

Pauker, Ana (1893–1960): Romanian Communist activist; worked for Comintern from 1925; jailed in Romania, 1935; freed in exchange with Soviet Union, 1940; worked at ECCI; member of Romanian CP Politburo, 1944; foreign minister, 1947–52; expelled from the party, 1952.

Pavelić, Ante (1889–1959): fascist leader of wartime Croatia.

Pedro. *See* Gerö, Ernö.

Pieck, Wilhelm (1876–1960): long-time leader of KPD; member of ECCI from 1928; member of ECCI Presidium and Secretariat from 1931; president of GDR, 1949.

Pijade, Moša (1887–1957): Yugoslav Communist theorist, journalist, vice president of Antifascist Council of National Liberation (AVNOJ).

Pollitt, Harry (1890–1960): member of ECCI from 1924; general secretary of British CP, 1929–39, 1941–56; member of ECCI Presidium from 1931.

Ponomarev, Boris Nikolaevich (1905–95): on ECCI staff; one of Dimitrov's deputies in OMI; member of CPSU CC, 1956; candidate member of Politburo, 1972–86.

Popov, Blagoi (1902–68): Bulgarian Communist; member of Bulgarian Politburo, 1931–32.

Poskrebyshev, Aleksandr Nikolaevich (1891–1965): on CPSU CC staff from 1924; chief of Special Sector of CC from 1929; major general of Red Army, 1939; close aide of Stalin's.

Prestes, Luis Carlos (1898–1970?): Brazilian army officer who became Communist official; member ECCI, 1935–43; secretary general of Brazilian CP from 1936; repeatedly under arrest.

Prieto, Indalecio (1883–1962): Spanish socialist; at various ministerial positions in Spain in 1930s; war minister of Spanish Republic, 1937–38.

Pyatnitsky, Osip Aronovich (1882–1938): Old Bolshevik; treasurer of Comintern from 1921; member of ECCI Secretariat from 1923; held key positions on ECCI; arrested in 1937, killed.

Rákosi, Mátyás (1892–1971): in Béla Kun government, Hungary, 1919; secretary of ECCI, 1920–23; illegal work for Comintern in Europe, 1923–25; arrested in Budapest, given life sentence, 1925; freed in exchange with Soviet Union, 1940; member of ECCI, 1940–43; general secretary of Hungarian CP, 1945–53; first secretary of Hungarian CP, 1953–56; ousted 1956, 1962.

Rammette, Arthur (pseud. Charles Dupuy): member of PCF Politburo, 1932–35; to USSR, 1940?; worked on ECCI staff; later at Institute No. 301; editor of French radio programs.

Sémard, Pierre (1887–1942): general secretary of PCF, 1924–29; member of ECCI, 1924–31; arrested in France, 1939; shot by the Germans, 1942.

Shcherbakov, Aleksandr Sergeyevich (1901–45): first secretary of Moscow committee of CPSU, 1938–45; secretary of CPSU CC from 1941; chief of Main Political Administration of Red Army, 1942; later chief of Sovinformburo.

Sheng Shicai [Sheng Shih-tsai]: Soviet-sponsored warlord in control of Xinjiang in the 1930s and 1940s.

Shuklin, ?: head of OMI Secretariat of CPSU CC, 1944–45.

Shvernik, Nikolai Mikhailovich (1888–1970): member of CPSU CC from 1925; candidate member of Politburo from 1939; member of CPSU CC Presidium, 1952–53, 1957; chair of USSR Supreme Soviet Presidium from 1946.

Sikorski, Władysław (1891–1943): general, premier of Poland; premier of Polish government in exile; killed in a plane crash, 1943.

Slánský, Rudolf (1901–52): member of Politburo of Czechoslovak CP from 1928; general secretary of Czechoslovak CP, 1945–51; arrested, executed, 1952.

Sobottka, Gustav (1886–1953): veteran German Communist, member of KPD CC.

Soong, T. V.: prime minister of Chinese Nationalist government.

Stepanov. *See* Mineff, Stojan.

Sukharev, Konstantin Petrovich (1899–?): headed ECCI Liaison Service, 1941; later head of ECCI internal management administration.

Šverma, Jan (1901–44): member of Politburo of Czechoslovak CP from 1929; candidate member of ECCI from 1935; returned to Slovakia, 1944.

Tanev, Vasil (1897–1941): Bulgarian Communist.

Thälmann, Ernst (1886–1944): German Communist leader; alternate member of ECCI, 1924; member of ECCI, 1925–43; chairman of KPD from 1925; arrested in Germany, 1933; executed in Buchenwald, 1944.

Thorez, Maurice (1900–1964): member PCF CC from 1924; member of ECCI from 1928; member of ECCI Presidium, 1931–43; deserted French army, 1939; returned to France from USSR as leader of PCF, 1944; served in government, 1945–47; secretary general of PCF until 1964.

Timoshenko, Semion Konstantinovich (1895–1970): Soviet people's commissar for defense, 1940–41, then deputy commissar.

Tito, Josip (Broz) (pseud. Walter) (1892–1980): active in CPY in 1920s and 1930s; member of CPY Politburo from 1934; member of Comintern Balkan Secretariat from 1935; secretary general of CPY, 1937–66; marshal, head of government, then president of Yugoslavia.

Togliatti, Palmiro (pseuds. Ercoli, Alfredo) (1893–1964): member of PCI CC from 1922; member of ECCI Presidium from 1924; member of ECCI Politsecretariat, 1926–35; member ECCI Secretariat from 1935; ECCI representative in Spain, 1937–39; general secretary of PCI after World War II.

Tréant, Maurice (pseud. Legros) (1900–1949): Soviet-trained official of PCF, relieved of party duties during World War II.

Trilisser, Mikhail (Meer) Abramovich (pseud. Moskvin) (1883–1940): prominent in both secret police and Comintern in the 1920s and 1930s; head of OMS and member of ECCI Presidium, candidate member of ECCI Secretariat, 1935; arrested, 1938; shot, 1940.

Ulbricht, Walter (1893–1973): member of KPD CC from 1923; member of KPD Politburo from 1935; KPD representative to ECCI, 1925–29; candidate member of ECCI, 1928–43; member of Free Germany Committee, 1941–45; general secretary of SED CC, 1950–71.

Uribe, Vicente (1902–61): member of PCE Politburo from 1932; minister of agriculture of Spanish Republic, 1936–39.

Vasilevsky, Aleksandr Mikhailovich (1895–1977): chief of General Staff of Red Army from 1942; marshal of Red Army from 1943; minister of USSR armed forces, 1949–53; Soviet first deputy minister of defense, 1953–57; member of CPSU CC, 1952–61.

Vlahović, Velimir (Veljko) (pseud. Ivan Pavlovich Vlasov) (1914–75): Yugoslav representative in KIM, 1939–41; editor in chief of ECCI press department, 1941–43.

Voroshilov, Kliment Efremovich (1881–1969): member of CPSU CC, 1921–61; people's commissar of defense, USSR, from 1925; member of CPSU CC Politburo, 1926–60; marshal of Red Army, 1935; member of State Defense Committee (GKO), 1941–45; chairman of Presidium of Supreme Soviet of USSR, 1953–60.

Walter. *See* Tito, Josip.

Wang Jiaxiang [Chon Li-wang/Chia-hsiang] (pseud. A. G. Kommunar) (1906–74): student, then instructor at KUTV, 1925–30; member of CCP Politburo from 1934; CCP representative to ECCI, 1937–38; Chinese ambassador to USSR.

Wang Jingwei [Wang Ching-wei] (1883–1944): Chinese Nationalist, headed Japanese-sponsored government of northern China in 1930s and 1940s.

Wang Ming (1904–74): joined CCP Politburo, 1931; CCP representative to Comintern; on ECCI Presidium, 1932; member of ECCI Politsecretariat, 1933; member of ECCI Presidium and candidate member of ECCI Secretariat, 1935; returned to China, 1937; returned to Moscow, sided with CPSU against Mao.

Warski, Adolf (Warszawski) (1868–1937): member of Polish CP leadership, arrested, 1937.

Yezhov, Nikolai Ivanovich (1895–1940): member of CPSU CC, 1935–39; candidate member of Politburo from 1937; member of ECCI from 1935; people's commissar of internal affairs, 1936–38; arrested, 1939, later shot.

Yves. *See* Duclos, Jacques.

Zápotocký, Antonin (1884–1957): general secretary of Czechoslovak CP, 1922; candidate member of ECCI from 1935; in German concentration camp, 1939–45; prime minister of Czechoslovakia, 1949; president of Czechoslovakia, 1953.

Zarski, Tadeusz (1896–1934): Member of Polish CC, 1923–29; arrested in USSR, 1934, tried, sentenced to death.

Zhang Guotao [Chang Kuo-t'ao] (1897–1979): one of founders of CCP; commander of 4th Army, 1934–36; candidate member of ECCI Presidium, 1928–31; member of ECCI from 1935; excluded from CCP, April 1938.

Zhang Wentian (Luo Fu [Lo Fu]) (1900–1976): member of CCP from 1925; member of CCP CC Politburo, 1934–56; general secretary of CCP CC, 1935–40.

Zhang Xueliang [Chang Hsüeh-liang] (1901–94?), warlord of Manchuria in 1930s.

Zhdanov, Andrei Aleksandrovich (1896–1948): secretary of CPSU CC from 1934; member of Politburo from 1939; member of ECCI from 1935.

Zhou Enlai [Chou En-lai] (1898–1976): leading Chinese Communist; foreign minister, 1949–58; prime minister, 1949–76.

Zhu De [Chu Teh] (1886–1976): member of CCP Politburo from 1934; a commander of the Long March, 1934–35; commander-in-chief of Chinese Red Army, 1931; commander of 8th Army, 1937–45; vice president of People's Republic of China, 1954; marshal of People's Republic, 1955.

Zhukov, Georgy Konstantinovich (1896–1974): chief of General Staff of Red Army, 1941; first deputy people's commissar of defense, 1942; marshal of Red Army, 1943; USSR minister of defense, 1955–57; member of CPSU CC, 1953–57; member of Politburo, 1956–57.

Zinoviev, Grigory Yevseyevich (1883–1936): Close associate of Lenin's before and after 1917 revolution; chairman of ECCI, 1919–26; member of CPSU Politburo from 1919; in opposition to Stalin from 1925; ousted from Politburo, 1926; major defendant in 1936 show trial, sentenced to death and executed.

Index

Many of the persons listed here are obscure figures whose first names are not known and cannot be given.

273